THE PERMISSION SEEKER'S
GUIDE THROUGH THE LEGAL

Clearing Copyrights, Trademark
Entertainment and Medi

JOY R. BUTLER

Sashay Communications, LLC

Published by Sashay Communications, LLC
2200 Wilson Boulevard, #102-329, Arlington, VA 22201
www.sashaycommunications.com

Cover and Interior Book Design by Shane Felux

Publisher's Cataloging-In-Publication Data
(Prepared by The Donohue Group, Inc.)

Butler, Joy R.
    The permission seeker's guide through the legal jungle : clearing copyrights, trademarks and other rights for entertainment and media productions / Joy R. Butler.

    p. ; cm. -- (Guide through the legal jungle)

    Includes index.
    ISBN-13: 978-0-9672940-1-8
    ISBN-10: 0-9672940-1-0

1. Intellectual property--United States--Popular works. 2. Mass media--Law and legislation--United States--Popular works. I. Title.

KF2979 .B85 2007
346.7304/8

GUIDELINES AND CAUTIONS
FOR THE USE OF THIS BOOK

This book is designed to help you identify legal issues that arise in your productions. There are certain guidelines you should keep in mind as you use this book or any other book on legal issues.

The law is complex. To make this book easy to follow, discussions of legal principles have been simplified. This book covers only principles of United States law. Each principle of law is subject to differing interpretations and may have numerous exceptions. As this book provides a broad overview of the law, it may not cover an interpretation or an exception that applies to your specific legal situation.

The author and the publisher have made their best efforts to ensure that the information presented in this book is as complete and as accurate as possible. However, the entertainment and media businesses are fluid. Industry customs and laws change constantly. Always make sure that you are relying on the most up to date information.

Furthermore, every legal situation is unique. Neither this book nor any book is an adequate substitute for seeking legal advice from an attorney familiar with the circumstances of your particular situation. If you have a specific legal problem, you should consult an attorney.

As a result of the above, the author and the publisher cannot assume any responsibility or liability to any person or entity for any loss or damage caused, or alleged to be caused, by the information presented in this book.

ACKNOWLEDGMENTS

Numerous people helped me in completing this book project.

Thank you to the current and former law school students who worked as my research assistants. They are Grace E. Ahn, Jason Baum, Vikrant D. Bhatia, Matthew Scott Brown, Candice Bruno, Jesse L. Campbell, Cecille H. Chen, Alex E. Colon, Toya L. Gavin, Marques Johnson, Lyndsey J. Kuykendall, Sum Mehrnama, Javad Namazie, Elaine Tran, and Derrell Winder. Much success to you in your legal careers.

I also thank and acknowledge all the attorneys from the entertainment and intellectual property bars who generously shared their time and legal expertise by reviewing and offering comments on portions of the book. These attorneys are Erin G. Austin, Barbara I. Berschler, Tony Brackett, Maureen Cohen Harrington, Kurt R. Klaus, Alan Lewine, Gerard J. Lewis, Jr., M. Melisse Lewis, Leigh Ann Lindquist, John Davis Malloy, Aoi Nawashiro, Laura Possessky, Diana Michelle Sobo, and Bruce V. Spiva.

Finally, thanks to my mother, Elaine Randall Butler, who waded through two drafts of the entire manuscript and applied her thirty-two years of English literature and composition experience to the editing and proofreading of the book.

SUMMARY TABLE OF CONTENTS

TABLE OF CONTENTS

Part Five: Seeking Permission to Use Specific Materials   249

PART ONE

Overview of Rights Clearance Issues

Part One explains what rights clearance entails and why you should even bother to clear rights in your production. Part One includes a rights clearance checklist which poses a series of questions about your production and then refers you to subsequent sections of this book for more details on rights issues relevant to your production

Chapters in Part One:

GUIDE TO USING THIS BOOK | 1

1.1. Who Should Read This Book?

If you produce, acquire, distribute, or otherwise work with media productions, this book is for you. It offers detailed analysis and practical advice to help you identify and eliminate rights clearance problems in your media productions.

I use the term media production broadly to encompass film, video, television programs, newspapers, magazines, posters, comic books, paintings, CDs, websites, computer games, photographs, sculptures, fine art, advertisements, and a host of other media through which people communicate and express themselves.

If this list omits the type of media production on which you are working, don't worry! While each type of media production has the potential of posing unique clearance issues, the same themes and questions appear repeatedly across all media. Regardless of your particular project, you should find helpful information in *The Permission Seeker's Guide Through the Legal Jungle* to assist you through the rights clearance process.

1.2. What Does It Mean to Clear Rights?

As a media producer, you may borrow from other media or from real life. The borrowed item may be a few measures from a song, a line from a poem, an illustration, or a clip from a television program. An element borrowed from real life may be the image of a real person, a common grocery store product, or a true story. Typically, there are people or organizations who possess rights in these borrowed items. Depending upon the borrowed item and how you use the borrowed item in your production, the person's rights in that borrowed item might be classified as a copyright, a trademark, a right of publicity, a right of privacy, the right not to be defamed, or other right.

When you clear rights, you verify that your production contains no material that violates the rights of another person or that violates any relevant laws. There are other terms used to describe the process of clearing rights. They include vetting the production, getting permission, and licensing. Clearing rights in a production requires all of the following:

- determining if you need consent to use a particular item in your production

- identifying who holds the rights in those items for which you need permission

- obtaining permission to use the item

As the list suggests, the law sometimes allows you to use the item without the permission of the rights holder. This allowance comes with a huge caveat. Application of the law to rights clearance questions is subjective and fact specific – even fickle at times. Having the rights holder's permission is always preferable.

1.3. How to Use This Book

Use this book as a reference tool for your rights clearance questions and work. You can read the book from cover to cover for a grounding in the laws and business practices within the rights clearance process. Alternatively, you can go directly to the section that addresses your question of the moment. This reference book includes six parts:

Part One. Overview of Rights Clearance Issues
Part Two. Relevant Rights and Laws
Part Three. Clearance Issues for Specific Producers
Part Four. Process of Clearing Rights and Seeking Permission

Part Five. Seeking Permission to Use Specific Materials
Part Six. Minimizing Your Risks and Protecting Yourself

Part One provides an overview of the rights clearance process. It includes a detailed checklist to help you spot clearance and permission issues in your media production and then refers you to subsequent sections of this book for greater explanation. If you have a specific media production in development, use Part One for an idea of the copyright, trademark and other rights issues that confront you.

Part Two provides a detailed overview of the laws most relevant to the rights clearance process. These laws include copyright, trademark, right of publicity, right of privacy, defamation, obscenity and indecency. Read all of Part Two if you want a more complete understanding of how these laws impact your production. Alternatively, you can read specific sections of Part Two to supplement your understanding of the areas highlighted for your particular media production in the Part One checklist.

Part Three builds on Part Two. Many of the concepts and procedures discussed in this reference book apply to all sectors of media. However, there are special considerations for certain areas of media. Part Three explains some of these special considerations and provides examples of how the concepts explained in Part Two are applied to specific types of productions.

Parts Four and Five are for those who already know which rights need to be cleared and seek guidance on how to go about clearing those particular rights. Part Four explains the general procedure for clearing rights with tips on how to locate rights holders, request permission, and negotiate rights agreement.

Part Five goes into greater detail on procedures for obtaining rights to use specific categories of material. The categories of materials discussed include literary material, visual art, music, stock images and footage, film clips, online materials, computer software, and people's names and images.

Part Six has suggestions for minimizing your liability by obtaining errors and omissions insurance, using disclaimers, and implementing common sense operational procedures.

The book also includes an Appendix with resources and sample forms.

1.4. Approach Used by This Book

Ask an attorney whether your use of material in your production will create trouble for you. The attorney's answer is likely to be "It depends". While the answer is frustrating to producers, it is the truth. Clearance questions are incredibly fact specific. What applies to one situation may not always apply in another situation that seems similar.

The answer to any rights clearance question depends on the specific material you want to use and how you want to use it. This book provides examples from real-life situations and legal battles to illustrate the results that can come about from particular sets of circumstances. For attorneys and others who may want to read the entire opinion from the real-life examples, I do include legal citations for most of the cases discussed. The legal citations provided typically do not include complete prior and subsequent case histories.

While the real-life examples offered throughout this book provide insight into how your own situation might play out, they do not provide definitive answers. Rights clearance issues are often more art than science. By way of analogy, think of what happens when you ask two separate people whether they like a sculpture, a book or a film. Each person may give you a different opinion on the merits of the film. One person's opinion who views the film as brilliant may be completely inconsistent with another person's opinion who views the film as a waste of good tape. Similarly, separate courts or separate attorneys can – and often do - look at the same or similar rights clearance questions and reach different conclusions.

1.5. Why You Should Clear Rights

At this point, perhaps you are thinking that clearing rights sounds like a lot of trouble, and you are questioning whether you should even bother.

1.5.1. Not Clearing Rights Is A Gamble

Failing to clear rights is a gamble that subjects you and your production to risk. That risk may lead to one or more outcomes:

Nothing May Happen. It is possible that Lady Luck will be on your side and allow you to ignore all rights issues without experiencing any negative consequences. Perhaps the rights holder never becomes aware of your use or, if he does become aware, he may not care about or disapprove of the use. This game is exclusively for those producers who enjoy a good game of Russian Roulette.

I analogize the risk of ignoring rights clearance to the risk of driving a car with your eyes closed. If you drive your car with your eyes closed for twenty seconds, you may hit something – but it is also possible that you will get through the experience without damaging any property or injuring yourself. But what if you drive with your eyes closed on a regular basis. You make entire road trips this way. Sooner or later, you are going to crash. It is the same scenario for rights clearance. If you produce on a regular basis and you ignore rights issues, there will eventually be consequences.

Lawsuit or Injunction If the rights holder notices your use and does care, it may seek to prevent the distribution of your production by obtaining an injunction or restraining order through the courts. Alternatively or in addition, the rights holder may sue you in order to recover money damages for any harm she suffered as a result of your unauthorized use.

Inability to Secure Distribution Even if you are willing to take the risk that nothing may happen as a result of your failure to address rights clearance issues, there may be additional individuals or entities associated with your production who are less willing to roll the dice.

Professional producers often seek distribution of their productions through a distribution company. Many distributors require assurances that your production has been properly cleared. If you can not provide these assurances, a distribution company may decline to accept your production. A distribution agreement might include the following terms to provide the distributor with this assurance:

- You make representations that all the material in your production is original and that any material that is not original has been properly licensed.

- You warrant, meaning that you guarantee, that the production has no clearance problems.

- You must give the distributor documentation to back up your representations. This documentation, often referred to as deliverables, includes contracts with performers, licensing agreements, copyright reports, and title reports.

- You indemnify the distributor. This means that you promise to reimburse the distributor for any money it loses due to a lawsuit or claim generated by clearance problems in your production

- You obtain errors and omissions insurance. Errors and omissions insurance covers producers for copyright, trademark and other claims associated with the material in a production. You are not going to be able to get an errors and omissions insurance policy if you have not taken steps to clear your production.

1.5.2. The Two Separate Risks of Not Clearing Rights

Using another person's material without authorization invokes two separate risks:

- the risk of being sued and

- the risk of losing a lawsuit and having to pay money damages or having the distribution of a production stopped by the court.

You must view these risks as separate and distinct. Many rights holders are extremely aggressive about protecting the use of their content. They may launch a lawsuit over your unauthorized use of their content even if there is a valid justification under the law for the unauthorized use. As a result, you still incur the expense and time of defending a legal action, even if you ultimately win the legal action. To eliminate this risk, producers sometimes find it worthwhile to secure a license for material even when it may arguably be legal to use the material without a license.

1.5.3. The Bad News

Here's the bad news. The proper clearance of rights can require much effort and paperwork. Clearing rights can become a nightmare if you start the process after you have already completed your production. At that point, you have made and implemented decisions about material to incorporate into the production. Undoing those decisions, if possible at all, is time-consuming and expensive. Rights clearance should begin during pre-production and continue throughout the production process. If you begin clearing rights only after production, you guarantee yourself the maximum in frustration and cost.

1.5.4. The Good News

Here's the good news. You have the power to exercise control over the process and minimize your trouble and costs. You exercise control by giving yourself a reasonable amount of time. The more time allowed for the clearance process, the more available options you have and the easier the process becomes. For example, you can substitute one music selection for another if you discover during pre-production that your first choice is outside your production budget.

CHECKLIST OF CLEARANCE ISSUES | 2

The following checklist can help you spot clearance and permission issues in your media production. By necessity, the discussion within the checklist is cryptic. The checklist refers you to subsequent sections of this book for greater explanation. The checklist is not an exhaustive list of every clearance issue relevant to your production. Each question may not be relevant to your production.

Subject Matter of the Production

Is the production based on real life? If the production is based on a true story, there may be issues of defamation and right of privacy. (Sections 6.2, 8.1, 8.2 and 10.2) Consider a life story rights agreement with your subject if he is still living. (Section 25.3)

Are the subjects of the true story still living? It is not possible to violate the right of privacy or to defame a person who is no longer living. However, it is still possible to violate the rights of any living family, friends and associates of your deceased subject if those persons factor into your production. (Section 5.3.4) Also, the right of publicity may still be relevant. Consider consulting agreements or releases with certain family, friends and/or associates of the subject. (Sections 25.3 and 25.4)

Does the production focus on a real-life crime? Son of Sam laws prevent criminals from selling rights to their life stories. (Section 9.3)

Does the production portray any living individuals or existing companies in a negative manner? If yes, right of privacy and defamation claims are possible. (Chapters 6 and 8)

On what information, documents, and other sources is the depiction of the true story based? Recording the sources on which you rely is part of developing an annotated script or outline of the production. (Section 13.4)

- **Is the depiction based on information in public records?** Using public records as a source provides insulation from right of privacy and defamation claims. (Sections 6.7.5, 8.4.6, and 8.4.7)

- **Is the depiction based on information in private records?** If yes, you should be able to show that you had legitimate access to the private records to avoid right of privacy claims. (Sections 6.3 and 6.7.2)

- **Is the depiction based on interviews with the subject of your production?** If yes, consider a life story rights agreement in which the subject expressly authorizes a story on his life and promises not to sue you for right of privacy, right of publicity, defamation or related claims. (Section 25.3)

- **Is the depiction based on interviews with family, friends and acquaintances of your primary subject?** A written agreement with each interviewee is advisable. Depending on the circumstances, the agreement could be a simple one-page release or a more extensive consulting agreement. (Chapter 25)

- **Is the depiction based on secondary sources such as other books, articles or films?** You must take only facts – and not expression - from the secondary sources in order to avoid claims of copyright infringement. (Section 3.4.2)

- **Can you document that the depiction is true?** Truth is a defense to defamation. (Section 8.4.5) It is not a defense to most right of privacy claims. (Section 6.7.3)

- **Are you covering an event that occurred in a public place or in front of a large number of people?** If yes, using the event as the subject of your production is unlikely to trigger a successful right of privacy claim. (Section 6.7.5) However, you must be cautious concerning any copyrightable material (such as music, poems, etc.) that you pick up during the coverage of the event. (Section 13.3)

If the production is based on an original idea, are there any stories, films, artwork or other material to which you had access and which are similar to your production? With respect to copyright, similarity in productions is okay as long as the two productions were created independently. Otherwise, substantial similarity can lead to claims of copyright infringement. (Section 3.5). However, there are certain elements – such as facts, themes, and stock characters - that are not copyrightable. (Section 3.4)

Is the production based on an underlying work or on pre-existing material? If developing your production from a pre-existing story, image or musical piece, your production may be a derivative work. If the pre-existing material is protected by copyright, and you are not the owner of that copyright, you may need permission to base a new production on the pre-existing material. (Section 17.2)

Did you employ or commission someone to prepare the production? If the creator is your employee, you own the production as a work made for hire. (Section 19.3.1) If the creator is a freelancer you retained, the freelancer should transfer rights to you through a written work made for hire, assignment or license agreement. (Sections 17.3 and 19.3.1)

If rights are granted as a license or assignment, does the grant cover all your intended uses for the production? The grant must cover all your intended uses in order for you to clear rights properly. (Section 19.3.2)

Did anyone else contribute or help with the creation of the production? You should have written agreements with all contributors and collaborators. Otherwise, there is the potential for a contributor to claim co-ownership in the production. Contributors include graphic artists, performing musicians, crew, illustrators, editors, and creative consultants. (Section 17.3)

Characters in the Production

Does the production include a depiction of any fictitious characters from other productions (*e.g.*, Scarlett O'Hara, Donald Duck, James Bond)? Fictitious characters can be protected by copyright and trademark. (Sections 3.3.3 and 21.4)

Does the production include characters based on real people? Even if the character is only loosely based on a real person or is a composite person, a successful claim is possible if people reasonably identify the character as a depiction of the real person. (Section 5.3)

- If the portrayal is unflattering, a defamation claim is possible. (Section 8.2)

- A right of publicity claim is possible if the real person is famous and the production uses the person's identity in a commercial manner. (Section 7.1 and 7.2)

- A right of privacy claim is possible if you wrote the portrayal using private information to which you had no legitimate access. (Sections 6.3 and 6.5)

People Appearing in Your Production

Are there actors, models, musicians, or other performers in the production? You should obtain a written agreement from every such person waiving right of publicity and other claims. In the written agreement, the person should grant rights to you in the person's performance, appearance or contribution. These are usually talent agreements or releases. (Sections 17.3 and 25.1)

Are there people (other than professional talent specifically hired to be in your production) whose images, names, or personal information somehow find their way into your production? Ideally, you should obtain a release from each such person. (Section 25.4)

Does the production incorporate the image or name (or other identifiable trait) of a famous person? There is a potential right of publicity claim if you are using the famous person's name or image in a commercial context. (Sections 7.1 and 7.2)

If there is a descriptive caption or narration used with an image, does the caption or narration accurately describe the image? Mischaracterizing an image can give rise to false light or defamation claims. (Sections 6.4, 8.1 and 8.2)

Location

Are there any distinctive locations or buildings that appear in the production? Buildings can be protected by both trademark and copyright law. (Section 26.1)

Do any store or company signs appear in the production? Trademark infringement is a potential claim. (Section 4.4.3)

Music Incorporated into Your Production

This portion of the checklist is most relevant to audiovisual, website and software productions, which are the types of productions most likely to incorporate music. This portion of the checklist may also apply to literary material that includes lyrics.

For rights clearance issues that arise in the production of music, see the section on Recording Music later in this checklist.

Did you commission original music specifically for the production? You should have written agreements with the songwriter as well as the musicians performing the music. (Section 22.5.1)

Does the production use pre-existing songs? Normally, unless the songs are in the public domain, you must obtain a synchronization license to incorporate the song into your production. (Section 22.5.2)

Does the production use pre-existing sound recordings? Normally, unless the sound recording is in the public domain, you must obtain a master use license to incorporate the sound recording into your production. (Section 22.5.2)

Will a soundtrack of the production be released? You need either (i) outright ownership of the songs and sound recordings included on the soundtrack or (ii) mechanical licenses for the songs as well as permission from the copyright owner of the sound recordings. (Section 22.6)

Are you using music in an internet production? There are specific rules depending on whether you offer streams or downloads of the music. (Section 22.7)

Are you seeking an easier option for licensing songs and sound recordings? Consider licensing music for your production from a production music library. (Section 22.5.3)

Literary, Visual and Audio-Visual Material Incorporated into Your Production

Is there artwork in the production? If unlicensed artwork appears in your production, copyright infringement claims are possible. (Section 3.5) Depending on the subject matter of the artwork, other claims are possible.

Is there text from any literary work (e.g., books, poems) used in the production? Unless fair use applies, you should obtain permission for the use. (Section 3.7)

Does the production include any clips of films, television programs or other audio-visual productions? You need permission from numerous rights holders including the following:

- The producer of the audio-visual production (Section 23.1.2)
- A synchronization and/or master use license for any music in the clip (Section 23.4)
- Releases from union actors appearing in the clip (Section 23.5.1 and 23.5.2)
- Permissions for other copyrightable elements in the clip such as choreography, special effects, and visual art (Section 23.1.1 and 23.4)
- Permissions from members of the Directors Guild and the Writers Guild who worked on the audio-visual program from which the clip is taken. (Section 23.5.3 and 23.5.4)

Are you seeking an easier option for licensing visual images and audio-visual material? Consider licensing stock images and stock footage for your production. (Sections 21.2 and 23.2) You might also consider using a film poster rather than a clip of the actual film. (Section 23.6.2)

Appearance of Company Names and Products

Are there any real company names or real products that appear in the production? If a viewer could reasonably conclude that the manufacturer of the product is affiliated with or has endorsed the production, a trademark infringement claim is possible. (Section 4.4.3)

Recording Music

Are you the original creator of the song? If yes, you are the copyright owner and you need no permission to record the song. (Section 3.2). If you are not the copyright owner of the song, you need a license to record the song unless the song is in the public domain. If the song has been commercially recorded, you can record and distribute the song pursuant to a compulsory mechanical license. (Section 22.6)

Are there instrumentalists and/or vocalists who perform on the recording? You should obtain a written agreement from all performers granting to you rights in their performance. (Section 12.1 and 17.3)

Does your music production include samples (or clips) from any pre-existing songs or recordings? Samples normally require the permission of both the copyright owner of the song and the copyright owner of the sound recording. (Section 12.2)

Do you intend to play the song via the internet? If you are not the copyright owner of the song, you need a public performance license which you can obtain directly from the songwriter or from a performing rights organization (PRO). The PROs for songs in the United States are ASCAP, BMI and SESAC. (Section 22.4 and 22.7)

Do you plan to incorporate the recording into an audiovisual production (film, TV program, CD-ROM, multimedia program)? You need a separate synchronization license for the song. (Section 22.5)

Other Issues

Is there any material in the production that might be interpreted as obscene? Distribution of obscene material is illegal. (Section 9.1)

Is the title of your production similar to or the same as another production's title? Normally, the title of a single production is not protectible as a trademark and you can use a title even if it is similar to another production's title. An exception applies if the title has acquired secondary meaning. (Sections 4.4.1)

Does the title of your production incorporate someone else's trademark? Your title can trigger trademark infringement claims (Sections 4.4.1 and 27.2)

PART TWO
Relevant Rights and Laws

Part Two includes an overview of the laws that are relevant to rights clearance issues. Before launching into Part Two, I want to highlight an element that will come up repeatedly in the discussion of media-related laws. It is the First Amendment to the United States Constitution which reads as follows:

> Congress shall make no law respecting an establishment of religion, or prohibiting the free exercise thereof; or abridging the freedom of speech, or of the press; or the right of the people peaceably to assemble, and to petition the government for a redress of grievances.

It is the freedom of speech and of the press that have the greatest impact on media and entertainment productions. There is a constant balancing act between the producer's right to use and disseminate material as a means of expressing himself and the individual's interest in protecting his rights under copyright, trademark, privacy, defamation and other media-related laws. Sometimes the individual's rights give way to the First Amendment. Sometimes the reverse happens and the First Amendment gives way to the individual's rights.

Chapters in Part Two:

COPYRIGHT BASICS | 3

3.1. United States Copyright Law and Copyright Registration

United States copyright protection springs from the United States Constitution which gives Congress the right to promote:

> the Progress of Science and useful Arts, by securing for limited Times to Authors and Inventors the exclusive Right to their respective Writings and Discoveries (U.S. Constitution, Art. 1, sec. 8).

The words Authors' Rights to their Writings refers to copyright law. Congress relies on this constitutional power when it enacts and amends copyright laws. The words Inventors' Right to their Discoveries refers to patent law, a topic not treated in this reference book.

3.1.1. Copyright Act of 1976

The Copyright Act of 1976 governs current copyright law. As the name implies, Congress passed the Copyright Act in 1976. However, the law did not go into effect until January 1, 1978. If you ever want to read the Copyright Act in its entirety, you can find it in Title 17 of the United States Code starting at Section 101.

The Copyright Act has its own jargon. It refers to all creations as *works* regardless of whether the creation is a song, poem, film, book, architectural design, poster or other artistic creation. It refers to the creators of all works as *authors* regardless of whether the creator is a poet, instrumentalist, sculptor, filmmaker, architect, or other creative individual.

3.1.2. Copyright Act of 1909

Prior to the enactment of the Copyright Act of 1976, the Copyright Act of 1909 governed U.S. copyright law. The 1909 Act is still relevant in determining whether works created prior to January 1, 1978 are in the public domain.

Most of the discussion about the copyright statute in this reference book concerns the Copyright Act of 1976 which is the current law. It is the Copyright Act of 1976 to which I refer when I mention the Copyright Act. When I mean the prior act, I refer to it as the 1909 Act.

There are a number of distinctions between the Copyright Act and the 1909 Act. For rights clearance purposes, the most significant distinctions are how a copyright begins and how long a copyright lasts.

- How Copyright Begins. Under the Copyright Act, copyright protection begins as soon as you create the work. Under the 1909 Act, federal copyright protection began upon publication of the work. Separate state laws normally protected unpublished works.

- How Long Copyright Lasts. Under the Copyright Act, copyright protection generally lasts for the life of the author plus seventy years. Under the 1909 Act, copyright protection lasted for an initial term of twenty-eight years with an option to renew for an additional twenty-eight years.

Sections 3.1.3 and 3.6 contain more discussion about the creation and duration of copyrights.

3.1.3. Copyrighting Your Work

Registration Is Not Required. Under the Copyright Act, any original work of authorship is copyrighted as soon as it is *fixed in a tangible medium of expression*. This language comes directly from the Copyright Act. Your work is *fixed in a tangible medium of expression* as soon as you write it down or record it. As a result, as soon as the writer jots a short story into a notebook, the poet types a haiku on the keyboard of a laptop computer, the composer hums a song into a tape recorder, or the filmmaker rolls the camera for scene one - a valid copyright is created.

In contrast, if the writer tells a short story orally without writing the story down, if the poet performs the haiku impromptu at a poetry jam, if the composer sings a piece that exists only in his memory, or if a theatrical troupe renders a live performance of a scene that is not written down - there is no valid copyright in that short story, haiku, song or scene because they do not exist in tangible form. Once the performance is complete, they are no more - until the next performance.

Benefits of Copyright Registration. While you do not need to register your copyright with the Copyright Office in order to have valid copyright protection, registration does offer several benefits:

Benefit One: Notice.   Registration of a copyright puts the world on notice that you claim the copyright in a particular work.

Benefit Two: Easier Identification of Copyright Owner.   Tracking down the individual authorized to grant permission is often the most difficult part of rights clearance. If you are a copyright owner seeking to generate licensing revenue in your work, you want to be easy to locate and contact. The conservative producer declines to use a work for which he cannot locate the rights owner. Being difficult to locate may lead to missed licensing opportunities. Producers can more easily identify and locate the rights owner of registered works.

Benefit Three: Enforcement Tools.   Registration provides additional mechanisms for enforcing a copyright. These tools include the ability to file a copyright infringement lawsuit and eligibility for statutory damages and attorneys' fees.

• Ability to File a Copyright Infringement Lawsuit.   Registration is a prerequisite to filing a copyright infringement lawsuit.

Not having registered does not mean a copyright owner cannot sue an infringer. It just means the copyright owner must first register his work prior to filing the lawsuit. In this situation, the copyright owner – anxious to initiate suit – might register on an expedited basis.

A copyright registration is effective on the date the Copyright Office receives your complete application. However, it normally takes about six months for the Copyright Office to process the application and mail the certificate of registration.

If you request and receive expedited registration, the Copyright Office will attempt to process your application and issue a certificate of registration within five business days. The expedited registration costs an additional $685. You can find more information on expedited registration in the Copyright Office's information circular 10 on special handling, available on the Copyright Office's website.

   • Eligibility for Statutory Damages.   A copyright owner who has registered his copyright in a timely manner can pursue statutory damages in a copyright infringement lawsuit. Damages refers to the amount of money awarded to you through the court when you win a lawsuit. The person you sued pays you the amount of the damage award. As part of the lawsuit, you have to convince the court how much your damage award should be.

As the name implies, statutory damages are set by statute. In this case, the applicable statute is the Copyright Act which currently sets statutory damages for copyright infringement at $750 to $30,000 for each act of infringement. The amount can go up to $150,000 if the copyright owner shows the infringer acted willfully. The court has great discretion regarding where within that range to set damages.

If not eligible for statutory damages, the copyright owner must pursue money damages based on the amount lost as a result of the infringement plus the infringer's profits. Calculating an amount acceptable to the court can be difficult.

For example, suppose a producer includes the painting of an unknown artist in the set decoration of a major motion picture without the artist's permission. The artist has never licensed or sold a painting. Even if use of the painting is clearly infringement,

winning an infringement lawsuit can be a hollow victory if the artist cannot rely on statutory damages. Without statutory damages,
the artist must explain to the court how much money, if any, she
lost as a result of her painting's appearance in the motion picture
and how much of the motion picture's profits are attributable to
the use of the painting. These are not easy questions to answer and
often require the artist to present expert testimony and statistical
and economic data. The resulting damage award may not justify
the expense of presenting the case.

• Eligibility to Receive Attorneys' Fees.   A copyright
owner who has registered his copyright in a timely manner is eligible to have the infringer pay the copyright owner's legal costs for
the copyright infringement lawsuit. If the alleged infringer is a
person or individual with adequate financial resources, an attorney
may agree to take the copyright infringement case on contingency.
An attorney working on contingency gets paid only if the copyright
owner receives a monetary payment from the infringer. Attorneys
generally only want to accept contingency cases if there is a high
probability of the case reaching a resolution where the attorney is
paid.

Without eligibility for attorneys' fees, the copyright owner may
not be able to interest an attorney in taking the case on contingency
and will have to pay out of pocket to obtain legal representation.
For a copyright owner with modest financial resources, the possibility of shifting your legal costs to a financially stable infringer
can be the deciding factor in whether you pursue or abandon a
legitimate infringement claim.

Importance of Timely Registration. Statutory damages and attorneys' fees are available only for those works registered in a timely
manner. Your copyright registration is timely if you

- register your work within three months of the publication date or

- register your published or unpublished work before the date
  copyright infringement begins.

The first test of timeliness is tied to the publication date. In general, a work is published if it is available for distribution to the general public. However, as discussed further in Section 3.6.3, pinpointing the date of publication is not always straightforward.

Resources for Registering Your Copyright. Copyright registration is generally a straightforward process. To register your copyright, you must send three items in the same package to the Copyright Office:

- A completed application. The Copyright Office has several different application forms for registering copyrights. The nature of your work determines which form you should use.

- Copies of your copyrighted work. The copies are referred to as a deposit. While the number of copies to be submitted varies depending on the status of the work, the requirement is usually one copy for unpublished works and two copies for published works.

- The filing fee which is currently $45.

You can find detailed forms and step-by-step instructions for registration of your copyright on the Copyright Office's website.

Group Registration. One way to avoid multiple filing fees is to register your unpublished works as a collection on one form. You may use group registration under the following circumstances:

- You assemble the elements in an orderly form for submission to the Copyright Office. For example, you might place all your unpublished sound recordings on one CD or all your unpublished short stories in one binder.

- The works included in the group have a single title that identifies the collection as a whole. For example, you might name your short stories Carla Brown's Short Stories, Spring 2008.

- The copyright owner of all the works in the collection is the same.

3.1.4. Alternatives to Copyright Registration

Copyright owners frequently ask about alternatives to formal copyright registration so this section includes a discussion of two of those alternatives:

- the poor man's copyright

- registration with the Writers' Guild of America

The Poor Man's Copyright. Has anyone ever told you to copyright your work by sending a copy of it to yourself by registered or certified mail – and then not opening the envelope? This is a technique often referred to as the "poor man's copyright". A variation on the poor man's copyright is having a copy of your work notarized.

The usefulness of these techniques as an alternative to formal copyright registration is questionable, and many attorneys frown on their use. These techniques do not establish a copyright in your work because as already discussed in Section 3.1.3, you have a valid copyright as soon as your work is fixed. Nor does a poor man's copyright provide any benefits you obtain from registering your copyright with the Copyright Office.

What a poor man's copyright may do is help you prove the date on which you created your work. This could be important if someone accuses you of copying. A poor man's copyright method might help you show that your work was created prior to the work of another person's and, as a result, show that you could not have copied from that person's work. Still, if you are trying to convince someone that you hold a valid copyright in a particular work, producing a certificate of registration issued by the Copyright Office is much more persuasive.

Registration with the Writers' Guild of America. The Writers' Guild of America (WGA) offers a script registration service for literary works. WGA membership is not required to use the service. While WGA registration establishes the completion date of your work which may be useful in a copyright infringement action, it does not provide any of the benefits of registration with the Copyright Office. Nevertheless, one might use WGA registration for treatments, outlines, story ideas, and similar materials that are normally not eligible for copyright protection.

Also, you might use WGA script registration as an intermediate step to keep unpublished material confidential until the material is ready for publication and registration with the Copyright Office. Deposits filed with the Copyright Office are available to the public. Material filed with the WGA is not.

3.2. The Copyright Owner's Rights

The Copyright Act lists six exclusive rights that a copyright owner has in his work. The exclusivity means that only the copyright owner, or a person authorized by the copyright owner, may exercise these rights.

3.2.1. Exclusive Right to Reproduce the Copyrighted Work in Copies or Phonorecords

The copyright owner has the exclusive right to make copies of his work. When you incorporate a copyrighted work into a production and then produce multiple copies of your production, you are making copies of the copyrighted work. For example, suppose you have written a book you plan to publish. Your book includes photographs taken by someone other than yourself. Each time you produce a copy of the book, you also make copies of the photographs inside your book. Normally, you need the permission of the copyright owner of those photographs in order to make copies.

The exclusive reproduction right mentions both copies and phonorecords. The term phonorecord is part of the Copyright Act's own special jargon and refers to audiocassettes, compact discs, and other physical objects onto which sound can be recorded. The "sound" on phonorecords typically consists of musical performances and spoken word performances.

3.2.2. Exclusive Right to Prepare Derivative Works Based on the Copyrighted Work

The copyright owner has the exclusive right to prepare derivative works. A derivative work is a new work based on or originating from another pre-existing work. You can think of a derivative work as a spin-off product or as an adaptation. For example, if you write new lyrics for the melody of a song or translate the song into another language, you have created a derivative work of the song.

3.2.3. Exclusive Right to Distribute Copies or Phonorecords of the Copyrighted Work to the Public.

The copyright owner has the exclusive right to sell or otherwise distribute copies of the copyrighted work. The exclusive right to distribute is distinct from the exclusive right to make copies.

Remember that book we discussed in Section 3.2.1 above – the one you published that includes photographs taken by someone other than yourself. In that example, the copyright owner of the photographs gave you permission to make copies of the photographs. That gives you the necessary authority to produce copies of your book. If you want to get your books - and the photographs inside - to the public, you also need permission to distribute the photographs.

As a producer clearing rights in a copyrighted work, you normally want permission both to reproduce and to distribute the work.

3.2.4. Exclusive Right to Perform the Copyrighted Work Publicly

The exclusive right of public performance is relevant only to works that can be performed. Such works include songs, plays, films and choreography. Note that the copyright owner does not have a right to control private performances of his work – only public performances. Disagreements on what constitutes a *public performance* versus what constitutes a *private performance* have sparked many lawsuits.

The Copyright Act describes a performance as public if the performance takes place before a number of people substantially larger than the number of people within a family circle. From that guidance, we can make the following statements with some certainty:

- There is no public performance when a family of four watches a DVD of a favorite film at home. While it is a performance of the DVD, it is a private and not a public performance.

- There is a public performance if I take the same DVD and show it to an auditorium filled with 300 strangers.

There are many situations that fall in between the two examples just described. It is those in-between situations that have motivated lawsuits concerning what qualifies as a public performance. Court opinions do tell us that there can be a public performance even if:

- attendees at the public performance must pay to enter;

- the performance takes place in a semi-public place such as a social club;

- only a small number of people actually hear or see the performance, as long as it is possible for a substantial number of people to have heard or seen the performance;

- the people viewing or hearing the performance are geographically dispersed as in the case of a radio broadcast received in numerous private homes; or

- the people see or hear the performance at different times as in the case of a performance rendered through a website.

3.2.5. Exclusive Right to Display the Copyrighted Work Publicly

The exclusive right to display a work in public is most relevant to visual creative works such as paintings and sculptures. The same guidelines regarding the meaning of "publicly" discussed under the exclusive public performance right in Section 3.2.4 apply to the public display right.

3.2.6. For Sound Recordings, the Exclusive Right to Perform the Copyrighted Work Publicly by Means of a Digital Audio Transmission

The exclusive right of public performance by means of digital audio transmission is applicable only to sound recordings. See Section 22.1 for a definition of sound recordings and an explanation of how they differ from songs. Copyright owners of sound recordings do not have an exclusive public performance right. This means that when a recording of a song is performed publicly, the copyright owner of the song is entitled to royalty income for that performance. The owner of the sound recording is not.

In 1995, Congress passed the Digital Performance Right and Sound Recordings Act which gave copyright owners of sound recordings a limited public performance right. The right applies only to public performances of sound recordings that are digitally transmitted. This right applies primarily to performances of sound recordings on the internet. See Sections 22.4 and 22.7.2 for further discussion of the sound recording public performance right.

3.3. What's Copyrightable?

Copyright protection subsists in original works of authorship fixed in any tangible medium of expression.

That language comes directly from the Copyright Act. Here's what it means in plain English.

The work must be original. The originality requirement does not mean that the work must be novel or unique. A work is original as long as the creator of the work did not copy it from another source. Copyright protection even covers a work that is similar or nearly identical to another work - provided that each of the works is created independently and is not copied from the other.

The work must be written down, recorded, or otherwise fixed. See Section 3.1.3 for a discussion of the requirement that a copyrighted work be fixed in a tangible medium of expression.

Some categories of works entitled to copyright protection are obvious. They include books, magazines, newspapers, poems, songs, plays, photographs, paintings, sculptures, films, and designs. Some categories of works entitled to copyright protection are less obvious. Below I discuss a few of the less obvious categories most relevant to media producers.

3.3.1. Letters Are Copyrightable

Copyright law protects letters, whether or not they are published. In most circumstances, the writer of the letter is the copyright owner of the letter. The recipient of the letter exercises control over the tangible copy which he may keep, sell, or discard. However, the recipient does not have the right to reproduce, publish, or exercise any of the copyright owner's other exclusive rights in the letter.

Media productions have been enjoined for including extensive verbatim passages of letters. For example, an unauthorized biography of J.D. Salinger was enjoined after the author included extensive verbatim passages of Salinger's unpublished letters without Salinger's permission. (*Salinger v. Random House*, 811 F.2d 90 (2nd Cir. 1987)).

3.3.2. Speeches Are Copyrightable

Speeches to the extent that they constitute original works of authorship and to the extent that they are fixed in a tangible medium of expression, are protected by copyright. This includes political speeches. The exception is the political speech that qualifies as a federal government work and is therefore in the public domain. See Section 3.9.4 for a discussion of federal government works and the public domain.

Accordingly, using any complete speech or a substantial excerpt thereof without the permission of the speech maker or speech writer may be copyright infringement. For example, Jesse Jackson obtained an injunction against the unauthorized distribution of video cassettes containing a recording of his entire 1988 Democratic National Convention speech. (*Jackson v. MPI Home Video*, 694 F. Supp. 483 (N.D. Ill. 1988)).

3.3.3. Fictional Characters Are Copyrightable

Fictional characters can be protected by copyright law. Most courts have ruled that characters are entitled to copyright protection outside of the work in which they appear. This means that you cannot freely take Forrest Gump, Mickey Mouse, Darth Vader, Harry Potter or Captain Kirk and incorporate that character into your production.

A smaller number of courts have ruled that fictional characters are only protected by copyright within the work in which they appear. In other words, it is the film or book or artwork that is protected as a whole - not the character independently. Under that view, you can place a Harry Potter-like character into your production without running afoul of copyright law - provided that your production does not include any copyrightable elements from the Harry Potter stories.

Fictional characters receiving copyright protection are characters that are well formed. The less developed the character, the less likely it is to be protected by copyright. Visually-expressed characters - such as animated characters and comic book characters - are more developed and, therefore, easier to protect under copyright law than characters that are expressed through words only.

Under certain circumstances, fictional characters may also be subject to trademark protection. See chapter 4 for a discussion of trademarks.

Examples of fictional characters protected by copyright

James Bond. James Bond is a copyright-protected character. Hence, a Honda commercial infringed the James Bond character when it lifted several aspects of James Bond films including plot, sequence, settings, pace, and dialogue style. Like James Bond, the character in the Honda commercial was a young, tuxedo-clad,

British-looking man with a beautiful woman at his side and with a grotesque villain in hot pursuit. Both James Bond and the Honda man exude uncanny calm under pressure and exhibit a dry sense of humor and wit. (*MGM v. Honda*, 900 F. Supp. 1287 (C.D. Cal. 1995)).

Rocky. A writer, who had prepared an extensive outline for a sequel to *Rocky,* sued Sylvester Stallone and MGM Studios when a sequel was made without his input. The writer lost the suit because the court found that his outline - which incorporates the characters created in the previous *Rocky* films – infringes those films and is not entitled to copyright protection. According to the court, the physical and emotional characteristics of Rocky Balboa and the other *Rocky* characters are set forth in tremendous detail in three previous *Rocky* movies and, as a result, are entitled to copyright protection. (*Anderson v. Stallone*, 91 U.S.P.Q.2d 1161 (C.D. Cal. 1989)).

Freddy Krueger. Freddy Krueger is a well-recognized character who is readily identifiable with the *Nightmare on Elm Street* films and thus copyrightable. He has distinctive physical traits which include a face scarred and distorted by severe burns, a battered fedora hat which partially obscures his burned face, and a dirty red and green striped sweater. He speaks in a low, rasping terrifying voice; and wears on his right hand a leather glove whose fingers consist of razor-sharp knives. According to a court, Freddy Krueger is a fictional character entitled to copyright protection. (*New Line Cinema Corp v. Bertlesman Music Group*, 693 F. Supp. 1517 (S.D.N.Y. 1988)).

3.4. What's Not Copyrightable?

Copyright protection is not available for everything. The Copyright Act specifically excludes ideas, procedures, processes, systems, methods of operation, concepts, principles, and discoveries. As a media producer, you should also know that facts, names, titles, scenes-a-faires, and stock characters are not copyrightable.

3.4.1. Ideas, Plots, and Concepts Are Not Copyrightable

Copyright law does not protect ideas, plots, or basic story concepts. It only protects the way in which those ideas are expressed or developed. Separating the "idea" from the "expression of the idea" is often subjective and not necessarily intuitive. Here are some examples that provide guidance of where the idea turns into the expression of the idea.

Switching Lives. Have you seen a movie in which a child and an adult magically switch bodies and live each others lives for a short period of time. During the experience, each gains a greater appreciation for the other's difficulties. That is an idea for a movie. The idea has been expressed in a number of different movies including *Freaky Friday, 18 Again!, Vice Versa, and Like Father, Like Son.*

Survivor versus I'm A Celebrity! CBS tried to stop ABC from airing its new reality show, *I'm a Celebrity! Get Me Out of Here* claiming that *I'm a Celebrity* is a celebrity version of the CBS hit show, *Survivor.* The court refused to issue the injunction finding that the programs had similarities but the similarities came from the fact that both shows were based on the idea of putting people in wilderness situations. The court also noted that the concept and feel of the shows was different and that *I'm A Celebrity* was already in development when *Survivor* first aired.

3.4.2. Facts Are Not Copyrightable

Facts by themselves are not copyrightable. Copyright protection requires at least a minimal level of originality. If you research and write down facts, the result of your efforts is not original. You did not independently create the facts. Hence, the facts by themselves are not subject to copyright protection regardless of the research time and effort you spent gathering them.

Separating Fact from Expression. Producers working on historical subjects must consciously separate non-copyrighable fact from copyrightable expression while preparing their productions. For example, to write a book or screenplay based on actual events, you might conduct research by reading existing books and other works covering the same events. While you can freely copy and use facts from those existing works, you can not take any of the copyrightable expression from the resource. Consider the following example.

A.A. Hoehling authored *Who Destroyed the Hindenburg?* Hoehling spent considerable effort reviewing investigative reports, articles and books and conducting interviews. Another author later published *The Hindenberg* covering the same series of events. *The Hindenberg* became the basis of a motion picture. Hoehling filed and lost a copyright infringement lawsuit. The second author had used only facts and other non-copyrightable elements from Hoehling's book. (*Hoehling v. Universal City Studios*, 618 F.2d 972 (2d Cir. 1980)).

The outcome would be different if the second author had used Hoehling's protectible expression. There can still be expression in the presentation of facts. With a historical or fact-based work, you are in danger of taking the expression if you copy verbatim or paraphrase very closely.

For example, author Jack Robinson infringed a fact-based work when he wrote *American Icarus: The Majestic Rise and Tragic Fall of Pan Am*, a manuscript about the rise and fall of Pan Am Airlines. Robinson used as a research source a biography of the Pan Am Airlines founder written by author Robert Daley. There was no problem with Robinson's use of factual and historical material from the biography.

However, Robinson used over twenty-five to thirty percent of the exact words and phrases from the biography, duplicating Daley's organization, writing style, punctuation, details, scenes, events, and characterizations. (*Robinson v. Random House*, 877 F. Supp. 830 (S.D.N.Y. 1995)).

Compilation of Facts May Be Protectible. A group of facts may be protected as a compilation. A compilation is a collection of pre-existing materials that are selected, coordinated, or arranged in such a way that the resulting work as a whole constitutes an original work of authorship. A compilation copyright protects the manner and order in which the facts are presented - but not the individual facts themselves.

3.4.3. Names, Titles and Short Phrases Are Not Copyrightable

Names, titles, and short phrases lack the originality and creativity required for copyright protection. Although they have no protection under copyright law, under certain conditions, names, titles, and short phrases may be protected by trademark law. See the discussion in Section 4.4.1

3.4.4. Scenes-A-Faire and Stock Characters Are Not Copyrightable

Scenes-a-faire are incidents or settings that naturally flow from a common theme, setting or plot premise. Stock characters are similar in concept. They are stereotypical characters that you expect to encounter in a particular genre of work.

For example, how many of the following elements were in the last action movie that you saw or thriller that you read?

- a protagonist with an objective that must be achieved by a set deadline in order to prevent the end of the world, an assassination, or other catastrophe
- a villain with a nefarious scheme
- a character who is affiliated with the police department, military, government or other para-military organization
- a chase scene
- an explosion
- a physical fight between the protagonist and the villain
- the betrayal of the protagonist by a close friend or co-worker who is actually working with the bad guys

These are scenes-a-faire and stock characters for an action story. You expect to encounter one or more of these elements in any action story you read or see.

3.4.5. Procedures and Processes Are Not Copyrightable

Procedures and processes are not copyrightable. If you write down a list of the steps for an activity, your written list is not copyrightable. For example, a recipe that lists ingredients and basic cooking directions is not protected by copyright.

3.4.6. Pre-1972 Sound Recordings Are Not Copyrightable

See Section 22.1 for a definition of sound recording and an explanation of how they differ from songs. With the exception of certain foreign sound recordings, there is no federal copyright protection for sound recordings made prior to February 15, 1972. However, this does not necessarily mean you are free to use any pre-1972 sound recording in any way you please. Pre-1972 sound recordings can still be protected by state law - either statutory or common law. Potential protection varies by state and comes in a number of forms including unfair competition, common law copyright, misappropriation of property, and anti-bootlegging laws.

3.5. Copyright Infringement

3.5.1. What Is Copyright Infringement?

Copyright infringement occurs when someone exercises one of the copyright holder's exclusive rights without permission. All the following activities, if done without the permission of the copyright owner, are copyright infringement:

- downloading a song from an unauthorized website
- playing CDs at a club open to the public if the club does not have a public performance license

- using the image of a copyrighted painting as the cover of a popular novel

- translating an English-language book into German and distributing copies of the German translation

3.5.2. Proving Infringement

To win a copyright infringement lawsuit, the copyright owner must prove that

- he is the valid owner of the copyright in the work,

- the work is original,

- the alleged infringer copied protectible elements of the work, and

- there is a substantial degree of similarity between the copyright owner's work and the alleged infringer's work.

Ownership of the Copyright. This it where prior copyright registration pays off. When you register a copyright, the Copyright Office issues you a certificate of ownership which is presumptive evidence you own the copyright in the work. As discussed above in Section 3.1.3, registration is not required for you to have a valid copyright. Registration is required before you can file a lawsuit alleging copyright infringement.

Copying of the Work. The accused infringer must have copied protectible elements from the work. Most claims of copying fall into one of two categories - verbatim copying or substantial similarity.

Verbatim Copying. With verbatim copying, it is normally easy to ascertain whether copying took place. The producer is accused of incorporating the copyright owner's material into his own work without authorization. The material might be artwork, a song, a poem, a film clip, or something else. For example, it may be one of the following situations:

- A character from the producer's production recites a copyrighted poem.
- The producer's CD contains a sample from a copyrighted song.
- The producer's book contains copyrighted photographs.
- The producer's website includes a copyrighted article.

Assuming that the incorporated material is in fact copyrightable material, the only question in determining the producer's liability is whether the producer's unauthorized use qualifies for fair use or for another exception to copyright protection. I discuss these exceptions to copyright protection in Section 3.9.

Substantial Similarity. Instead of incorporating a verbatim copy of the copyright owner's material, a producer may borrow some expressive elements from the copyrighted work. If the producer ends up with a production that is substantially similar to the copyright owner's work, the producer is liable for copyright infringement. Proving infringement claims based on substantial similarity is less straightforward than proving copyright infringement based on verbatim copying. The next Section contains an in-depth discussion of substantial similarity.

3.5.3. More About Substantial Similarity

Without verbatim copying, to prove copyright infringement, the copyright owner must show that

- the producer had access to the copyright owner's work, and
- the similarities between the copyright owner's work and the producer's work are substantial.

When Does Substantial Similarity Exist? Substantial similarity exists if the average person recognizes the copy as being taken from the copyrighted work. The existence of substantial similarity is dependent on the particular circumstances of each situation.

Which Version of the Work Is Relevant? Many producers generate draft or intermediate versions prior to the completion of the version that is ultimately released. Which version is relevant for the purposes of copyright infringement claims? Typically, the distributed version is the version a court examines when determining substantial similarity. There are cases that apply this strategy to films. The same strategy would likely be applied to other types of productions. A court weighing substantial similarity generally ignores preliminary or intermediate versions.

Similarities between the copyrighted work and earlier versions of the production are relevant when determining whether the alleged infringer had access to the work.

What If There Are Similarities and Differences? There may be both similarities and differences between your production and a copyrighted work. The fact that there are differences does not necessarily cancel out the fact that there are similarities. Sometimes, with a fact-based work, trivial differences are enough to avoid infringement. For other works that are very creative, even significant differences are not enough to avoid copyright infringement.

Examples of Substantial Similarity Cases. Here are some real-life examples of cases in which courts looked at the question of substantial similarity. Note in particular the factors that influenced each court's decision.

Starman and Wavelength. *(Wavelength Film Company v. Columbia Pictures Industries, 631 F. Supp. 305 (N.D. IL 1986))*

Situation: *Wavelength* is a 1983 film. *Starman* is a 1984 film. Both movies focus on aliens who are stranded on earth and are being pursued by hostile governmental authorities. In both films, the aliens eventually return home with the help of friendly humans. The *Wavelength* producers sued the *Starman* producers for copyright infringement.

Court Ruling: *Starman* does not infringe *Wavelength*. The court ruled that no reasonable jury could find the two motion pictures to be substantially similar and dismissed the case before it reached the trial stage.

What Factors Influenced the Court:

- The alien characters are portrayed differently. In *Starman*, there is one alien, a man in his mid-thirties who communicates verbally and speaks fifty-two languages. In *Wavelength*, there are three aliens who are pre-teen children who communicate only telepathically.

- In *Starman*, the alien develops a mature love relationship with the lead human protagonist. In *Wavelength*, the aliens develop a parent-child relationship with the lead protagonists.

- In *Starman*, the action takes place throughout the western portion of the United States. In *Wavelength*, all action takes place in California.

- In *Wavelength*, the three aliens murder several people. In *Starman*, the alien harms no one and, in fact, restores life to his lover and to a dead animal.

- Many of the similarities described by the *Wavelength* producers as copying are actually unprotectible as scenes-a-faire. The scenes-a-faire for a motion picture about a stranded alien include the alien arriving on earth in a spaceship, humans showing fear of the alien, governmental authorities pursuing the alien, humans befriending and helping the alien, and the alien leaving earth on a spaceship.

Fort Apache (a book) and Fort Apache, The Bronx (a movie)
(Walker v. Time Life Films, Inc., 784 F.2d 44 (2nd Cir 1986)).

Situation: *Fort Apache* is a book published in 1976 loosely based on the author's real-life experiences. *Fort Apache, The Bronx* is a 1981 film. Both works recount the experiences of policemen battling the violence and urban decay of the 41st Precinct of the New York City Police Department, nicknamed Fort Apache. The book's author sued the producers of the film for copyright infringement.

Court Ruling: The book and film are not substantially similar. The court dismissed the case without a trial.

What Factors Influenced the Court:

- The court concluded that differences in the plot and structure far outweigh similarities. The film revolves around several interrelated story lines including a manhunt for a police killer, a police officer's affair with a drug addicted nurse, and the moral dilemmas of officers. The book is in diary form and moves from one event to another with little plot or story line.

- Many of the similarities alleged by the book's author are unprotectible as scenes-a-faire. According to the court, scenes-a-faire for a work about police officers in a high-crime urban area include the depiction of cockfights, drunks, stripped cars, prostitutes and rats; Irish-American policemen who frequently drink; disgruntled police officers; and foot chases of fleeing criminals.

- The book is an account of actual events. Actual events are facts which are not copyrightable.

Star Wars and Battlestar Galactica. *(Twentieth Century-Fox Film v. MCA,* 715 F.2d 1327 (9th Cir. 1983)).

Situation: *Star Wars* is a 1977 film. *Battlestar Galactica* is a film and television series released in 1978. Both *Star Wars* and *Battlestar Galactica* take place in the fictitious future in which democratic rebels battle a totalitarian regime in an intergalactic war. The *Star Wars* producers sued for copyright infringement.

Court Ruling: The court concluded that reasonable minds could differ on whether the similarities in the two films are substantial. The case was sent to trial.

What Factors Influenced the Court: The court did not make a determination on whether there was substantial similarity. It left that question to a jury. Here are some of the similarities alleged by the *Star Wars* producers in their legal documents:

- The central conflict of each story is a war between the galaxy's democratic and totalitarian forces.

- In *Star Wars* the young hero's father had been a leader of the democratic forces, and the present leader of the democratic forces is a father figure to the young hero. In *Battlestar*, the young hero's father is a leader of the democratic forces.

- An entire planet, central to the existence of the democratic forces, is destroyed.

- The heroine is imprisoned by the totalitarian forces.

- There is a romance between the hero's friend (a cynical fighter pilot) and the daughter of one of the leaders of the democratic forces.

- A friendly robot, who aids the democratic forces is severely injured (*Star Wars*) or destroyed (*Battlestar*) by the totalitarian forces.

- There is a scene in a cantina (*Star Wars*) or casino (*Battlestar*) in which musical entertainment is offered by bizarre, non-human creatures.

- The climax consists of an attack by the democratic fighter pilots on the totalitarian headquarters.

- Each work ends with an awards ceremony in honor of the democratic heroes.

Jaws and The Last Jaws/Great White. *(Universal City Studios v. Film Ventures,* 543 F. Supp. 1134 (D.C. Cal. 1982)).

Situation: *Jaws* is a book by Peter Benchley published in 1974 and subsequently made into a 1975 film. *Great White* is a film released around 1980. Both *Jaws* and *Great White* tell the story of a great white shark which terrorizes the inhabitants of a coastal town on the Atlantic seaboard. The *Jaws* producers sued the *Great White* producers for copyright infringement.

Court Ruling: There is substantial similarity in the basic story lines, the major characters, the sequence of events, and the interplay and development of the characters and the plot. The court granted a preliminary injunction prohibiting further exhibition of *Great White* and impounding all copies of the film.

What Factors Influenced the Court:

- All the major characters in *Great White* have substantially parallel characters in *Jaws*. Major characters include a local politician who plays down the news of the shark in the interest of local tourism, a salty-English accented skipper, and a local shark expert.

- The movies contain several parallel scenes:

   o The shark bumps a boat and knocks a child into the water who is subsequently rescued before the shark attacks him.

   o An empty boat of a local fisherman killed by the shark

is found floating in the water by the major characters who warn the politician about the dangers of the shark.

o There is a false shark alarm caused by a broken surfboard which looks like the fin of a shark (*Great White*) and a bathing cap which looks like the head of a shark (*Jaws*).

o The shark attacks a dinghy and is shown consuming the occupant.

o The characters attempt to capture the shark by lowering raw meat off the pier which results in the shark grabbing the meat and breaking off part of the pier.

o Both movies conclude with the shark being killed by the detonation of an explosive which the shark has swallowed.

PAC-MAN and K.C. Munchkin. (*Atari v. North American,* 672 F.2d 607 (7th Cir. 1982)).

Situation: PAC-MAN and K.C. Munchkin are both video games in which the player guides a central character, called the gobbler, through a maze. Monster-characters pursue the gobbler through the maze and the gobbler must avoid colliding with them. The player accumulates points as the gobbler gobbles dots, power capsules, fruit symbols, and monsters. PAC-MAN was introduced into the arcade market in 1980. KC Munchkin was introduced into the retail market in 1981. The makers of PAC-MAN sued the makers of K.C. Munchkin for copyright infringement and other claims.

Court Ruling: Despite variations in the appearance of the maze and the characters, there is substantial similarity between PAC-MAN and KC Munchkin. The court issued a preliminary injunction forbidding further distribution of K.C. Munchkin.

What Factors Influenced the Court: The court found substantial similarity in the video games' characters and plot structures including the following similarities:

- The main character of both games is a gobbler. The gobbler is round (yellow in PAC-MAN and blue-green in K.C. Munchkin) with a V-shaped mouth which opens and closes in mechanical fashion as it travels the maze.

- Both games have monsters (four in PAC-MAN and three in K.C. Munchkin) that roam in centipede fashion on three "limbs" throughout the maze and chase the gobbler. They are about equal in size to the gobbler, but are shaped like bell jars.

- The monsters have highly animated eyes, which "look" in the direction the monster is moving.

- The monsters are stationed inside a corral portion of the maze and exit into the maze at the start of the game.

- If captured by a monster, both the Munchkin gobbler and the PAC-MAN gobbler fold back and disappear by exploding into a star-burst.

- When the gobbler consumes an object called a power capsule, there is a role reversal in which the gobbler turns into the hunter, and the monsters become vulnerable. Upon a role reversal, the monsters reverse direction and turn blue (PAC-MAN) or purple (K.C. Munchkin).

- When this period of vulnerability is about to end, the monsters warn the player by flashing a different color alternately blue and white in PAC-MAN and its original color in K.C. Munchkin.

- If the gobbler catches a monster, the monster's body disappears, and the player sees only its eyes (PAC-MAN) or eyes and feet (K.C. Munchkin).

- It is possible for an "eaten" monster to regenerate and again become a threat to the gobbler.

Mohawk Manhattan. *(Kerr v. New Yorker Magazine*, 63 F. Supp 2d 320 (S.D.N.Y. 1999)).

Situation: Artists, Thomas Kerr and Anita Kunz, separately prepared pictures depicting a male figure with a Mohawk haircut in the shape of the Manhattan skyline. Kerr's drawing, *New York Hairline*, appeared in various newspapers and postcards. Illustrator Anita Kunz later prepared a drawing *Manhattan Mohawk* which appeared on a cover of *New Yorker Magazine*. Kerr sued Kunz and *New Yorker Magazine* for copyright infringement.

Court Ruling: There is no copyright infringement. Although based on the same idea of a male figure with a skyline, the drawings are not substantially similar.

What Factors Influenced the Court: The court found the expressions of the idea to be completely different and specifically noted the following:

- Kerr's image is in black-and-white and made with pen and ink and crosshatching. Kunz's image is in color, with a fully-realized background.

- Kerr's figure appears in three-quarter profile, with two eyes visible, and meets the viewer's eyes. Kunz's figure appears in a true profile, with only one eye visible and looks downward.

- Kerr's figure wears a leather jacket and goatee giving him an aggressive and street smart appearance. Kunz's image has very smooth lines and rounded contours.

- The buildings that make up Kunz's skyline appear in a different order, and they are more differentiated than the buildings in Kerr's skyline.

- Kunz's figure wears four earrings and a chain stretching from a pierced nostril to its ear and has bare, non-realistically sloped shoulders. Kerr's figure is more conservative in appearance.

3.6. How Long Does a Copyright Last?

Copyrights do not last forever. Once the copyright expires, the work falls into the public domain and anyone may use it without authorization from the creator. Determining the copyright duration of a work can be tricky because copyright law has changed many times. As a result of these changes, different copyright durations apply to different works depending upon the specific work's date of publication or date of creation.

3.6.1. Current Copyright Act

A copyright in a work created on or after January 1, 1978, lasts for the life of the author plus seventy years. For works created as a work made for hire or created anonymously or under a pseudonym, the copyright lasts for the shorter of 95 years from first publication or 120 years from creation. For an explanation of a work made for hire, see Section 19.3.1.

3.6.2. 1909 Copyright Act

The 1909 Copyright Act governs the duration of copyright in works created prior to January 1, 1978. Under the 1909 Copyright Act, a copyright lasted for an initial term of twenty-eight years. Copyright owners could renew the term for an additional period of twenty-eight years. To keep up with changes in the current Copyright Act, the duration of the 1909 Copyright Act renewal term increased and is currently sixty-seven years. The initial term of twenty-eight years plus the current renewal term of sixty-seven years combine to give works created prior to 1978 a potential copyright duration of up to ninety-five years.

Renewal for works published prior to 1964 required that the copyright owner file a renewal application. Renewal is automatic for works published between 1964 and 1977.

The following chart summarizes copyright duration.

Creation/Publication Date of the Work	Duration of Copyright
Created on or after Jan. 1, 1978	Life of author plus 70 years [1]
Published between 1964 - 1977	28 years plus 67-year automatic extension for a total of 95 years [2]
Published between 1923 - 1963	28 years plus 67-year potential renewal term for a total of up to 95 years

[1] The shorter of 95 years from first publication or 120 years from creation for works made for hire, anonymous and pseudonymous works.

[2] If the copyright owner does not file a renewal application filed, the work falls into the public domain after the initial 28-year period.

3.6.3. Publication

Publication within copyright law can be a complicated concept. In order for a work to be considered published, the copyright owner must authorize the publication and make multiple copies of the work available to the public. The public performance or public display of a work does not necessarily qualify as a publication of the work.

Publication is most significant for works created prior to 1978 and initially governed by the 1909 Copyright Act. Under the 1909 Copyright Act, federal copyright protection normally began upon publication of the work. In contrast, under the current Copyright Act, copyright protection begins upon creation of the work.

Nevertheless, publication does maintain some significance for works created under the current Copyright Act. For purposes of rights clearance, the most significant impact of publication on works created after 1978 includes the following:

- A work created prior to March 1, 1989 is in the public domain if it was published without proper copyright notice. However, the copyright owner could save the work from the public domain if she implemented one of the saving provisions listed in the Copyright Act.

- The duration of the copyright in certain works is tied to the publication date. The duration of copyrights in works made for hire and in works published anonymously or under a pseudonym is either 95 years from first publication or 120 years from creation, whichever period is shorter.

Real-Life Example Illustrating Importance of Publication Date. Here is a real-life copyright dispute in which the publication date became crucial. Folk artist Woodie Guthrie is the composer of the song, "This Land Is Your Land". In 2004, two brothers, Gregg and Evan Spiridellis, working as JibJab Media produced and widely distributed via the internet a short film in which animated figures of President George W. Bush and Democratic Presidential candidate, John Kerry, traded insults to the tune of "This Land Is Your Land". Ludlow Music which claimed the exclusive copyright to "This Land Is Your Land", objected to the use and sent a series of cease and desist letters to JibJab.

JibJab initiated a lawsuit in which it requested the court to rule that the use of "This Land Is Your Land" in the short Bush-Kerry film is protected by the First Amendment and the Fair Use Doctrine. JibJab and Ludlow Music settled the suit before the court ever made a ruling.

A dispute over the song's publication date lead to the settlement. According to JibJab's argument, "This Land Is Your Land" entered the public domain in the 1970s. Since Woody Guthrie wrote the song in 1940, it falls under the 1909 Copyright Act. Under the 1909 Copyright Act, copyrights lasted for an initial term of twenty-eight years beginning on the date of publication. Copyright owners who filed a timely renewal application could extend the duration of the copyright for a subsequent term.

JibJab argues that Guthrie's sale in 1945 of the song as sheet music was a publication which triggered the initial copyright term. An initial term commencing in 1945 would expire twenty-eight years later in 1973. There was no renewal application filed for the song in 1973. Under this analysis, "This Land Is Your Land" fell into the public domain in 1973.

Ludlow argues that the copyright term began on the copyright registration filing date in 1956. An initial term commenced in 1956 would expire in 1984. Ludlow filed a renewal application for the song in 1984. As discussed in Section 3.6, works published between 1923 and 1963 have a renewal term of 67 years if the copyright owner files a timely registration. Under Ludlow's analysis, "This Land Is Your Land" is protected by copyright until 2051.

Despite its argument, Ludlow still chose to settle the lawsuit without a trial. As part of the settlement, JibJab remains free to continue distributing the animation. (*JibJab Media v. Ludlow Music*, Complaint filed in N.D. Cal. July 29, 2004).)

3.7. Fair Use of Copyrighted Works

The Fair Use Doctrine allows you to use a reasonable portion of a copyrighted work without running afoul of copyright law. Within all areas of media, there is constant debate over when a particular use qualifies as a fair use.

3.7.1. Fair Use Four Factor Test

There is no bright line rule to determine what qualifies as fair use. Instead, courts use a four-factor test to make the determination. No single factor is determinative.

Factor One: Purpose and Character of the Use. The first factor is the purpose and character of the use. When claiming fair use, how you use the work is important.

Favored Uses for Fair Use. The Copyright Act lists favored uses for fair use. The favored uses are criticism, comment, news reporting, teaching, scholarship and research. While each activity on this favored list is not always a non-profit use, the list does strongly hint at copyright law's preference that fair use be for non-profit purposes. The Copyright Act's list of favored uses serves only as an example of purposes for which fair use is most appropriate. Keep the following in mind:

- A non-profit use does not guarantee your use is a fair use.

- A for-profit or commercial use does not guarantee your use is not a fair use.

- A use on the favored use list does not guarantee your use is a fair use.

- A use outside the favored use list does not guarantee that your use is not a fair use.

Even if your unauthorized use fits into one of the favored use-categories listed in the Copyright Act, you must still weigh the remaining three factors for each individual case of fair use.

Transformative Use. Copyright law favors uses that are transformative. Your use of a copyrighted work is transformative if your use is creatively different from the way in which the copyright owner used it. As a general rule, the transformed work can not serve as a substitute for the original work. Here are some examples of uses that might be considered transformative:

Original Work	Transformative Use
video	using a clip of the video with voice-over narration to provide illustrative or historical context for a point you are making
photography	using low-resolution, thumbnail of photograph as part of an online index
book	creating a parody of the book

magazine cover	a commemorative poster containing thumbnail pictures of hundreds of previous magazine covers

Factor Two: Nature of the Copyrighted Work. There is a hierarchy of copyright protection. Some works are closer to the core of intended copyright protection than others. The more originality and creativity embodied in a work, the more protection it enjoys. An animated cartoon and a symphony are examples of works that might fall at the top of the hierarchy and receive the most protection copyright has to offer. Fact-based works like encyclopedias and biographies are at the bottom of this hierarchy and are sometimes referred to as having thin copyrights.

Copyright law also draws a distinction between published works and unpublished works. An author has a right to control the first publication of her work. As a result, the scope of fair use is narrower for unpublished works than for published works.

Here are some broad generalizations that you can apply to your analysis of factor two of the fair use test:

- Your use of a fact-based work stands a better chance of being viewed as a fair use than your use of a highly creative work.

- Your use of a work with limited availability stands a better chance of being viewed as a fair use than your use of a work that is widely available.

Factor Three: Amount of the Work Used. There is a copyright myth that you are in a fair use safe harbor if you use fewer than eight bars of a song or fewer than 250 words of a book or fewer than five seconds of a film. This is untrue! Use of a small amount of a copyrighted work has been deemed by courts as infringement. There is no set amount of a copyrighted work that guarantees fair use. However, it is true that the less of a copyrighted work you use, the more inclined a court will be to view your use as a fair use.

The quality of what you take is just as important as the quantity. If you use the best part, the most notable part, or the most famous part of a copyrighted work, your use may be viewed as infringement even though you may have used only a small portion of the copyrighted work. In the fair use analysis, the best part of the copyrighted work is often referred to as the heart of the work.

Factor Four: Effect on the Copyright Owner's Ability to Market the Work. If your use competes with the original copyrighted work or damages the copyright owner's ability to market the work, your use is less likely to be viewed as a fair use.

An Extra Factor: Good Faith. While it is not one of the four factors listed in the Copyright Act, the Fair Use Doctrine does carry an underlying principle of good faith and fair dealing. Fair use claimants who employ deception do not favorably impress courts.

3.7.2. Fair Use Four-Factor Test In Action

Elvis Presley Documentary. (*Elvis Presley Enterprises v. Passport Video*, 349 F.3d 622 (9th Cir. 2003)).

   Situation: Passport Entertainment produced *The Definitive Elvis*, a sixteen-hour video series chronicling the life of Elvis Presley. The video series, which retailed for $99, included copyrighted video, pictures and music including footage from the *Ed Sullivan Show* and the *Steve Allen Show*. The producer did not obtain authorization for inclusion of the copyrighted material. Various copyright owners sued the producer

   Court Ruling: The video infringes a number of copyrighted works. The court issued an injunction prohibiting additional sales of the video series.

Court's Application of the Four Fair Use Factors:

- Factor One. Purpose and Character of the Use: The use is commercial and only somewhat transformative. The use of a few seconds of video clips used for reference purposes while a narrator or interviewees explain their context in Elvis' career is transformative. In contrast, the use of over one minute of Elvis' *Hound Dog* performance is an entertainment use and not a transformative use.

- Factor Two. Nature of the Copyrighted Work: Although some of the footage might be classified as newsworthy, the photos, music, and portions of the television footage used in the documentary are creative in nature and, as a result, eligible for a high degree of copyright protection.

- Factor Three. Amount of the Work Used: The documentary uses substantial amounts of several works including almost all of Elvis' appearance on the *Steve Allen Show* and 35% of Elvis' appearance on the *Ed Sullivan Show*.

- Factor Four. Market Effect: The court was more concerned with the market effect on the film and television clips than it was about the market effect on the still photos and music. In the court's view, the documentary could serve as a substitute for footage of Elvis. Furthermore, in its marketing material, Passport said every film and television appearance of Elvis is represented, suggesting that the documentary could replace the original film and television programming.

The Seinfeld Aptitude Test. (*Castle Rock Entertainment v. Carol Publishing Group*, 150 F.3d 132 (2nd Cir. 1998)).

Situation: Carol Publishing Group published *The Seinfeld Aptitude Test*, a trivia quiz book by Beth Golub about the television series *Seinfeld*. The 132-page book contains 643 trivia questions, each based on a fictional situation in a *Seinfeld* episode. For example, one question asks "What candy does Kramer snack on while observing a surgical procedure from an operating-room balcony?"

The *Seinfeld* producers sued for copyright infringement.

Court Ruling: The *Seinfeld Aptitude Test* infringes the *Seinfeld* television series. The court issued an injunction preventing further distribution of the book. Defendants paid the *Seinfeld* producers $403,000 in damages.

Court's Application of the Four Fair Use Factors:

• Factor One. Purpose and Character of the Use: The book has no transformative use. Instead of commenting on or analyzing *Seinfeld*, it merely repackages the television program in quiz book form to entertain *Seinfeld* fans.

• Factor Two. Nature of the Copyrighted Work: *Seinfeld* episodes are creative and fictional and are at the top of the hierarchy for copyright protection.

• Factor Three. Amount of the Work Used: The trivia book takes too much material from the television program. The 132-page book contains 643 trivia questions drawing from 84 of the 86 *Seinfeld* episodes that had been broadcast at the time. As an instructional aside, the court noted that a book drawing material and a few fragments of dialogue from each of 84 television programs - perhaps comprising the entire season line-up on broadcast television - might qualify as a fair use.

• Factor Four. Market Effect: The book potentially competes with the copyrighted work. It fills a market niche that the *Seinfeld* producers might want to develop themselves or license others to develop.

President Ford's Memoirs. (*Harper & Row v. Nation Enterprises*, 471 U.S. 539 (1985)).

Situation: Publishers, Harper & Row, and Reader's Digest planned to release *A Time to Heal: The Autobiography of Gerald R. Ford*. Prior to the book's release date, *Nation*, a political commentary magazine, acquired a copy of the manuscript from an undisclosed source. Using the manuscript, *Nation* printed an article about Ford's pardon of Nixon scooping an article scheduled to appear in *Time Magazine*. The 2,250 word *Nation* article used between 300 and 400 words of verbatim quotes from the manuscript. Harper & Row sued *Nation* for copyright infringement.

Court Ruling: The case went all the way to the U.S. Supreme Court which concluded that *Nation*'s use of verbatim quotes from the manuscript was copyright infringement and not a fair use.

Court's Application of the Four Fair Use Factors:

- Factor One. Purpose and Character of the Use: Although *Nation* used the quotes for news reporting, the court gave more weight to what it viewed as *Nation*'s bad faith. *Nation* had knowingly used a stolen copy of the manuscript to scoop the authorized first publication of the book.

- Factor Two. Nature of the Copyrighted Work: *Nation*'s fair use argument was weakened because it used an unpublished work. Quotations that might qualify as fair use in a review of a published work may not be fair use in the review of an unpublished work.

- Factor Three. Amount of the Work Used: Although the *Nation* article used only 300 - 400 words of an entire book, those words comprised the heart and most interesting parts of Ford's memoirs and served as the focus of the entire *Nation* article.

- Factor Four. Market Effect: *Nation*'s unauthorized use had a direct impact on Harper & Row's ability to market the manuscript. *Time Magazine* had agreed to pay Harper & Row $25,000 for the exclusive right to print an excerpt about Ford's pardon of Nixon. After the *Nation* article appeared, *Time Magazine* cancelled its license agreement with Harper & Row.

Using Thumbnails of Full-Sized Photos. (*Kelly v. Arriba Soft, Corp.* 280 F.3d 934, (9th Cir. 2002)); opinion later withdrawn and replaced by 336 F.3d 811 (9th Cir. 2003)).

Situation: Arriba Soft Corp. operates an internet search engine that displays its results in the form of small pictures rather than as text. Arriba obtained its database of pictures by copying images from other web sites. Visitors to Arriba's search engine could access the full-sized photo by clicking on the thumbnail. Arriba provided access to the full-sized photo by inline linking or framing the originating site. As a result, although the image was directly from the originating web site and not copied onto Arriba's site, the user typically would not realize that the image actually resided on another web site. The Arriba database included photos by Leslie Kelly, a professional photographer who specializes in images of the American West. Kelly sued Arriba for copyright infringement.

Court Ruling: The court considered the use of the thumbnail images separately from the use of the full-sized images. The creation and use of the thumbnails in the search engine is a fair use. The display of the full-sized image is a violation of Kelly's exclusive right to publicly display his works.

Court's Application of the Four Fair Use Factors:

- Factor One. Purpose and Character of the Use: Thumbnail use was transformative. Arriba's search engine functions as a tool to help index and improve access to images on the internet. The thumbnail images do not serve as a substitute for Kelly's images because they are of much lower resolution. In contrast, the full-sized images Arriba provided could serve as a substitute for Kelly's original work.

- Factor Two. Nature of the Copyrighted Work: Kelly's works are creative.

- Factor Three. Amount of the Work Used: Arriba used the entire work. This was reasonable within the context of creating a picture-based index. It was not reasonable in displaying a full-sized copy of the work.

- Factor Four. Market Effect: Kelly uses his photographs to attract traffic to his web site where he sells advertising space as well as books and travel packages. In addition, Kelly sells and licenses his photographs to other web sites and to a stock photo database, which then offer the images to its customers. Arriba's use of thumbnail versions of Kelly's images did not harm the market for Kelly's images or the value of his images. Arriba's offering of full-sized versions of Kelly's images did compete with and harm the market for Kelly's images. With access to the full-sized photos through Arriba, people had no need to visit Kelly's website.

Other Noteworthy Aspects of this Case: The court later decided that it should not have addressed the issue of the full-size images for legal technical reasons. Neither Arriba nor Kelly had requested a judgment on the full-sized images. The court withdrew its opinion and replaced it with one that rendered no analysis on the full-size images. Nevertheless, the court's analysis in the original opinion provides valuable insight on how a court would apply the Fair Use Doctrine to the use of full-sized photos on the internet.

3.8. Parody of Copyrighted Works

3.8.1. What Is Parody?

Copyright law defines parody as a form of commentary that borrows liberally from an existing work to produce a new work that, at least in part, makes fun of the existing work. To qualify as a parody, your commentary must be about the existing work or its author. If you are borrowing from one work in order to comment about something else, the result is satire – not parody – and may be copyright infringement of the work from which you borrow.

3.8.2. Applying the Four-Factor Fair Use Test to Parody

I discussed the Fair Use Doctrine and the four-factor fair use test in Section 3.7. You may wish to review that section. Courts apply the same four-factor test to cases involving parody. The nature of parody requires that the test be more flexible.

Factor One: Purpose and Character of the Use. The Copyright Act lists favored uses for fair use. The favored uses are criticism, comment, news reporting, teaching, scholarship and research. While the list does not specifically include parody, parody is a form of commentary and criticism. Courts consider parody as a favored use under fair use.

Courts applying the fair use test favor uses that are transformative and can not serve as substitutes for the original work. By their very nature, parodic works are transformative. They are new works originating from pre-existing works and are typically poor substitutes for the original work they critique.

Factor Two: Nature of the Copyrighted Work. There is a hierarchy of copyright protection. Highly creative works are at the top of the hierarchy and receive the most copyright protection. Fact- based works receive less protection. Whether a work is highly creative or fact-based holds less significance in a parody case because parodies almost invariably copy popular, well-known, highly, creative works.

Factor Three: Amount of the Work Used. The producer of a parody can be more liberal in the amount borrowed from a copyrighted work. The parody should borrow just enough to conjure up the original in the minds of the audience. Copyright law is often more forgiving of parodies that use the heart, best part or most famous part of the copyrighted work. Copyright law recognizes that the heart is the section that most readily makes the audience think of the copyrighted work.

Factor Four: Effect of Use on the Copyright Owner's Ability to Market the Work. Typically, the parody is not a replacement for the copyrighted work. Copyright owners often claim that the parody damages the reputation of their works and thus affects the ability to market it. This argument is usually unsuccessful.

3.8.3. Examples of Real-Life Parody Cases

The Pretty Woman Case. (*Campbell v. Acuff-Rose Music*, 510 U.S. 569 (1994)).

Situation: Roy Orbison and William Dees are the writers of the classic rock ballad, *Oh, Pretty Woman*. In 1989, 2 Live Crew, a popular rap music group, released a song called *Pretty Woman* on its *As Clean As They Wanna Be* album. 2 Live Crew referred to the song as a parody of the Orbison/Dees 1964 hit. Prior to releasing the album, 2 Live Crew requested a license for the use of the song. Even though 2 Live Crew offered to give all authorship and credit for the parody to Dees and Orbison and to pay a license fee for the use, Acuff-Rose, the music publisher, refused to grant the license. 2 Live Crew released the song anyway. Acuff-Rose sued the group and its record company, Luke Skyywalker Records, for copyright infringement.

Court Ruling: This case went all the way to the U.S. Supreme Court which ruled that 2 Live Crew's version of the song could be protected as a parody.

Court's Application of the Four Factors:

- Factor One. Purpose and Character of the Use: 2 Live Crew's version does comment on and criticize the Dees and Orbison original. The original contains the romantic musings of a lonely man who spots a pretty woman walking down the street. The 2 Live Crew version adds to those musings degrading taunts and a bawdy demand for sex. 2 Live Crew's version can be taken as a comment on the naivete of the original and a rejection of its sentiment.

- Factor Two. Nature of the Copyrighted Work: Dees and Orbison's *Pretty Woman* is a creative work.

- Factor Three. Amount of the Work Used: The parody is not a verbatim copying of the original. 2 Live Crew copies the opening bass riff of the original and the first line of the Orbison lyrics. Thereafter, 2 Live Crew departs markedly from the Orbison lyrics. 2 Live Crew also produces distinctive sounds, interposes "scraper" noise, overlaying the music with solos in different keys, and alters the drum beat.

- Factor Four. Market Impact: The court noted that 2 Live Crew's version might compete with a non-parody rap version of the song. It also noted that neither side had submitted evidence addressing the issue.

The Cat NOT in the Hat! (*Dr. Seuss Ents., L.P. v. Penguin Books USA, Inc.*, 109 F.3d 1394 (9th Cir. 1997)).

Situation: In 1995, Alan Katz and Chris Wrinn wrote and illustrated *The Cat NOT in the Hat!*, a rhyming summary of highlights from the O.J. Simpson double murder trial. Katz and Wrinn's book mimics the style of *The Cat in the Hat*, a famous children's book first published in 1957 by Theodor S. Geisel under the pseudonym Dr. Seuss. Katz and Wrinn described their book as a parody of *The Cat in the Hat*. Neither the authors nor their publishers requested permission from Seuss Enterprises, which owned rights in most of Geisel's works. After seeing a pre-publication advertisement promoting *The Cat NOT in the Hat!*, Seuss Enterprises filed suit for copyright and trademark infringement.

Court Ruling: *The Cat Not in the Hat!* does not qualify as a parody of *The Cat in the Hat*. The court granted an injunction prohibiting distribution of the 12,000 copies printed by the publisher.

Court's Application of the Four Fair Use Factors:

- Factor One. Purpose and Character of The Use: Use of the Dr. Seuss trademarks and copyrighted works made no commentary on the substance or style of *The Cat in the Hat!*. In a filing submitted to the court, Penguin and Dove characterized *The Cat NOT in the Hat!* as follows:

> The [book] is a commentary about the events surrounding the Brown/ Goldman murders and the O.J. Simpson trial, in the form of a Dr. Seuss parody that transposes the childish style and moral content of the classic works of Dr. Seuss to the world of adult concerns . . .

Completely unconvinced, the court categorized the explanation as "pure shtick".

- Factor Two. Nature of the Copyrighted Work.: *The Cat in the Hat!* is a creative work.

- Factor Three. Amount of the Work Used.: Penguin and Dove appropriated the Cat's image, copying the Cat's Hat and using the image on the front and back covers and in the text thirteen times.

- Factor Four. Market Effect.: The court did not discuss the market effect.

The Wind Done Gone Case. (*SunTrust Bank v. Houghton Mifflin,* *(268 F.3d 1257* (11th Cir. 2001)).

Situation: Alice Randall is the author of *The Wind Done Gone*, a story that presents *Gone With the Wind* from the viewpoint of a slave. Randall uses the story line and the characters of *Gone With the Wind* but very little of the actual text. The Estate of Margaret Mitchell sued *The Wind Done Gone* publisher for copyright infringement and related claims.

Court Ruling: Randall's use of elements of *Gone With the Wind* is protected as a parody.

Court's Application of the Four Fair Use Factors:

- Factor One. Purpose and Character of the Use: The for-profit purpose of the *The Wind Done Gone* is outweighed by its transformative nature. Randall criticizes the fictional world of *Gone With the Wind*. Randall's story transforms *Gone With the Wind* into a very different tale by flipping *Gone With the Wind*'s traditional race roles, and portraying powerful whites as stupid.

- Factor Two. Nature of the Work: *Gone With the Wind* is a creative work.

- Factor Three. Amount of the Work Used: Approximately the last half of *The Wind Done Gone* tells a completely new story that, although involving characters based on *Gone With the Wind*'s characters, features plot elements not found in the original.

- Factor Four. Market Impact: *The Wind Done Gone* has little impact on the market for *Gone With the Wind*.

What Other Factors Influenced the Court: The Mitchell Estate does not grant licenses for use in works that mention homosexuality or miscegenation. Randall's book refers to both. Copyright is not designed to limit self-expression.

Demi Moore, Vanity Fair & Leslie Nielson. (*Leibovitz v. Paramount Pictures Corporation*, 137 F.3d 109 (2nd Cir. 1998)).

Situation: In August 1991, Vanity Fair released an issue with a cover photograph of the actress Demi Moore, who was pregnant at the time. Moore appeared in the photograph nude and in a pose similar to the pose used in Botticelli's *Birth of Venus*. The issue of Vanity Fair was one of the magazine's best selling issues.

In connection with the promotion of the 1994 film *Naked Gun 33 1/3*, Paramount produced a similar photograph - imposing the head of Leslie Nielson on the body of a nude, pregnant woman. While Moore wears a serious expression in her photograph, Nielson wears a mischievous smirk. Annie Leibovitz, a well-known photographer who took the photograph of Moore, sued Paramount for copyright infringement.

Court Ruling: The *Naked Gun 33 1/3* advertisement qualified as a parody entitled to the fair use defense.

Court's Application of the Four Fair Use Factors:

- Factor One. Purpose and Character of the Use: The commercial nature of Paramount's use is a strike against it; however, the commercial use is outweighed by other factors. The ad can reasonably be perceived as ridiculing pretentiousness or as interpreting the Leibovitz photograph to extol the beauty of the pregnant female body, and, expressing disagreement with that message.

- Factor Two. Nature of the Copyrighted Work: Leibovitz's photograph exhibits creative expression. Although the basic pose of a nude, pregnant body is free for anyone to use, Leibovitz is entitled to protection for artistic elements such as lighting, the resulting skin tone of the subject, and the camera angle.

- Factor Three. Amount of the Work Used: Paramount took great efforts to match the creative expression in Leibovitz's photograph. The Paramount model was carefully posed so that her posture, hands, and jewelry, match those of Moore in the Leibovitz photograph. Paramount then used computer digital enhancement to make the skin tone and shape of the model's body more closely match those of Moore.

- Factor Four. Market Impact: Leibovitz conceded that the Paramount photograph does not interfere with any potential market for her photograph.

3.9.   When Permission Is Not Required to Use a Copyrighted Work

In some instances, the law allows you to use copyrighted works without the copyright owner's permission. There is a huge caveat. Application of these laws is subjective, fact-specific, and even fickle at times. For works subject to copyright protection, having the copyright owner's permission is always preferable.

3.9.1.   Fair Use

The Fair Use Doctrine allows you to use a reasonable portion of a copyrighted work without running afoul of copyright law. For an in-depth discussion of the Fair Use Doctrine and its application, see Section 3.7.

3.9.2.   Parody

If your use of a work qualifies as a parody, you are not liable for copyright infringement. Parody involves the use of a copyrighted work as a target of a joke or commentary. For an in-depth discussion of parody, see Section 3.8.

3.9.3.   De Minimis Use

A use is *de minimis* when you use such a small or trivial amount of the copyrighted work that it cannot amount to infringement. Courts often look to the amount of the copyrighted work that is copied, as well as the length of time the copyrighted work appears in the allegedly infringing work and its prominence in that work.

When determining whether there is a *de minimis* use, courts sometimes rely on the regulations for royalties to be paid by public broadcasting entities' use of published pictorial and visual works. The regulation distinguishes between a featured display and a background and montage display, setting a higher royalty rate for a featured display. A court might be inclined to view your use as a *de minimis* use if it is similar to a background or montage use. The regulation defines a featured display as a "full-screen or substantially full screen display for more than three seconds," and defines a background or montage display as "[a]ny display less than full-screen, or full-screen for three seconds or less."

3.9.4. Works in the Public Domain

People sometimes use the term public domain incorrectly to signify that a work is available to the public. Any book at the store is available to the public. That does not necessarily mean that the book is in the public domain. For purposes of copyright law, being in the public domain means that the copyright in the work has expired – or that no copyright ever existed in the work. While there is no official list of works in the public domain, there are unofficial lists, a few of which are listed in the Appendix.

Federal Government Works. Works created by federal government employees or commissioned as works made for hire are in the public domain. This includes the text of speeches and official papers by federal officials *while in office*. State and local government works may be protected by copyright. There are a few caveats to the use of federal government works as public domain works:

- If the insignia of the government or an office such as the seal of the President, the seal of the FBI, or the Seal of NASA is integrated in the work, the use may be prohibited by applicable federal regulations.

- If the federal government licensed a freelancer or contractor to create the work, the freelancer or contractor retains the copyright unless there is a written agreement that says otherwise.

- An organization that appears to be part of the federal government may actually not be. Some agencies are only quasi-governmental entities.

- The federal government works are free for use for copyright law purposes. However, depending on the specific material and how you plan to use it, there may also be privacy, publicity and other rights issues that you need to address.

Works with Expired Copyrights. Copyrights last for a speci-fied period of time. Once the copyright expires, the work falls into the public domain. Section 3.6 provides guidelines on the duration of copyright. Determining whether a copyright has expired may require you to conduct some investigation.

Effect of the Sonny Bono Act On the Public Domain. In 1999, Congress passed the Sonny Bono Act which amended the Copyright Act and extended copyright duration by twenty years. The current general copyright duration is the life of the author plus seventy years. Prior to the Sonny Bono Act, the gen-eral copyright duration was the life of the author plus fifty years. Unless copyright law changes again, no works under copyright protection on January 1, 1999 will fall into the public domain as a result of an expired copyright until January 1, 2019.

Searching the Copyright Office's Records. The Copyright Office does not maintain a list of public domain works. Instead, you can use its records to determine a work's publication date and whether the copyright owner adhered to the formalities re-quired for maintenance of the copyright. The Copyright Office has records dating back to 1870. You can access records from 1978 through the present on its website.

The Copyright Office's Information Circular No. 22 is avail-able through the Copyright Office's website and provides instruc-tions on searching Copyright Office records. If you do not want to do the search yourself, you can retain a private search service or the Copyright Office to conduct the search.

Circumstances Leading to the Expiration of Copyright. The purpose of your search and investigation is to find information to help you determine whether one of the following situations exist which would place the copyrighted work in the public do-main. You should read this list in conjunction with Section 3.6 which discusses the duration of copyright and the publication of copyrighted works.

- Maximum Copyright Term. The copyrighted work was published prior to 1923.

- No Renewal Application. The copyrighted work was published or copyrighted prior to January 1, 1964 and the copyright owner did not file a renewal application after a twenty-eight-year period.

- Publication Without Proper Copyright Notice Under 1909 Act. The copyrighted work was published prior to January 1, 1978, and the copyright owner did not include a proper copyright notice. This is not applicable to the distribution of unpublished versions of the work or for versions of the work distributed without the copyright owner's authorization. Also, works published after March 1, 1989 do not require a copyright notice.

- Publication Without Proper Copyright Notice Under Current Copyright Act. The copyrighted work was published between January 1, 1978 and March 1, 1989, without a proper copyright notice, and the copyright owner did not take preventive measures within five years of publication to cure the improper copyright notice. This is not applicable to the distribution of unpublished versions of the work or for versions of the work distributed without the copyright owner's authorization.

Avoiding Pitfalls. There is ample room for error when trying to determine the copyright status of a work. Here are some tips for avoiding the pitfalls:

- The name on the copyright notice is not always the current owner. The original copyright owner may have transferred or sold the copyright.

- Copyright searches prove a positive. They cannot prove a negative. Your copyright search can prove that the work is protected by copyright. It cannot prove with 100% certainty that the work is not protected by copyright.

- You cannot assume that a work is in the public domain just because it does not come up in a copyright search. Works created after 1978 do not require registration in order to be protected by copyright law. As a result, those works may not be listed in any databases or sources you are searching.

- For songs, exercise caution with respect to the particular arrangement you are using. The original copyrighted work may be in the public domain, but a new musical arrangement that adds new elements to the song may be protected by copyright.

- For textual works, exercise caution with respect to translations of public domain works. The translation has a separate copyright. While the original work may be in the public domain, every translation may not be.

- Photographs and other visual artwork are listed in the Copyright Office's records by title. If you do not know the title of the artwork for which you are searching, you may have difficulty locating it in the records.

- Just because a production is in the public domain does not mean that all the material within that production is in the public domain. For example, a film may be in the public domain but music included in the film may still be protected by copyright.

- A work may be in the public domain within the United States but not in the public domain in other countries. This is relevant if you distribute your production outside the United States.

Works Placed in the Public Domain by Copyright Owners. Some copyright owners may deliberately place their work into the public domain prior to the expiration of copyright protection. Any producer may use such material in any way they choose.

There are also hybrid situations in which a copyright owner may place her work somewhere in between the public domain and full copyright protection. Some organizations provide standard ways and licenses or statements for copyright owners to reserve some rights but not all. Organizations, such as The Free Software Foundation and the Open Source Initiative provide such statements for software.

Creative Commons, a non-profit organization, focuses on music, images, text, and video. It offers copyright owners free documentation to assist them in placing their works in the public domain. Copyright owners that want to retain some rights can use one of a number of free Creative Commons licenses that relax the Copyright Act's exclusive rights.

For example, if a copyright owner adopts a Creative Commons Attribution License, anyone could copy, distribute, display, perform and develop derivative works from the copyright owners work as long as the copyright owner receives attribution – or credit for the work. If a copyright owner adopts a Creative Commons Noncommercial License, anyone can use the copyright owner's work for a non-commercial purpose. If you believe the material falls under an open license, read the licensing information to determine what rights you may freely exercise and whether there are any conditions with which you must comply.

3.9.5. First Amendment

The First Amendment encompasses the Fair Use Doctrine so cases often refer to both fair use and the First Amendment.

The First Amendment is a defense to a copyright infringement claim in situations where the copyrighted work is the only source of information, and the information found in the copyrighted work is vital to the public's understanding of certain events. A First Amendment defense typically fails in cases which do not involve unique and extraordinary historical events.

The First Amendment discourages anyone from using copyright law as a shield from unwelcome comment or as a method to censor individual opinion. It is not the purpose of copyright law to limit free speech.

Cases in which First Amendment concerns beat copyright concerns

Filming of Kennedy Assassination. Reproduction of frames of the Zapruder film in the book, *Six Seconds in Dallas,* inquiring into the assassination of President Kennedy is fair use. There is a public interest in having the fullest information available on the murder of President Kennedy. The sketches made it easier for readers to understand the author's assassination theory. (*Time Incorporated v. Bernard Geis Assoc.,* 293 F. Supp. 130 (S.D.N.Y. 1968)).

Outfoxed. Robert Greenwald is the producer of the political documentary *Outfoxed: Rupert Murdoch's War on Journalism.* The documentary is highly critical of the Fox Network's news coverage. Certain that Fox would refuse to license material for use in the documentary, Greenwald decided to claim fair use for material taped from Fox News. He did proceed with the advice of an attorney and had legal counsel lined up in the event Fox decided to file a lawsuit. While Fox released a statement condemning Mr. Greenwald's use of its material, Fox has not launched a lawsuit.

Rodney King Beating. A First Amendment defense to copyright infringement was successfully applied to newsgatherers' and commentators' use of the videotape of the Rodney King beating. *Holliday v. Cable News Network.,* CV92-3287 (C.D. Cal. June 11, 1993) (transcript of oral opinion)

Case in which copyright concerns beat First Amendment concerns

Train Wreck. A news clipping service's unauthorized use of copyrighted footage of an airplane crash and train wreck was not protected by the First Amendment. There were other depictions of the accident available. (*Los Angeles News Service v. Tullo,* 973 F.2d 791 (9th Cir. 1992)).

3.9.6. Public Performances

Some public performances do not require the consent of the copyright owner. Section 110 of the Copyright Act lists a number of exceptions to a copyright owner's exclusive public performance right.

If there is an exception, you do not need permission from the copyright owner and you do not need to pay any royalties to the copyright owner. The exception most relevant to media producers is the exception for a non-profit public performance of a song or literary work. To rely on the exception, your public performance must meet the following requirements:

- None of the performers, promoters, or organizers may receive direct or indirect payment or benefit for the performance.

- If attendees pay for admission to the public performance, the proceeds must be used exclusively for educational, religious, or charitable purposes.

TRADEMARK BASICS | 4

4.1. What Is a Trademark?

When you see golden arches, do you think of McDonald's Restaurants? When you hear the phrase JUST DO IT!, do you think of Nike? The golden arches symbol and the short phrase JUST DO IT! are both trademarks.

Companies use trademarks to create brand identities and to distinguish their goods and services. Trademark law protects any element that uniquely identifies a product or service. In addition to words and short phrases, trademarks can also be logos, graphic symbols, designs, sounds, shapes, colors and even smells.

Trademark law distinguishes between trademarks which identify goods and service marks which identify services. A good is a physical product. Throughout this book, I use the words "good" and "product" interchangeably in my discussion of trademarks.

For example, PEPSI is a trademark that identifies a soda product and REEBOK is a trademark that identifies athletic footwear. Examples of service marks include GREYHOUND for bus transportation services and H&R BLOCK for income tax preparation services.

The legal process for acquiring and protecting trademarks is virtually identical to the process for acquiring and protecting service marks. For the purposes of this reference book, I treat trademarks and service marks as functionally identical. Sometimes trademarks are simply referred to as marks. Unless I indicate otherwise, I use the terms mark and trademark interchangeably to refer to both trademarks and service marks.

4.2. Obtaining Trademark Rights

In the United States, registration is not required in order to establish trademark rights. You acquire trademark rights by being the first person to commercially use a protectible trademark within a particular geographic area. In order for a trademark to be protectible, it must meet certain criteria most notably:

- The trademark must be distinctive.

- The trademark must not create a likelihood of confusion with a pre-existing trademark.

4.2.1. What Makes a Trademark Distinctive?

Trademark law protects only those trademarks that are distinctive. In trademark jargon, the distinctiveness of a trademark is measured according to where it falls on a scale consisting of five categories. From most distinctive to least distinctive, the five categories are fanciful, arbitrary, suggestive, merely descriptive, and generic.

- Fanciful. Fanciful trademarks are made-up words such as KODAK or EXXON.

- Arbitrary. Arbitrary trademarks are ordinary words used completely out of context such as APPLE for the name of a computer.

- Suggestive trademarks hint at but do not directly name the good or service. They require some use of your imagination to come up with the nature of the actual goods or services. Examples include the trademark, SURFVIVOR used to identify beach-themed products and the trademark, CHICKENT OF THE SEA used to identify tunafish.

- Merely Descriptive. A merely descriptive trademark indicates a characteristic, function, use or other attribute of the good or service. Trademarks primarily based on a geographic location or a surname also fall into the category of merely descriptive trademarks. Descriptive trademarks receive little or no trademark protection. There is an exception for a descriptive trademark that has acquired secondary meaning. Secondary meaning exists if the public clearly associates the trademark with the good or service. CHAP STICK and AMERICAN AIRLINES are protectible trademarks which began as descriptive and overtime developed secondary meaning.

- Generic. A generic term is the common name of the good or service itself such as soap or hairspray. Generic trademarks never receive trademark protection. For example, if you use the term "java" to sell your brand of coffee beans, that is a generic use of "java" and you will receive no trademark protection for that use. However, note that "java" becomes an arbitrary trademark when used to describe a product completely unrelated to coffee – such as a computer programming application.

Determining where a particular trademark falls on this scale of distinctiveness is often subjective. For example, one person may categorize a trademark as suggestive while another categorizes the same trademark as merely descriptive.

4.2.2. When Is There A Likelihood of Confusion?

A likelihood of confusion exists when a consumer might confuse your proposed trademark with an existing trademark already being used to identify a similar good or service. There are eight questions a court frequently asks in a likelihood of confusion case. These questions are often referred to as the Polaroid factors after the legal case, *Polaroid Corp. v. Polarad Electronics Corp.*, 287 F.2d 492 (2d Cir. 1961), that first used them:

- How distinctive is the pre-existing trademark?

- How similar are the trademarks?

- How similar are the goods or services identified by each trademark?

- Are the goods or services marketed to the same customer base?

- If the goods or services are not similar, what is the chance that one trademark owner will eventually expand into the business of the other trademark owner?

- Have consumers actually been confused by the similarity in the trademarks?

- Was the accused trademark infringer acting in good faith when he did he choose a similar trademark or was he attempting to benefit from the good will associated with the pre-existing trademark?

- How much attention do customers pay to the trademark in this good/service category when making a purchase?

Real-Life Application of the Likelihood of Confusion Test. Application of the likelihood of confusion test is best illustrated through a real-life example.

Entrepreneur Media, Inc. uses the federally registered mark ENTREPRENEUR in connection with its magazine *Entrepreneur* and related publications. Scott Smith operated a company named EntrepreneurPR, a magazine named *Entrepreneur Illustrated*, and a website with the domain name EntrepreneurPR.com. Both *Entrepreneur* and *Entrepreneur Illustrated* target small businesses. Entrepreneur Media filed a trademark infringement lawsuit against Scott Smith and EntrepreneurPR.

The case spawned several rulings over a six-year period. Ultimately, the court found that there is a likelihood of confusion and that Smith was liable for infringement of the ENTREPRENEUR trademark. The court ordered Smith to pay Entrepreneur Media monetary damages of over $669,000 plus the cost of Entrepreneur Media's attorney fees.

The court specifically addressed seven of the eight factors in finding that Scott Smith's use of Entrepreneur Illustrated creates a likelihood of confusion with the trademark, ENTREPRENEUR:

- How descriptive is the pre-existing trademark? At one point in the proceeding, an appeals court ruled that the word "entrepreneur" is a descriptive term which can not be infringed. However, Entrepreneur Media was given an opportunity to refute this ruling. Later in the proceeding, Entrepreneur Media succeeded in proving the distinctiveness and strength of its trademark. At the time of the lawsuit, Entrepreneur Media had used the trademark continuously for over twenty-five years. Also, *Entrepreneur* magazine had a total audience of approximately 2 million readers per issue. Its companion website, entrepreneur.com, had 2 -3 million monthly visitor sessions.

- How similar are the trademarks? The trademarks are substantially similar in appearance, sound and meaning in that the dominant portion of both trademarks is the word "entrepreneur".

- How similar are the goods or services identified by each trademark? The goods are similar. Entrepreneur Media and Smith both use their trademarks in connection with magazines featuring articles about small businesses and with public relations services.

- Are the goods identified by the trademarks marketed to the same customer base? Yes, the marketing channels overlap. Both Entrepreneur Media and EntrepreneurPR target small businesses.

- Is there actual consumer confusion? There was actual confusion among consumers. Evidence showed that consumers believed that by signing up for Smith's EntrepreneurPR's services, they would be featured in *Entrepreneur* magazine.

- Was the accused infringer acting in good faith? Evidence indicated that Smith intentionally used the EntrepreneurPR trademark in a manner to mislead consumers. For example, Smith released press releases on *Entrepreneur* magazine's masthead with the phrase PR firm. This implied that EntrepreneurPR was the public relations firm for *Entrepreneur* magazine.

4.2.3. Benefits and Process of Trademark Registration

You do not have to register your trademark in order to have valid rights. However, federal registration of your trademark does give you a number of benefits including the following:

- Nationwide exclusivity for your trademark. Without federal registration, you have trademark rights only in those states in which you use the trademark.

- Notice to others. A federal trademark registration places others on notice that you are the owner of the trademark.

- Increased damage awards. With federal registration, you are eligible to collect attorneys' fees and increased monetary damages from an infringer if you file and win a trademark infringement lawsuit.

- Incontestability. After five years your federal registration qualifies for incontestability which makes it difficult for anyone to claim that your trademark is not valid.

You file an application for federal trademark registration with the United States Patent and Trademark Office (PTO). Unfortunately, registration of a trademark with the PTO is not as straightforward as registration of a copyright with the Copyright Office. This book does not offer a detailed description of the trademark registration process.

Here is a brief and simplified outline of the steps in the process:

- Submission of Application. You submit a completed application to the PTO including samples of how you use the trademark, the applicable filing fee, and the date on which you began using the trademark.

- Review by PTO. A trademark examiner at the PTO checks your application to make sure it is complete and that your trademark qualifies for federal registration. The PTO may reject your application for a number of reasons including that your proposed trademark is not distinctive or that it is likely to cause confusion with a pre-existing trademark.

- Office Action. If the trademark examiner finds a distinctiveness, likelihood of confusion, or other problem with your application, she sends you a letter explaining the problem. The letter is called an Office Action. You have six months in which to respond to the Office Action.

- Publication. Once the trademark examiner is satisfied with the application, the trademark is published in the *Official Gazette*, an official publication of the PTO. Anyone who believes that registration of your trademark would harm his or her rights has thirty days in which to object to the registration. Most objections will come from a trademark owner who believes that your trademark is too similar to his trademark and that your use of the trademark creates a likelihood of confusion.

- Registration or Third Party Objection. If no one objects, the PTO registers your trademark. If someone does object, there is a proceeding before the PTO to resolve the dispute. The PTO proceeding is similar to a lawsuit in federal court so having representation by a trademark attorney is highly recommended.

If you are not yet using the trademark but you have a bona fide intention of doing so, you can reserve a trademark by filing an intent-to-use application. The application process is substantially the same as the steps outlined above – except that you do not have to submit examples of how you are using the trademark with the initial application.

Once granted, an intent-to-use application reserves the trademark for six months. The reservation can be extended for five additional periods of six months each provided you have a legitimate reason for the delay in your commercial use of the trademark. An intent-to-use application must be followed by an additional application once you begin to use the trademark.

Even if everything goes smoothly, it can take a year or more for a trademark to be accepted for registration. You can find additional information on the federal trademark registration process at the website of the PTO.

4.3. United States Trademark Law

Trademarks are protected by a combination of federal and state laws. Unlike copyrights and patents, there is no specific language in the United States Constitution giving Congress power to regulate trademarks. The federal government's power to regulate trademarks comes from the Commerce Power which gives Congress the power to regulate interstate and international commerce.

As a result, federal trademark laws are only applicable to those trademarks that are used in interstate commerce. You are using your trademark in interstate commerce if you are marketing or selling your good or service in more than one state or across national lines. For trademarks used only within one state, state laws do provide some protection.

4.3.1. Lanham Act (The Trademark Act of 1946)

The Lanham Act is the workhorse of federal trademark protection. The Lanham Act was signed by President Truman on July 5, 1946, and took effect one year later on July 5, 1947.

The Lanham Act protects both registered and unregistered trademarks. The Lanham Act prohibits you – without the consent of the trademark owner – from using in commerce any registered trademark in a manner likely to confuse consumers.

The Lanham Act also prohibits using either federally registered or unregistered trademarks in a false advertising context or as a false designation of origin. Many states include similar advertising and false designation provisions in their unfair competition laws.

4.3.2. Federal Anti-Dilution Laws

Anti-dilution laws have two primary purposes. They prevent a trademark's distinctiveness from being weakened as a result of being used to identify another's good or service. They also prevent the trademark's reputation from being tarnished through an association with an undesirable good or service. Dilution claims are generally available only for trademarks considered famous.

There are both federal and state laws that protect trademarks from dilution. The federal version is the Federal Trademark Dilution Act.

For example, the use of the DISNEY trademark with a pornographic production might dilute the strength of the DISNEY trademark. When there is dilution, a trademark owner can prevent someone else from using his trademark even if there is little or no likelihood of consumers confusing the two trademarks.

Often, it is dilution, and not the likelihood of confusion, that is the issue when media productions are challenged for their use of trademarks. In those cases, the trademark owner claims that while the public knows there is clearly no connection between its good and the media production, the use of its trademark in the media production makes the public associate its trademark with a new and different source. This new association damages the ability of the trademark to provide a unique identification for the goods or services offered by the trademark owner.

4.3.3. State Trademark Laws

You can register a trademark at the state level. While state registration provides some protection, it does not provide nearly as many benefits as federal registration. The process for state registration which varies by individual state is generally simpler than the process for federal trademark registration.

For the protection of trademarks, most states have laws that parallel the federal Lanham Act and the federal anti-dilution laws. Many trademark infringement lawsuits include a combination of claims based on federal law and state law.

4.4. How Productions Use Trademarks

When clearing rights, you must confirm that nothing in your production infringes another person or organization's trademark.

There are at least four ways in which a production might use a trademark:

- in the title of the production
- as a reference in the dialogue or text of the production
- in the form of a brand-name product that appears in the production
- as the subject of the production

4.4.1. Trademarks and Title Selection

People often erroneously speak of copyrighting a title. As discussed above in Section 3.4.3, titles lack the required creativity and originality to qualify for copyright protection. However, in certain circumstances, trademark law can protect titles.

No Trademark Protection for Titles of Most Single Works. As a general rule, the title of an individual work does not have enforceable trademark rights. In contrast, the title of a series can have enforceable trademark rights. When Jack Canfield and Mark Victor Hansen wrote *Chicken Soup For the Soul* in 1993, there were initially no enforceable trademark rights in the book title. Since that time, over 100 books have been released in the *Chicken Soup* series. Since *Chicken Soup*, once the title of single work, is now a title of a series of books, it qualifies for trademark protection and federal trademark registration.

While the title of a single book, play, film, or other creative work generally has no enforceable trademark rights, there is an exception if the title of the single work has achieved secondary meaning. Secondary meaning signifies that the title is well-known or famous. Examples of titles with secondary meaning might include *West Side Story*, *The Sound of Music*, and *Gone With the Wind*.

Avoiding Trademark Problems When Selecting A Title. Even though the title of your single production may not be protectible, your title may raise objections from another trademark owner. When possible, you should avoid selecting titles that are the same as or confusingly similar to another production in active circulation.

In order to make a successful objection to your title under trademark law, a third party must show

• that it has valid trademark rights in a trademark that is identical or similar to your title and

• that there is a likelihood that consumers will confuse your production with the third party's product or service.

In this situation, confusion means that a consumer might believe the trademark owner endorses, sponsors or is in some way affiliated with your production.

Giving a title to a media production is a form of expression. As a result, titles receive great protection under the First Amendment. If your title has at least some artistic relevance to your production, and your title is not explicitly misleading as to the content of your production, it will be difficult for someone else to prevent your use of that title.

A title report can help you evaluate whether your title creates any trademark infringement issues. A title report prepared by a professional search company lists productions with similar titles to your proposed title. The title report also includes trademarks of non-entertainment-related goods and services that are similar to your proposed title. Most title reports cover a search of the Copyright Office's records, the Trademark Office's records, and other entertainment databases. Some distributors and insurers require that producers submit title reports.

Successful challenges to titles

Dairy Queen. The title *Dairy Queens* for a satirical documentary about beauty pageants in rural Minnesota dairy country infringes DAIRY QUEEN, a trademark for a chain of frozen dairy stores. The Court issued an injunction preventing use of the title for the documentary. (*American Dairy Queen Corp. v. New Line Productions, Inc.,* 35 F. Supp. 2d 727 (D. Minn. 1998)).

Spike Lee v. SpikeTV. Viacom planned to use SpikeTV as the name for its cable network. Viacom described the network as "unapologetically male, . . . aggressive and irreverent." Filmmaker, Spike Lee sued. During the proceedings, Lee submitted evidence indicating that he had a reputation for irreverence and aggressiveness and that a number of people would associate SpikeTV with Spike Lee. A court ordered Viacom to refrain from launching the SpikeTV Network. The parties eventually reached a settlement that allowed Viacom to use the SpikeTV name. (*Spike Lee v. Viacom*, No. 110080/2003 (N.Y. Sup. Ct. June 12, 2003)).

Unsuccessful challenges to titles

CNN v. World Beat. CNN used *World Beat* as a title for a new weekly international music program and for a portion of the CNN website. A record company that features reggae music had previously registered WORLD BEAT as a trademark. The record company filed and lost a trademark infringement suit against CNN. According to the Court, CNN's use is not infringing. While the trademarks are both used in the same general field of music, the services they describe - a televised music program versus recordings of reggae music - are not sufficiently similar to create a likelihood of confusion. The court also noted that the term "world beat" is often used to describe a specific genre of music which makes it a relatively weak trademark. (*Richards v. Cable News Network*, 15 F. Supp. 2d 683 (E.D. Pa. 1998)).

Ginger Rogers. The film, *Ginger and Fred*, tells the story of two fictional Italian cabaret performers who imitate Ginger Rogers and Fred Astaire and become known in Italy as Ginger and Fred. Ginger Rogers sued the producers and distributors of the film for false advertising and for violation of her privacy and publicity rights. Rogers lost. According to the court, the names Ginger and Fred are genuinely relevant to the subject matter of the film and were not used for commercial advertisement. In contrast, a title such as *The True Life Story of Ginger and Fred* would have been actionable since it would be an explicit misleading statement about the content of the film. (*Rogers v. Grimaldi*, 875 F.2d 994 (2nd Cir. 1989).

4.4.2. References to Trademarks

As a general rule, the dialogue or text of your production can refer to a trademark as long as the reference does not falsely imply that the trademark owner or the good is somehow sponsoring, endorsing or affiliated with your production. The physical appearance in your production of a product that carries a trademark or brand name merits additional analysis. See Section 4.4.3 below.

4.4.3. Product Appearances

The brand names we see at stores identify specific products. Those brand names are trademarks. Products with brand names have a way of popping up – sometimes unexpectedly – in visual productions. Just imagine the number of products that might appear in a film scene in which the character opens the refrigerator or in a photograph taken in a gift shop.

Several court rulings say the unauthorized appearance of a brand-name product in a production is okay as long as:

- The producer is not using the brand or product in a way that promotes the production. In other words, the producer is not feeding off the reputation of the brand to increase awareness of his production which would be trademark infringement.

- The appearance of the product does not make people think that the manufacturer of the product is in anyway sponsoring or supporting the production.

- The appearance of the product does not dilute the brand name. In other words, the appearance does not tarnish the reputation of or decrease the value of the brand name.

In one real-life example, Disney's direct-to-video production of *George of the Jungle 2*, the villains use CATERPILLAR-brand bulldozers in an attack on the good guys. The bulldozers appear in about eight minutes of scenes and are referred to as "deleterious dozers" and "maniacal machinery". Caterpillar tried but failed to prevent the release of the video on trademark infringement and dilution claims. In denying the injunction, the court concluded that consumers would not be confused into believing that Caterpillar had sponsored the film, and that consumers would not be influenced by the film in making decisions about purchasing Caterpillar equipment. (*Caterpillar v. Walt Disney Company*, 287 F. Supp.2d 913 (C.D. Ill. 2003)).

Nevertheless, placing products in your production without permission does carry some risk. Keep in mind that the court rulings I have mentioned in this section exist because a trademark owner sued a producer. The more attention placed on the product in your production, the greater the risk. The risk of some product appearances is often minimal. However, if a trademark owner views your production's treatment of its trademark as negative, the trademark owner may take some action.

Not all producers have the resources or the desire to defend themselves in a lawsuit. The more conservative approach is to obtain authorization for all trademarks that appear in your production or at least for all trademarks that are highlighted or featured in some manner. The good news is that many trademark owners want their products featured in entertainment productions and will grant permission at no charge. In some cases, they will even pay for an appearance of their product in your production.

4.4.4. Trademark as Subject Matter of Production

You may make a trademark the subject of your production. Here is where we once again encounter the First Amendment. A trademark owner is not entitled to quash an unauthorized use of the trademark by someone who is using the trademark to communicate an idea or express a point of view about the product.

For example, there is no trademark infringement by a series of seventy-eight photographs entitled *Food Chain Barbie*. The series, developed by Utah photographer Thomas Forsythe, depicts Barbie doll in various absurd and often sexualized positions. Forsythe describes his work as a parody that criticizes the way in which Barbie doll products objectify women. The BARBIE trademark in the titles of Forsythe's works and on his website are permissible as they accurately describe the subject of the photographs. (*Mattel Inc. v. Walking Mountain Productions*, 353 F.3d 792 (9th Cir. 2003)).

4.5. When Permission Is Not Required to Use a Trademark

4.5.1. Fair Use of Trademarks

Trademark fair use does not use the same four-factor test used for copyright fair use. There are two types of trademark fair use: (i) traditional or classic fair use and (ii) nominative fair use.

Classic trademark fair use recognizes that anyone may use a trademark in its descriptive sense. For example, Apple Computer owns a registered trademark for APPLE in connection with computers goods. That does not mean it can prevent others from using the term "apple" to describe apple sauce, an apple orchard, or apple juice.

When you use a trademark to refer to or describe the trademark owner's goods or services, that is a nominative fair use of the trademark. Your use of a trademark qualifies as a nominative fair use if all the following conditions apply:

- You can not readily identify the good or service without using the trademark.

- You use the trademark only to the extent necessary to identify the good or service.

- Your use does not suggest sponsorship or endorsement by the trademark owner.

In one real-life example of nominative fair use, *USA Today* newspaper used the trademark, NEW KIDS ON THE BLOCK, which is the name of a musical group. *USA Today* used the trademark when conducting a poll in the paper to determine the most popular member of the musical group. There was no other satisfactory way for *USA Today* to identify the band and the newspaper did not suggest that the group endorsed or sponsored the poll in any way. (*New Kids on the Block v. News America Publishing. Inc.*, 971 F.2d 302 (9th Cir. 1992))

4.5.2. First Amendment

The First Amendment prevents a trademark owner from using trademark law to limit public discourse. Some trademarks develop iconic status or come to represent cultural ideas and concepts beyond their association with the product or service they identify. Producers may use these iconic trademarks within a social commentary.

BARBIE doll, a trademark owned by Mattel, is one example of an iconic trademark. For many people, Barbie Doll represents society's view of the perfect woman. As a result, Mattel has been unsuccessful in preventing artists and producers from using the name and image of Barbie Doll in productions that comment on and criticize the concept of an ideal woman.

4.5.3. Trademarks as Parody

Parody is a form of commentary that borrows liberally from an existing work to produce a new work that at least in part, makes fun of the existing work.

For your use of a trademark to qualify as a parody, your production must comment on the trademark. It is not a qualifying parody use if you incorporate the trademark into your production in order to comment on something else.

Al Franken's book title, *Lies and the Lying Liars Who Tell Them: A Fair and Balanced Look at the Right*, is a parody mocking Fox News Network and Bill O'Reilly. Fox, which owns a registered trademark for the term FAIR & BALANCED, complained that Franken's use of the term "fair and balanced" would make consumers mistakenly believe that Fox was associated in some way with the book. In denying Fox's request for an injunction, the court concluded that Franken's use is a parody and that the use creates no likelihood of consumer confusion.

In addition, the frequent use of the phrase by the press and media makes the trademark relatively weak. (*Fox News Network v. Penguin Group,* 03 cv 6162 (S.D.N.Y., August 22, 2003)(transcript of preliminary injunction hearing).

COMMON ELEMENTS OF PRIVACY, PUBLICITY AND DEFAMATION LAWS

5.1. Overview of Privacy, Publicity and Defamation Laws

In a privacy, publicity, or defamation action, a defendant causes personal harm to an individual. This makes privacy, publicity, and defamation distinct from copyright and trademark. Copyright and trademark actions concern a violation against someone's personal property - albeit intangible rather than tangible property.

This chapter highlights common traits shared by privacy, publicity, and defamation. Each area is then discussed in greater depth in the following chapters.

- The Right of Privacy is the right to be left alone and the right to have others stay out of your personal affairs.

- The Right of Publicity is the right to prevent others from commercializing or profiting from your identity.

- Defamation occurs when you make a false statement about a person and the statement damages that person's reputation.

5.2. Governed by State Law

Unlike copyright and much of trademark law, the right of privacy, the right of publicity and defamation are governed by state law. As a result, these laws vary significantly from state to state.

5.3. Identification Is Required

One factor common to all privacy, publicity and defamation actions is the requirement that the individual be identifiable in the media production about which he is complaining. If your production includes the person's name or image, the person is normally identifiable. Your production can identify someone even without using the person's name or image. If your audience can identify the person, there is potential for liability.

5.3.1. Identification Through the Use of a Nickname or a Former Name

A person can be identified through the use of his former name or his nickname. For example, Kareem Adbul-Jabbar, recognized as one of the greatest professional basketball players of all time, was born Ferdinand Lewis ("Lew") Alcindor and used that name throughout his college basketball career and into his early years in the National Basketball Association. After converting to Islam, he began using the name Kareem Abdul-Jabbar. During the 1993 NCAA men's basketball tournament, General Motors aired a television commercial that posed the trivia question:

Who holds the record for being voted the most outstanding player of this tournament?"

On the screen appeared the printed words:

Lew Alcindor, UCLA, '67, '68, '69.

The commercial then compares Alcindor's champion record to the General Motors Oldsmobile Eighty-Eight's champion record which had been listed as a Consumer Digest Best Pick for three years. The commercial concludes with a printed message on the screen that says

A Definite First Round Pick

Even though Abdul-Jabbar had not used the name Lew Alcindor for over ten years, the court would not dismiss his lawsuit against General Motors. The court decided it was possible for Kareem Adbul-Jabbar to be identifiable through the use of his former name, Lew Alcindor. The question of whether Abdul-Jabbar actually was identifiable by his former name was left for a jury to decide. (*Abdul-Jabbar v. General Motors*, 85 F.3d 407 (9th Cir. 1996)).

Compare the *Abdul-Jabbar* case with a case involving the sons of convicted spies, Julius and Ethel Rosenberg. In 1973, Doubleday published *Implosion Conspiracy*, a recounting of the trial and June 1953 execution of Julius and Ethel Rosenberg. The Rosenbergs had been convicted of conspiring to transmit national defense information to the Soviet Union. The Rosenbergs two sons, Robert and Michael, were adopted after the execution. The sons changed their name to Meeropol, the name of their adopted family.

Implosion Conspiracy refers to the sons as Robert and Michael Rosenberg. The name Meeropol does not appear in the book. The sons sued the publisher and the author for defamation and invasion of privacy. The court dismissed the lawsuit because the sons are not identifiable by the name Rosenberg. They had not used the name Rosenberg for twenty years. With the exception of a few intimate friends, they were known exclusively as Meeropol. (*Meeropol v. Nizer*, 381 F. Supp. 29 (S.D.N.Y. 1974)).

5.3.2. Identification Through the Depiction of Person's Property

A person can be identified through the depiction of his personal property. Race car driver, Lothar Motschenbacher, uses a distinctive red race car. The race car has a unique narrow white pinstripe and oval medallion. A nationally televised commercial for Winston cigarettes featured a photograph of the car. Even though Motschenbacher's facial features were not distinguishable in the picture, he was identifiable through the image of his distinctive race car. (*Motschenbacher v. R.J. Reynolds Tobacco*, 498 F.2d 821 (9th Cir. 1974)).

There is no action if the person's identity is not readily apparent from the depiction of the property. That is why a Missouri horse trainer lost his right of privacy action over a print advertisement featuring an image of his Appaloosa horse. The court decided that the horse trainer had no right of privacy claim because no one immediately identified him with the horse. (*Bayer v. Ralston Purina Co.*, 484 S.W.2d 473 (1972)).

5.3.3. Identification Through Voice

Some celebrities are recognized just by the sound of their voice. Television and film producers frequently use sound-a-like recordings. A sound-a-like recording is a new recording of a well-known song in which a vocalist imitates the performance of the artist who made the song famous. Use of a sound-a-like recording may be acceptable for a docudrama or biography on the life of the artist. However, you risk substantial liability if you use a sound-a-like recording in an advertising context without the celebrity's consent.

There are two well-known sound-a-like recording cases. One involves Bette Midler; the other involves Tom Waits.

After Bette Midler declined an offer to make a recording for a Ford commercial, Ford's advertising agency hired a singer to make a sound-a-like recording of Midler singing *Do You Want To Dance*. Midler sued Ford and the advertising company. She ultimately won $400,000 in damages. (*Midler v. Ford Motor Co.*, 849 F.2d 460 (9th Cir. 1988)).

In a separate case, Tom Waits, who has a well established policy of not performing in commercials, received over 2.5 Million Dollars in damages after a sound-a-like recording of Waits performing *Step Right Up* was used in a Frito Lay commercial. (*Waits v. Frito-Lay*, 978 F.2d 1093 (9th Cir. 1992)).

5.3.4. Identification of Person Through Focus on Another Person

Media focus on one person may reveal the identity of another person. This sometimes happens when the media's report on a subject brings out facts about the subject's relatives and associates. There may be liability for the producer if private personal facts are revealed about the relatives and associates.

5.3.5. Identification Through Illustration or Manipulated Image

A person can be identified through a manipulated image or an illustration. The original version of *Playgirl Magazine* February 1978 issue included an image of a nude black man seated in the corner of a boxing ring. The figure is seated on a stool in a corner of a boxing ring with both hands taped and outstretched resting on ropes on either side. The picture is an illustration falling somewhere between representational art and cartoon. The caption reads "Mystery Man" but the accompanying text refers to the figure as "The Greatest".

Does that description remind you of anyone? Boxing legend, Muhammed Ali, noted that the facial characteristics of the man in the image included his cheekbones, broad nose, wide set brown eyes, distinctive smile, and close cropped black hair. Ali successfully prevented *Playgirl Magazine* from distributing the issue. (*Ali v. Playgirl*, 447 F. Supp. 723 (S.D.N.Y. 1978)).

5.3.6. Identification Through Image or Personality Traits

A person can be identified through elements of his personality. A character in the *Spawn* comic book series had the name and tough guy persona of former professional hockey player, Tony Twist. The persona was sufficient to identify the hockey player even though the comic book character had no physical characteristics or life story details similar to those of Twist. (*Doe v. TCI Cablevision*, 110 S.W.3d 363 (Mo. 2003).

RIGHT OF PRIVACY | 6

6.1. *What Is the Right of Privacy?*

Broadly speaking, the right of privacy is a person's right to be left alone. Privacy can mean constitutional protection from the government's unreasonable search and seizure. It can also mean protection from the collection and control of personal information collected by mailing lists and credit bureaus. For rights clearance purposes, the right of privacy protects you from privacy invasions by other private individuals and organizations.

The right of privacy is often divided into four subcategories:

- disclosure of embarrassing private facts

- false light invasion of privacy

- intrusion

- misappropriation of name or likeness

State law governs privacy laws. As a result, privacy laws vary from state to state and not every state offers protection according to these four sub-categories. The right of publicity - a person's right to benefit commercially from his identity - is sometimes included with state privacy laws. However, publicity rights have evolved into their own area of law, and I treat them separately in the next chapter.

6.2. *Limitations on Privacy Rights*

6.2.1. Famous Individuals Have Limited Privacy Rights

The more famous a person is, the less ability that person has to claim privacy rights. This is due to the First Amendment. Events and personal matters surrounding a person in public life are matters of legitimate public interest. Famous individuals with limited privacy rights include celebrities and politicians. The category also includes private individuals whom for reasons sometimes beyond their control become famous for a short period of time. However, even famous individuals are entitled to some zone of privacy with respect to highly personal matters.

6.2.2. Deceased Individuals Have No Privacy Rights

Generally, a deceased person has no right of privacy. Some states do allow a deceased person's estate to bring an action for violation of the right of publicity. Also, media producers focusing on a deceased individual must still exercise caution so as not to violate the privacy rights of the deceased person's living relatives and associates.

6.3. Disclosure of Embarrassing Private Facts

6.3.1. Disclosure of Embarrassing Private Facts Defined

You have violated a person's privacy through the disclosure of embarrassing private facts if

- you disclose information about the person,
- the disclosure is made to the public, and
- the disclosure of such facts would offend the average person.

6.3.2. Elements of Private Facts Claim

Facts Must Have Been Private. The facts you reveal must actually have been private facts of which the public was not already aware. Hence, there is typically no liability for publication of truthful information contained in official records open to public inspection.

Similarly, most courts will not view your republication of information already made public by another media group as the disclosure of private facts – although such republication can still qualify as defamation if the information published is false.

Examples of facts that are private

- details about a person's sexual conduct
- a person's nude appearance
- a person's medical history

Examples of facts that are not private

- marital status
- age
- information available in public records
- person's normal appearance
- events that occur in public

Facts Must Be Disclosed to Public. A large number of people must learn the facts. Disclosure to a few people, such as a small group of co-workers, may not qualify as public disclosure. Facts revealed through national, regional or even local media outlets should meet the standard for public disclosure in most jurisdictions.

Facts Must Be Embarrassing. The facts revealed must be facts that would embarrass the person of average sensitivity. For example, if an individual is highly sensitive to facts concerning his marital status, and disclosure of those facts would not offend the typical person, a privacy claim would not be successful.

Facts Must Not Be Relevant to a Public Matter. If the private facts are relevant to a matter of legitimate public interest, they can be disclosed even if the disclosure results in embarrassment to a particular individual. This is the balancing test where an individual's right to privacy is weighed against the First Amendment. When hoping to rely on the First Amendment, you should verify that all information given in the media account is relevant to the topic of general public interest.

For example, the facts surrounding the commission of a crime are of public interest. In *Romaine v. Kallinger*, 537 A.2d 284 (N.J. 1988), there was no violation of plaintiffs' privacy rights by the publication of the book *The ShoeMaker* detailing the crime spree of Joseph Kallinger. Kallinger had held hostage and victimized the plaintiffs during a home invasion. The critical chapter of *The Shoe-Maker* describes the painful treatment, the humiliation and abuse plaintiffs suffered at the hands of Kallinger. While perhaps embarrassing to the victims, the facts surrounding the commission of the crime were relevant to a matter of legitimate public interest.

6.4. False Light

6.4.1. False Light Defined

You have committed false light invasion of privacy when you publish information about an individual which – although the information may be true on the surface – creates an inaccurate impression of a person. False light claims result from "half truths" when producers embellish a story or use a statement or photograph out of context.

6.4.2. Elements of False Light Claim

False light invasion of privacy requires a showing that

- You share certain information with the public or with a large number of people.

- The information you share attributes to an individual characteristics, conduct, or beliefs that are inaccurate.

- The inaccuracy would be highly objectionable to the typical person.

False light invasion of privacy claims sometimes arise in connection with the publication of photographs. As the following example portrays, while a picture may be worth a thousand words, any words that accompany the picture are just as important. The identical photograph of a married couple appeared in the magazines *Harper's Bazaar* and the *Ladies Home Journal*. In the photograph, the couple is sitting side by side at the confectionery and ice cream concession in the Los Angeles Farmers' Market. The husband has his arm around his wife and is leaning forward with his cheek against hers.

Ladies Home Journal's Use of the Photo Is Actionable. In the *Ladies Home Journal*, the photo carries the caption "instantaneous powerful sex attraction - the wrong kind of love." The accompanying article offers a philosophical and sociological discussion of love and divorce. It says that love based on physical attraction - the type of love the couple in the photo are alleged to have - does not last and frequently leads to divorce. The use of the photo was actionable as a false light invasion of privacy. (*Gill v. Curtis Publishing*, 38 Cal.2d 273 (1952)).

Harper's Bazaar's Use of the Photo Is Not Actionable. In *Harper's Bazaar*, the photo carries the caption "immortalized in a moment of tenderness". The article is a short commentary that the world cannot revolve without love. It is a permitted use of the couple's likeness as the photo was taken in a public place and neither the picture nor the caption is uncomplimentary to the couple. (*Gill v. Hearst Publishing Co.*, 40 Cal.2d 224 (1953)).

6.4.3. Similarities of False Light and Defamation

False light is the privacy subcategory most similar to defamation. You defame someone when you make a false statement that harms the person's reputation. A major distinction between false light and defamation is that success on a defamation claim requires harm to the individual's reputation. There is no such requirement for a false light claim.

Many courts apply to false light cases the constitutional standard of actual malice used in defamation cases. The actual malice standard applies to public figures and public officials but not to private individuals. Hence, a public figure must prove that you acted with actual malice when placing him in a false light. Actual malice exists if you realized or should have realized that the statement was false when making it. In contrast, a private individual does not need to show you acted with actual malice. The private person need only show that you were negligent when placing him in a false light. See Chapter 8 for a discussion of defamation, the actual malice standard, and an explanation of who is a public figure and who is a private individual.

6.5. Invasion of Privacy by Intrusion

6.5.1. Intrusion Defined

Intrusion is similar to physical trespass. Trespass is the act of intentionally entering the land of another without consent. In the media context, intrusion commonly arises within the context of newsgathering. It is often intrusion when a newsperson enters private property uninvited or uses hidden cameras and microphones or a long lens camera.

6.5.2. Elements of Intrusion Claim

Uninvited Entry. A successful intrusion claim requires proof that you intentionally intruded, either physically or otherwise, on someone else's physical space or private affairs. Media pursuit and filming in public places are generally not actionable as intrusion. See the discussion of anti-paparazzi claims in Section 9.6 and the discussion of acceptable and unacceptable newsgathering practices in Section 13.2.2.

Publication or Broadcasting Not Necessary. It is not necessary that you publish or broadcast the information you obtain in order to be liable for violation of privacy by intrusion. The act of intruding upon another's physical space or private affairs is sufficient for a successful intrusion claim.

6.6. *Misappropriation of Name or Likeness*

Misappropriation occurs when you use an aspect of a person's identity in such a way that you cause damage to the person's peace of mind and dignity. Misappropriation is similar to the right of publicity in that both claims allege that you have used some aspect of the person's identity. Misappropriation differs from the right of publicity in that the right of publicity focuses on commercial uses of the person's identity and compensates the person for economic harm. Traditionally, misappropriation focuses on emotional or mental harm. All state laws do not make a clear distinction between misappropriation and the right of publicity. Some state statutes mix elements of the two.

The newsworthy use of a private person's name or photograph is not actionable as long as the use is reasonably related to a matter of public interest. For example, Bob Dylan and Jacques Levy wrote and released a song called *Hurricane*. The song describes a celebrated murder trial, a matter of legitimate public interest. The song mentions one of the trial witnesses by name. The trial witness sued for invasion of privacy. She lost. According to the court, the song does not commercially exploit the woman's name and does not imply that she participated in the alleged conspiracy. (*Valentine v. CBS, Inc*, 698 F.2d 430 (11th Cir. 1983)).

6.7. *Defenses to Privacy Actions*

Here's a summary of defenses to claims that you have violated someone's right of privacy:

6.7.1. No Publication

If you have not released any information about the person, you have a defense to claims based on disclosure of private facts, false light, and misappropriation. The fact that you did not publish information you improperly obtained about a person is not a defense to an intrusion claim.

6.7.2. Consent

If the person consents to your actions by sharing personal information with you for your production or inviting you into his or her private space, there is no invasion of privacy. Obtaining such consent is a primary purpose of obtaining a release. Consent can be explicit or implied, written or verbal. See Section 25.4 for a detailed discussion about obtaining consents and releases.

6.7.3. Truth

If you can show that the information you published is true, you have a defense to a false light invasion of privacy claim. Truth is not a defense to any other privacy claims.

6.7.4. Person Not Identifiable

If the relevant remarks, photographs or other material can not be reasonably associated with a specific person, there is no actionable claim for invasion of privacy based on disclosure of private facts, false light, or misappropriation.

6.7.5. Information Was Not Private

If the information you published is from a public record or was otherwise generally known to the public, it was not private. This is a defense to a claim that you violated someone's privacy through the disclosure of private facts.

6.7.6. Newsworthiness

Newsworthiness is a common defense in a private facts case. Newsworthy is another way of saying the incident is a matter of public concern. In a lawsuit, the jury's assessment of what's newsworthy prevails. Newsworthiness may also be a mitigating factor in misappropriation and intrusion cases. A story's value as news rarely matters in a false light case.

RIGHT OF PUBLICITY 7

7.1. What Is the Right of Publicity?

The right of publicity allows each individual to control and profit from the commercial value of his or her own identity. The right covers all aspects of an individual's identity including name, likeness, voice, and personally identifying characteristics. The right of publicity evolved from the right of privacy and like the right of privacy, it is governed by state law. Many – but not all – states treat the right of publicity as distinct from the right of privacy.

7.2. When Has a Producer Violated a Person's Right of Publicity?

To win a right of publicity claim, a person must demonstrate that his identity has commercial value and that you used his identity without consent for commercial purposes.

7.2.1. Commercial Use Versus Non-Commercial Use

Right of publicity claims are limited to the commercial use of a person's identity. If you use the person's identity in a non-commercial context, there is no right of publicity claim. Broadly speaking, you are using a person's identity for a commercial purpose when you use the person's identity to sell something.

Your intention to make a profit from your production does not by itself make your use commercial. For example, even though news producers seek to make a profit, the use of a person's identity in the news is not categorized as a commercial use.

7.2.2. Right of Publicity for Deceased Individuals

An area in which privacy and publicity differ is in the rights allocated to deceased individuals. While there is no right of privacy for deceased individuals, several states allow the right of publicity to extend beyond death. These states include California, Florida, Indiana, Kentucky, Nebraska, Nevada, Oklahoma, Tennessee, Texas and Virginia. That means the individual's estate or heirs can object to the unauthorized commercialization of the individual's identity.

The duration of descendibility varies from state to state - ranging from ten to one hundred years to indefinitely. In deciding whether the right of publicity is descendible, many – but not all - courts apply the law of the state in which the deceased person last resided. For example, when the successors to the Marx Brothers' rights wanted to stop performances of a New York play imitating the Marx Brothers' comedic style, the law of California determined whether the Marx Brothers' right of publicity was descendible. California was the state of residence of the brothers at the time of their deaths. (*Groucho Marx Productions, Inc. v. Day & Night Co.*, 689 F.2d 317 (2nd Cir. 1982)).

7.3. *Defenses to Right of Publicity Claim*

Here is a summary of defenses to claims that you have violated someone's right of privacy.

7.3.1. Newsworthiness

The use of an individual's identity does not violate the right of publicity where the use reports on newsworthy items of public interest. The First Amendment protects such use. For example, California law provides that no prior consent is required for use of a name, voice, signature, photograph, or likeness in connection with any news, public affairs, or sports broadcast or account, or political campaign.

In one real-life application of this concept, publication in *People* of wedding photographs of Lyle Lovett and Julia Roberts was deemed to be newsworthy and not infringing on the couple's right of publicity (*Time, Inc. v. Sandcreek Partners, L.P.*, 825 F. Supp. 210 (S.D. Ind. 1993)).

7.3.2. Promotion of a Related Product

Court opinions suggest that you can use a person's identity to promote a related product. For example, a magazine may use celebrity photographs from current or prior issues as advertisements for the magazine itself.

The *San Jose Mercury News* published a story on the 1989 Super Bowl which included a picture of Joe Montana. Later the newspaper sold a poster which contained the picture of Montana from its Super Bowl coverage. Montana lost his lawsuit claiming that the newspaper violated his right of publicity. The newspaper has a constitutional right to promote itself by reproducing its news stories. (*Montana v. San Jose Mercury News, Inc.*, 40 Cal. Rptr.2d 639 (Cal. Ct. App. 1995)).

7.3.3. Incidental Use Exception

A producer may use a person's identity in a manner that is incidental. In other words, mention of the person is casual or sometimes even accidental. The use cannot be a disguised advertisement for the sale of a product or service.

There are two categories of incidental use: fleeting use of a person's identity and incidental use in the context of advertising.

Fleeting Use of a Person's Identity. A quick mention or glance of someone is not sufficient for a right of publicity claim. Here are some real-life examples applying this exception:

• A glimpse of a picture of interviewee's husband was not a right of publicity violation. (*Glickman v. Stern*, 19 Media L. Rep 1769 (N.Y.Sup 1991).

- The four-second appearance of a man in a documentary was not a right of publicity violation. *(Delan by Delan v. CBS,* 458 N.Y.S.2d 608 (1983)).

- During an interview with *Women's Wear Daily,* the president of a handbag manufacturing company mentioned that a fashion designer had joined the company.   *(Marks v. Elephant Walk,* 548 N.Y.S.2d 549 (1989))

In contrast, General Motors likely went beyond incidental use when it used Kareem Abdul-Jabbar's given name in a television commercial. The commercial posed the question on screen: "Who Holds the Record for being voted the most outstanding player of the NCAA tournament?". The commercial then displayed the answer - Lew Alcindor - on screen. Lew Alcindor is the former name of professional basketball player, Kareem Abdul-Jabbar.

Had General Motors limited itself to the "trivia" portion of its ad, General Motors might have successfully defended the reference to Lew Alcindor as an incidental use. Instead, the commercial compared Adbul-Jabbar/Alcindor's winning record to General Motor's record for winning Consumer Digest Best Pick for the Oldsmobile Eighty-Eight. The comparison arguably implied Abdul-Jabbar/Alcindor's had endorsed the commercial and General Motor's product. *(Abdul-Jabbar v. General Motors Corp.,* 85 F.3d 407 (9th Cir. 1996))

Advertising for News or Entertainment Media. Courts recognize an incidental use exception to the right of publicity in the context of advertising. In an advertisement, a producer may use another person's identity to illustrate the content of her production.

For example, Random House published *Case Closed,* a book by Gerald Posner that refutes the conspiracy theories about the Kennedy assassination. An advertisement for *Case Closed* appearing in the *New York Times* contained the names, photographs, and quotations of six authors who had authored books offering conspiracy theories for the Kennedy assassination.

Two of those authors sued Random House for violating their right of publicity. They lost. Even though *Case Closed* does not contain all the pictures or quotations of the authors reproduced in the advertisement, it does contain numerous references to the six authors' conspiracy theories and challenges both their research and conclusions. Hence, the use of the authors' names and photos illustrated the content of the book being advertised and was not a violation of the right of publicity. (*Groden v. Random House*, 61 F. 3d 1045 (2d Cir. 1995), and *Lane v. Random House*, 985 F. Supp. 141 (D.C. Cir. 1995)).

CHAPTER

DEFAMATION 8

8.1. What Is Defamation?

You defame someone when you make a false statement about the person and the statement harms the person's reputation. Public figures and public officials must prove that you made the statement with actual malice or with reckless disregard for the truth. Private figures need only show that you were negligent in making the statement.

Many states divide defamation into libel and slander. If you say the harmful false statement, you commit slander. If you write the harmful false statement or put it in another fixed form such as a film, broadcast, or a website, you commit libel. Defamatory actions against producers of media and entertainment usually allege libel.

As in the areas of privacy and publicity, there is no federal law that governs defamation. Each state applies its own laws to defamation claims. Defamation differs somewhat from privacy and publicity because certain U.S. Supreme Court rulings set specific guidelines on how states may structure their defamation laws.

8.2. Elements of a Defamation Claim

8.2.1. Communication to the Public

Before a producer is guilty of defamation, he must communicate the false statement to someone other than the person who is the subject of the statement. For the libel form of defamation, communication normally means that the producer has published the statement.

For example, suppose you say or write in a note to the board member of a non-profit organization, "You've embezzled funds from your organization." You don't share the accusation with anyone else. In that situation, there is no defamation even if the statement is false. You have shared the accusation only with the board member who is the subject of the statement. That is not a publication or a communication for purposes of defamation.

Once you repeat or share your accusation with additional people, there is the possibility of a defamation action. Since most producers share their productions with the public or with a group of some size, they normally satisfy the requirement of communicating the statement to the public.

The fact that you are repeating defamatory material published elsewhere is not a defense. A person who repeats a defamatory statement is generally as liable as the one who first made the statement.

8.2.2. False Statement of Fact

The statement must be false. A truthful statement - even if unflattering - is not defamatory. For purposes of defamation, it is not necessary that every element of the statement be true. It is sufficient for the statement to be substantially true. I discuss truth as a defense to defamation below in Section 8.4.5.

8.2.3. About the Person

Like privacy and publicity, the statement must be about the person who claims to have been defamed. See Section 5.3 for a detailed discussion of the statements and communications that may qualify as being about the person. If a group is so large that it is impossible to associate one particular member with the defamatory remark, the remark is not defamatory with respect to any particular individual and, therefore, there is no actionable defamation claim. For example, if you make a defamatory statement regarding all police officers, no single police officer can file a defamation claim. An individual can be successful in a defamation suit for a statements made against a group only if the size of the group is small or if the individual is singled out in some way.

8.2.4. Harmful to the Person's Reputation

The person claiming defamation must show that your statement injured him. The law recognizes different ways in which a person might suffer from defamation.

Actual Harm (or Actual Damages). Actual harm includes any form of harm. It can be economic harm (*i.e.*, the loss of money) or non-economic harm. Economic harm means the person has lost money or money-making opportunities as a result of the defamation. Forms of non-economic actual harm include impairment of one's reputation and standing in the community, personal humiliation, and mental anguish and suffering.

Special Harm (or Special Damages). Special harm refers to a monetary loss. For example, a person who loses a job or a business opportunity as a result of the defamatory statement has suffered special harm. Special harm is a subset of actual harm. It is more difficult to prove special harm than it is to prove actual harm.

Presumed Harm. Under the theory of presumed harm, the person need provide no proof whatsoever of having suffered as a result of the defamatory statement. The defamatory statement was so "bad" that the court presumes it damaged the person in some way.

U.S. Supreme Court's Requirements for Proving Harm. The Supreme Court has set the constitutional floor for damages a state must require in a defamation claim. Today, categorization of a defamatory remark as libel or slander is most relevant to the type of harm that the plaintiff must show. Defamation law can vary significantly by state law but here are some generalizations:

- If the person claiming defamation is a private individual and the subject matter of your production is not a matter of legitimate public concern, states may require that the private individual show only presumed harm. I discuss who qualifies as a private individual in Section 8.3.

- If the person claiming defamation proves you acted with actual malice, there is presumed harm. The court presumes the person has suffered harm as a result of the defamatory statement and he need not show any particular damages. See Section 8.2.5 for a discussion of actual malice

- If the defamatory statement is made in a production about a topic of legitimate public concern, the person claiming defamation must show he suffered actual harm as a result of the defamatory statement.

- In libel *per se* or slander *per se* cases (defined below), there is presumed harm. The court presumes the person has suffered harm as a result of the defamatory statement, and he need not show any particular damages.

- In libel *per quod* or slander *per quod* cases (defined below), the person claiming defamation must prove he suffered special harm.

Slander Per Se and Libel Per Se. With slander *per se* or libel *per se*, the statement has only one meaning and that meaning is clearly defamatory. There is no need for further analysis. Traditionally, the per se concept applied only to slander and included only four categories of statements. They four categories are statements that a person

- has committed a criminal act;

- has an infectious disease (such as venereal disease or leprosy);

- is incompetent in his trade or profession; or

- is unchaste.

A number of states have expanded the *per se* categories to any statement that is defamatory on its face. A number of states also apply the *per se* concept to libel.

With *per se* defamation, the plaintiff need not provide any proof that he suffered any particular harm as a result of the statement.

The court presumes the *per se* defamatory statement resulted in harm.

Slander Per Quod and Libel Per Quod. When a court must consider extraneous factors to reach a conclusion that a statement is defamatory, the statement is libel *per quod* or slander *per quod*.

For example, *Science*, the magazine, committed libel *per quod* when it published an article on lawsuits involving the controversial drug Bendectin. The article said that William McBride, an obstetrician with the Women's Hospital in Sydney, Australia, received $5,000 a day as an expert witness. The article then noted that Merrell Dow, on the other side of the lawsuit, paid witnesses "$250 to $500 a day, and the most it has ever paid is $1,000 a day."

Science's statement was not defamatory *per se* or defamatory on its face. However, the statement was defamatory *per quod*. After considering the total context of the article, the court determined that the statement could be interpreted with the defamatory meaning that McBride's testimony was for sale. (*McBride v. Merrell Dow*, 800 F.2d 1208 (D.C. Cir. 1986)).

8.2.5. Producer's Actual Malice or Negligence Required

The fear of defamation lawsuits should not discourage the media from releasing information that the public needs to hear. So that the defamation laws are not used to curtail public criticism, a person alleging defamation must prove that the producer made the defamatory statement with negligence or with actual malice. The relevant standard depends on the status of the person complaining of defamation.

Public Officials and Public Figures Must Show Producer Acted with Actual Malice. In order for a public official or a public figure to win a defamation claim against you, he must prove that you made the defamatory statement with actual malice. I discuss who qualifies as a public official or public figure in detail below in Section 8.3.

The actual malice standard is not just academic. A defamation plaintiff who must prove actual malice has a much more difficult time winning his lawsuit.

Actual malice is publication with knowledge that the offending statement is false or publication with reckless disregard of whether or not the statement is false. It is a subjective standard that depends on the producer's state of mind. Actual malice is very fact specific. Below are a few broad generalizations:

There is actual malice:

- if the producer had serious doubts about the truthfulness of the statements being published

- if there are obvious reasons for the producer to have doubted the veracity or the accuracy of his sources and informants

There is no actual malice:

- just because the producer failed to investigate; however, proof that a story was carefully researched and fact checked can establish that actual malice does not exist

- just because a producer fails to verify the accuracy of statements even if a prudent producer would have done so

- if the producer has a reasonable belief that the statements in the production are substantially correct

- if the producer publishes the statement in good faith

Cases in which actual malice was shown

The Wall Street Journal. The *Wall Street Journal* published an article about the MMAR Group, a securities firm, indicating that the company engaged in unethical and questionable business practices. MMAR sued for defamation. According to the court, the *Wall Street Journal* reporter acted with actual malice. The relationship between the reporter and MMAR had become openly hostile during the interview process as shown by (i) a letter sent by

MMAR's lawyer complaining about the reporter's competence and inappropriate questions asked by her, (ii) MMAR's refusal to grant an interview to the reporter, and (iii) the hostile tone of reporter's written questions submitted to MMAR. (*MMAR Group v. Dow Jones*, 987 F. Supp. 535, (S.D. Tex. 1997)).

Look Magazine. *Look Magazine* linked San Francisco mayor, Joseph Alioto, to organized crime in a September 1969 article. There was actual malice by *Look Magazine* because (i) the reporter relied on information from an individual whom the editor admittedly viewed as a "liar" and a "notorious hoodlum," (ii) federal and state law enforcement sources, who were actively investigating the matter, told the reporter and publisher they had no information on Alioto's connections to organized crime, and (iii) the reporter made no attempt to corroborate the story with people who were unbiased and readily available. (*Alioto v. Cowles Communications*, 430 F. Supp. 1363 (N.D. Cal. 1977)).

Case in which actual malice was not shown

Newspaper Political Ad. On the eve of a Trumball County, Ohio Commissioner election, a local newspaper published a political advertisement containing negative information about the incumbent. The incumbent had no time to respond to the ad and lost the election. There was no actual malice on the part of the newspaper because (i) the advertisement addressed the official conduct of a public official, (ii) the advertisement was submitted to the paper by a reputable person known to the newspaper employee, and (iii) the newspaper staff recognized the names of the people who had signed the ad as individuals with good reputations. (*Baldine v. Sharon Herald Co.*, 391 F.2d 703 (3rd Cir. 1968)).

Private Individuals Must Show Producer Was Negligent. In order for a private individual to win a defamation claim against you, he must show that you were negligent in making the defamatory statement. I discuss status as a private individual in detail below in Section 8.3.3.

Negligence is the absence of reasonable care. You are negligent if you are slipshod and careless in putting together your production. Negligence might consist of failure to follow journalistic standards or failure to investigate.

For example, the grandparents of a child at the center of a national child custody case were private individuals and not public figures in a defamation case against ABC. The distinction is important because ABC's reference to them as child abusers was negligent and unintentional. ABC aired a docudrama entitled *A Mother's Right: The Elizabeth Morgan Story*. In one scene, a four-year old child visits with her father and paternal grandparents at the office of a court-appointed psychiatrist. After being somewhat aloof, the child climbs into her grandfather's lap. In the next scene, a character remarks on the exchange by saying the child is being kind to her "abusers" so she won't be hurt again.

It is undisputed that the "s" that converted the singular *abuser* – referring solely to the father - into the plural *abusers* – including the grandparents in the reference - was included unintentionally. Negligence was sufficient for the grandparents to win a defamation lawsuit against ABC. As private individuals, the grandparents did not need to show that ABC had acted with actual malice.

8.3. Public Officials, Public Figures, and Private Individuals

Defamation cases distinguish between plaintiffs who are public figures or public officials and plaintiffs who are private individuals.

8.3.1. Who Is a Public Official?

A public official is someone who holds a position of considerable importance and is responsible for governmental affairs. Classifying someone as a public official is often quite easy. Most elected or appointed federal, state or territorial officials are public officials. It is more challenging to determine whether lower-level city and state officials qualify as public officials. The U.S. Supreme Court has not said how far down the lower ranks of government employees the public official designation extends and has not specified categories of persons who are or are not to be included.

Most courts classify a person as a public official if she has supervisory, management or policy making functions and has access to the media for rebuttal. For the actual malice standard to apply, the defamatory statement must relate to the person's official conduct and position.

Case where person classified as public official

Court-Appointed Psychologist. A court-appointed psychologist in a child custody case who had the power to determine visitation rights is a public official for purposes of a defamation suit against HBO's 1992 airing of *Women on Trial.* (*HBO v. Harrison*, 983 S.W.2d 31 (1998))

Case where person not classified as public official

Private Physician. Lazelle Michaelis was the coroner of Otter Tail County, Minnesota. Michaelis was also employed as a private physician and occasionally performed autopsies for the Becker County Coroner. Through her connection with the Becker County Coroner, Michaelis performed an autopsy on a young woman who had died under questionable circumstances. A news broadcast questioned Michaelis' competence as a coroner. Michaelis had performed the autopsy in her capacity as a private physician - not in her capacity as the coroner of Otter Tail County. As a result, she was not a public official with respect to the newscast's statements. (*Michaelis v. CBS, Inc.,* 119 F.3d 697 (8th Cir. 1997)).

8.3.2. Who Is a Public Figure?

The actual malice standard is also applied to public figures. A public figure is an individual

- who is famous or notorious,
- who generates public attention by his position alone, or

- who has placed himself into the midst of a public controversy.

Some people are public figures in all circumstances. Others are public figures in limited circumstances.

General Purpose Public Figure. A general purpose public figure is someone who occupies a position of great power or influence. Nationally recognized celebrities fall into this category.

Limited Purpose Public Figure. A limited purpose public figure is someone who has thrust himself to the forefront of a particular controversy in order to influence the outcome. Limited purpose public figures are subject to the actual malice standard when they are defamed with respect to the issues in which they have invited public scrutiny. They are still private individuals for all other topics.

In determining whether the person invited public scrutiny, a court will examine whether the person (i) is a voluntary participant in the controversy of public interest and (ii) has access to the media for a rebuttal.

People classified as limited purpose public figures

Gennifer Flowers. Gennifer Flowers was a limited purpose public figure in her defamation action against James Carville, George Stephanopoulus and Hillary Clinton. Her alleged affair with President Bill Clinton made headlines in *STAR*, a national tabloid, and Flowers held a press conference to corroborate her story during a presidential nomination campaign at which she played tapes of her conversations with Clinton. The court found that Flowers voluntarily injected herself into the fray. (*Flowers v. Carville*, 310 F.3d 1118 (9th Cir. 2002)).

Birth Defects Expert. William McBride, an obstetrician and expert on the study of birth defects, testified at an FDA hearing about the drug Bendectin's alleged links to birth defects, a topic which had sparked widespread public controversy. McBride had also testified as an expert witness for plaintiffs challenging the drug's safety. He was a public figure with respect to a *Science* magazine article concerning the drug. (*McBride v. Merrell Dow*, 800 F.2d 1208 (D.C. Cir. 1986)).

Playboy Model. Carol Vitale is a model who appeared as the centerfold in an issue of *Playboy* Magazine. *National Lampoon* did a parody of *Playboy*. The parody included a copy of *Playboy* magazine opened to the centerfold picture of Vitale. Vitale sued for defamation. As someone who had voluntarily posed for *Playboy*, an international magazine, she was a limited purpose public figure with respect to *Playboy* Magazine. (*Vitale v. National Lampoon*, 449 F. Supp. 442 (E.D. Pa. 1978)).

Prominent Sports Agent. Sports agent, A.J. Faigin, was a limited purpose public figure in a defamation claim against a former client who said Faigin unethically managed the client's funds. The court reached this conclusion in part due to claims made by Faigin. Faigin claimed he was a nationally known prominent sports agent in the mid 1980s, who through self-promotion had contact with the press regarding the athletes he represented. Faigin also claimed to have created or taken a lead in influencing all significant trends in football contract negotiations. (*Faigin v. Kelly*, 978 F. Supp. 420 (D. N.H. 1997)).

People classified as involuntary limited purpose public figures. In some jurisdictions, status as a limited purpose public figure can be thrust upon someone involuntarily.

Falsely Accused Man. Todd Erdmann was an involuntary limited purpose public figure. A sixteen-year old boy shot himself and then told police that Todd Erdmann, a man who reportedly had been stalking the boy's sister, had shot him.

Law enforcement took several actions in responding to the shooting report. Upon learning that Erdmann might have access to weapons, law enforcement placed the sister in protective custody. Police officers initiated a regional manhunt for Erdmann. A

SWAT Team evacuated the sister's place of employment, a prominent public building. The police also held a press conference in which Erdmann was described as armed and dangerous. The local news station covered the incident using information provided by the police. After the sixteen-year old confessed to making up the story and police cleared Erdmann of all charges, Erdmann sued the television station for defamation. Erdmann was a limited purpose public figure - albeit involuntarily - with respect to the incident which had become a public controversy in Wisconsin. (*Erdmann v. S.F. Broadcasting of Green Bay*, 599 N.W.2d 1 (1999)).

8.3.3. Who Qualifies As Private Individual?

A private individual is anyone who is not a public official or public figure. That's most people - but not necessarily most people who are the subjects of media productions.

People classified as private individuals

Relatively Unknown Model. An obscure model and actor who does not enjoy fame or celebrity is not a public figure. He is a private individual in his defamation action regarding the unauthorized appearance of his image on a book cover. (*Kennedy v. Ministries*, 10 Media LR 2459 (E.D. Pa. 1984)).

Regional Beauty Queen. A Mississippi woman received significant local publicity and fame through her involvement in beauty contests and her service and candidacy for local and state office. While she would be a public figure for statements related to those public activities as regional beauty queen and local politician, she was a private individual with respect to statements in a magazine article unrelated to those activities. (*Phyler v. Fiona Press*, 12 Media LR 2211 (N.D. Miss. 1986)).

Star High School Athlete. Although a high school athlete had received news coverage for his athletic accomplishments, he did not have general fame or notoriety within the state to be an all-purpose public figure. Furthermore, he was not a central figure in any public controversy as required for status as a limited purpose public figure. (*Wilson v. Daily Gazette*, 588 S.E.2d 197 (W. Va. 2003)).

Accused Child Abusers. The grandparents of a child at the center of a national child custody case were not public figures in a defamation case against an ABC docudrama accusing them of child abuse. The case became a public controversy which focused attention on women's plight in protecting children. The grandparents' public role was limited to responding verbally to accusations against them as child abusers and supporting their son, the child's father, by being physically present - but not participating in - the son's news meetings. They did not assume a role of special prominence in order to influence the outcome. (*Foritich v. Capital Cities/ABC*, 37 F.3d 1541 (4th Cir. 1994)).

8.4. Defenses to Defamation

Here is a summary of defenses to claims that you have defamed someone.

8.4.1. Elements of Defamation Not Satisfied

If applicable, you can argue that one of the elements required for a defamation claim does not exist. The required elements, as discussed above in Section 8.2, include that a statement be published, that the statement concern the person claiming defamation, that the producer have made the statement with negligence or with actual malice, and that the defamed person suffered some harm as a result of the defamation.

8.4.2. The Person Consented

People normally do not consent to being defamed. However, your subject might have signed a general release or life story rights agreement in which she agrees to appear in or to be the subject of your production. Such written agreements typically include a provision that the individual waives her right to file a lawsuit for defamation and other claims. I discuss obtaining consent in Section 25.4.

8.4.3. Opinion

A statement of opinion is constitutionally protected and can not be defamatory. Don't take this as *carte blanche* to make any statement you want hoping to pass it off as an opinion. Merely labeling a statement as opinion does not insulate the statement from being defamatory.

For your statement to qualify as an opinion, your audience must realize that your statement is not meant literally. In deciding whether your statement qualifies as an opinion, a court will consider

- the impression of the entire production (in which the statement appeared) taken as a whole,

- whether you used figurative or exaggerated language, and

- whether the statement can be proven to be true or false.

The most significant of these factors is whether the statement can be proven to be true or false. Suppose I say that James Smith is a jerk. Even though there may be a large group of people who agree with me that James Smith is a jerk, my statement about James can not be proven as true or false. It really is a statement of my opinion. However, if I say that James Smith embezzled funds from his employer, that is a statement that can be shown to be true or false. If it is a false statement, I have defamed James Smith.

In a real-life example, *Hustler* magazine expressed an opinion and was not alleging fact when it featured the founder of Women Against Pornography in its *Asshole of the Month* column. The court reasoned that readers should know thoughts expressed were opinion because *Hustler* is a magazine known for its pornographic content and the column is a vehicle regularly used by *Hustler* to lampoon its critics. (*Leidholdt v. L.F.P., Inc.,* 860 F.2d 890 (9th Cir. 1988)).

In contrast, in his autobiography, *Armed and Dangerous*, former Buffalo Bill, Jim Kelly, makes the following statements with respect to his relationship with his former agent:

- Kelly learned his lesson the hard way about whom to trust in business.

- His brothers did not like what they found when they looked at his business affairs.

- After finally seeing the light, Kelly fired his agent, gave his brothers control of his financial affairs, and filed a lawsuit against his agent.

Kelly never directly said that his agent improperly managed his financial affairs. In a subsequent defamation lawsuit filed by his former agent, Kelly portrayed the statements as opinion. The court agreed that the first statement expressed Kelly's subjective opinion about his former agent's trustworthiness. However, the second and third statements implied that his brothers found evidence of the agent's fraudulent activity and that the agent was cheating Kelly. They were statements that can be proven as true or false. If false, they would be defamatory.

The agent ultimately lost because the court in later proceedings determined that Kelly's statements were not substantially false and, therefore, not defamatory. (*Faigin v. Kelly,* 978 F. Supp. 420 (D. N.H. 1997)).

8.4.4. Name Calling

Insults and name calling by themselves are normally not actionable as defamation. Like an opinion, the context determines whether the statement is actionable.

8.4.5. Truth

If you are telling the truth, you are not defaming anyone. For purposes of defamation, truth means substantial truth. It is not required that every detail of your statement be accurate. Minor inaccuracies are immaterial as long as the slightly inaccurate version conveys the same impression about the person as the literal truth would.

In the song *Brain Damage*, rap artist Eminem talks about his childhood experiences with a school bully in elementary school. The song lyrics identify the bully by name and describe an assault in the bathroom in which the bully beat Eminem, banged Eminem's head against the urinal, broke his nose, and choked him. In a lawsuit, the plaintiff admitted that he had regularly "picked on" Eminem in fourth grade including an episode in which he pushed Eminem down. The court found the admission sufficient to dismiss the lawsuit since the song truthfully characterized the plaintiff as a bully. It did not matter that there was a dispute regarding whether the specific bathroom assault actually occurred as described in the song lyrics.

Lawyers may wish to know that the plaintiff actually alleged false light. False light shares many similarities with defamation including incorporation of the substantial truth doctrine. (*Deangelo Bailey v. Marshall Bruce Mathers III, a/k/a Eminem Slim Shady*, unpublished opinion, State of Michigan Court of Appeals, April 14, 2005).

8.4.6. Official Reporting Privilege

Under the official reporting privilege, there is no defamation when a journalist reports libelous statements that were made by others at a public meeting or court proceeding or in governmental reports, transcripts, and similar documents. The press frequently invokes the official reporting privilege. States may call this defense by different names including the record privilege, the reporter's privilege, the fair comment privilege, and the official proceedings privilege.

8.4.7. Neutral Reporting Privilege

A close cousin to the official reporting privilege is the neutral reporting privilege. Under the neutral reporting privilege, the press can repeat a statement even if the press member believes the statement to be false. It is the fact that the statement itself was made that is newsworthy.

Requirements for the neutral reporting privilege include (i) the statement relates to a preexisting public controversy or generates a public controversy in its own right, (ii) the statement is made by a public official, public figure, or by a prominent organization, and (iii) the statement is about a public figure, public official or prominent organization.

8.4.8. Plaintiff as Libel Proof

You are not guilty of defamation if you can show that the person about whom you made the statement is libel proof. One is libel proof when one's reputation can not get any worse. To establish a libel proof defense, you may need to show that there has been media coverage about the person's criminal or anti-social behavior. If there has been a great deal of media coverage, the individual may qualify as a public figure which means he has the additional burden of proving you made any defamatory statement with actual malice.

Examples of individuals deemed to be libel proof

Dr. Jack Kevorkian. Jack Kevorkian is a nationally recognized proponent of assisted suicide. He has admittedly assisted in the suicide of over 100 terminally-ill patients and was convicted for second-degree murder in connection with an assisted suicide. On the issue of assisted suicide, he is libel proof and had no claim against the American Medical Association which released letters and news releases saying Kevorkian engaged in "criminal practices", "continued killings" and "criminal activities". (*Kevorkian v. American Medical Assoc.*, 602 N.W.2d 233 (1999)).

Mafia Associate. John Cerasini, a mafia associate was libel proof. He had no defamation claim against producers of the film, *Donnie Brasco*, depicting his life - even if the film depicted him in some violent acts in which he had not participated. Cerasini had pled guilty in federal court to racketeering; conspiring to rob a bank; and possessing marijuana, cocaine and heroin with the intent to distribute them. Prior to the film's release, Cerasini's activities had been the subject of numerous newspaper articles. (*Cerasini v. Sony Corp.*, 991 F. Supp. 343 (S.D.N.Y. 1998)).

Elizabeth Taylor's Ex. Henry Wynberg had a reputation for taking financial advantage of Elizabeth Taylor. He also had convictions related to his treatment of women in general. He was libel proof and had no defamation action with respect to an unflattering *National Enquirer* article. Other articles regarding Wynberg's criminal convictions and reputation for misusing Taylor had appeared in the press for at least three years prior to publication of the *National Enquirer* article. (*Wynberg v. National Enquirer*, 564 F. Supp. 924 (C.D. Cal 1982)).

8.4.9. Retraction

If you retract a statement, you formally and explicitly disavow it and admit that the statement is false. Retraction is not actually a defense to defamation. However, it may decrease the damages the defendant must pay.

About thirty states have retraction statutes. Requirements for retraction vary significantly by state, but here are some broad generalizations. The retraction must be issued within a reasonable time of the defamatory statement. A reasonable time depends on the state law as well as the specific facts and circumstances. The retraction must also be as conspicuous as the original defamatory statement.

OTHER RELEVANT RIGHTS AND LAWS 9

9.1. Obscenity and Indecency

The First Amendment does not protect obscene material. It does protect indecent material. As a result, the distribution of obscene material may be banned while the distribution of indecent material may only be restricted.

9.1.1. When Is Material Obscene?

There is no constitutional protection for obscene material. While people are allowed to possess obscene materials, they are not allowed to communicate, distribute, sell or transport obscene materials. Material qualifying as obscene may be verbal or visual. That means obscenity laws impact writers, photographers, visual artists, filmmakers, internet sites, musicians, and the whole range of media producers.

Obscenity is governed by a mixture of federal and state law. The U.S. Supreme Court tells us what material qualifies as obscene. According to the Supreme Court, your production is obscene if it appeals to the prurient interest, describes sexual conduct in a patently offensive manner, and lacks value. Violent material, by itself, does not qualify as obscene. Within those parameters, Congress and individual states may pass laws prohibiting the distribution of obscene material.

Appeals to Prurient Interest. For a production to qualify as obscene, the average person, applying contemporary community standards, must find that the production, taken as a whole, appeals to the prurient interest. The Supreme Court defines prurient interest as "a shameful or morbid interest in nudity, sex, or excretion".

The community standard means that each individual state and local community can decide what is obscene. It is designed as an acknowledgement that the people of Boise, Idaho do not have to accept material found unobjectionable in Las Vegas, Nevada. However, in our increasingly global community, the community standard sometimes results in media productions being subject to the most conservative community within the United States – especially for material distributed via the internet.

Describes Sexual Conduct in a Patently Offensive Manner. The production must depict or describe sexual conduct in a manner that is patently offensive. To be patently offensive, the material has to do more than simply suggest sex. It must depict hard core sexual acts which can include sexual acts that are normal or perverted or actual or simulated, masturbation, excretory functions, or lewd exhibition of the genitals.

Lacks Value. The production, taken as a whole must lack serious literary, artistic, political, or scientific value.

9.1.2. Obscenity and Criminal Violations

Distributing obscene material can carry criminal penalties. Federal law prohibits the following:

- broadcasting obscene language via radio
- knowingly using obscene language or distributing obscene material via cable or subscription television
- transmitting obscene material to minors via the internet or other telecommunications device
- failing to maintain accurate records for every performer portrayed in a production which contains depictions of sexually explicit conduct and that travels through interstate commerce

These laws are especially stringent with respect to the use of children in obscene material and/or the distribution of obscene material to children. Any producer who thinks his production might be construed as obscene – especially if it includes minors – should consult with an attorney knowledgeable about obscenity law.

9.1.3. When Is Material Indecent?

Your production contains indecent material if it contains patently offensive sexual or excretory references that do not rise to the level of obscenity. Indecency laws are most relevant to producers whose productions are broadcast on free radio or television.

Since the First Amendment protects indecent programming, the government cannot ban it. The government – through the Federal Communications Commission (FCC) - can and does prohibit the broadcast of indecent programming between 6:00 a.m. and 10:00 p.m. Those are the hours during which children are most likely to be in the audience. Hence, the same programming that is actionable as indecent if broadcast during the day and evening between 6:00 a.m. and 10:00 p.m. is not actionable if broadcast during the late evening and early morning hours of 10:00 p.m. and 6:00 a.m.

9.1.4. The FCC's Enforcement of Obscenity and Indecency Laws

Enforcement actions are triggered by complaints received from the public about indecent or obscene broadcasting. The Federal Communications Commission (FCC) takes action – normally by levying a fine – against broadcasters who air programs containing indecent or obscene words, language or images. Broadcasters who transmit obscene material may also be subject to criminal penalties.

Currently, the FCC levies fines only against television and radio stations and their owners; however, Congress has received proposed legislation that would punish and fine the performers.

9.2. Idea Protection

As discussed in Section 3.4.1, copyright law does not protect ideas. It protects only the expression of the idea. While it is often difficult to protect a raw idea, some states do have misappropriation laws. Success under these idea misappropriation laws requires proof that

- you submitted the idea with the intention of selling it and
- the idea was used by the person to whom you submitted it.

Idea misappropriation cases are difficult to win – and even more difficult to win in a meaningful manner. One must prove the monetary value of the idea and, thus, the damage award that one should receive from the person who misappropriated the idea.

Ideas can also be protected by contracts such as non-disclosure agreements. However, most media companies refuse to sign non-disclosure agreements and, in fact, often require the individual pitching the idea to sign a submission agreement waiving the right to sue the media company for use of the same or similar idea.

9.3. Son of Sam Laws

A number of states have Son of Sam laws. They are designed to prevent criminals from profiting from their crimes by selling their life story rights. The laws derive their name from serial killer David Berkowitz who was referred to as the Son of Sam during his late 1970's New York killing spree.

Generally, Son of Sam laws require that any criminal who derives money from recounting the story of his crime for a television appearance, book, film, magazine article or other media vehicle, forfeit that money and make it available for retribution to the victims of his crime.

These state statutes have not stood up under constitutional scrutiny. The U.S. Supreme Court struck down New York's Son of Sam law finding it unconstitutional and a violation of the First

Amendment because the law punished people for the content of their speech. (*Simon & Schuster v. Members of the New York State Crime Victims Board*, 502 U.S. 105 (1991)).

The U.S. Supreme Court and the state courts do not object to the principle of preventing criminals from profiting from their crimes. They have rejected implementation of specific Son of Sam laws for the following reasons:

- The law penalizes a person for expressing himself or talking about a certain subject.

- The law applies to all revenue from any work that mentions the author's crime regardless of the purpose of the work itself or the extent to which the work relates to the crime.

- The law can be used against a person who was never prosecuted or convicted of the crime if the published work includes an admission to the crime.

Courts have suggested that it is possible to draft a Son of Sam law in a manner that is consistent with the First Amendment. For example, a law that targets all income of the criminal derived in connection with the crime might withstand constitutional scrutiny as such a law would not target speech. Instead, it would treat all income derived from the crime equally.

In response to the court actions, New York, California and other states have modified their Son of Sam laws in an attempt to make them consistent with the First Amendment. Nevertheless, the states have not yet come up with the perfect language and Son of Sam laws are still regularly struck down as unconstitutional.

9.4. Trade Secrets

A trade secret is confidential information of a particular company that gives the company a competitive advantage over other businesses. The primary benefit comes from the fact that other companies do not have the same information.

Specifically, a trade secret can consist of a practice, a method, a design, computer software, a customer list, a database, a compilation of information, or other know-how. To qualify as a trade secret, the information must

- not be known to the public;
- give the holder of the information some economic benefit based on the fact that the information is not generally known to the public; and
- be treated by the owner as a secret.

Trade secrets are based on state law and they can theoretically last forever.

Within the context of rights clearance issues, trade secrets are most common in the area of software development. Employees, consultants, and business partners of computer-related companies often sign non-disclosure and confidentiality agreements in which they agree not to disclose nor use the trade secrets of the company. If you are a software developer, and you employ someone to work on your production, you should verify that the person is not incorporating into your production any elements that another party might view as its trade secret.

Trade secrets also come up in the context of blogs and electronic bulletin boards. These are online sites that often allow visitors to post information. Companies have filed lawsuits against operators of blogs and electronic bulletin boards complaining that the companies' trade secrets have been posted.

9.5. Anti-SLAPP Statutes

There are companies and individuals who use lawsuits as a form of intimidation to stop people from speaking out on issues of public interest. Such lawsuits are referred to as Strategic Lawsuits Against Public Participation – or SLAPPs. A SLAPP suit might be in the form of a defamation or right of privacy action. Other forms in which SLAPPs may appear – and which are not discussed in this book – include conspiracy, intentional infliction of emotional distress, and interference with contract. SLAPP suits may also include a request for a temporary restraining order or an injunction. A number of states have passed anti-SLAPP laws to prevent such abuse of the judicial process. If you believe a lawsuit filed against you is a SLAPP, you can file a complaint under the anti-SLAPP statute. If the person suing you cannot show that his case has a probability of winning, the court will "strike" the other person's complaint, and dismiss the lawsuit. If you win the anti-SLAPP lawsuit, you become eligible to receive reimbursement from the person who sued you for your attorneys' fees and costs.

9.6. Anti-Paparazzi Laws

Paparazzi is an Italian word for a kind of buzzing insects. Americans have adopted the term to refer to a category of photographers and reporters who make their living by taking and selling sensational facts and pictures about celebrities. The paparazzi are often criticized for the aggressive and harassing techniques they use in their persistent pursuit of celebrities. Paparazzi have argued with celebrities they are following and have even been accused of assaulting celebrities and causing celebrities to have traffic accidents.

There are standard criminal and civil penalties available to celebrities who want to take action against reporters who cross the line of acceptable behavior. For example, a celebrity could file a criminal or civil action against an overzealous paparazzo for false imprisonment, invasion of privacy, or assault.

California is one state that has taken the extra step of passing laws targeted directly at paparazzi misconduct. California's anti-paparazzi laws triple the damages that can be awarded to a celebrity in a suit against a member of the paparazzi. The law also denies photographers the right to profit from photographs taken during altercations. There have also been a few unsuccessful attempts to pass federal anti-paparazzi legislation.

Anti-paparazzi laws risk challenge as unconstitutional as they may impede legitimate newsgathering activities and may violate the First Amendment.

9.7. Blind-Sided from Left Field

There is the rights clearance problem that leaves you and your lawyer saying "Wow, I never saw that coming!"

My favorite example of this phenomenon is a case involving the motion picture *Spider-Man*. *Spider-Man* includes a scene set in Times Square during a fictional World Unity Festival. In order to generate revenue, Sony, the producer of the film, implemented a very creative product placement campaign. It superimposed the advertisements of various companies on the Times Square billboards so that the movie audience saw the ads of the film's sponsors and not the billboard ads actually posted in Times Square. The owners and licensees of the billboards sued for several trademark and trespass related claims.

In the rights clearance arena, it is normally a risk-minimizing move to replace another entity's trademarks and copyrighted property with material which you have permission to use. One would normally think that Sony replacing the Times Square ads with ads of companies who had expressed a desire to be in the film would be a good move! The *Spider-Man* lawsuit illustrates that there are certain risks that a producer cannot anticipate. Fortunately for the producers and distributors of *Spider-Man*, the court dismissed the billboard owners' claims. (*Sherwood 48 Associates v. Sony*, 76 Fed. Appx. 389 (2nd Cir. 2003)).

PART THREE
Clearance Issues for Specific Producers

In Part Three, I discuss unique clearance issues for specific categories of media producers. Part Three builds on Part Two which summarized the laws most relevant to the rights clearance process. These laws include copyright, trademark, right of publicity, right of privacy, defamation, obscenity and indecency. Although many of the concepts discussed in Part Two apply to all media, they can arise in unique ways within certain types of media productions.

Chapters in Part Three:

CLEARANCE ISSUES FOR PUBLISHERS AND WRITERS

In this chapter, I highlight the following situations which are somewhat unique to books and other printed material:

- using a fictional work as the subject matter of your book
- telling a person's life story
- protecting recipes through copyright
- publishing a periodical with material provided by freelancers
- triggering libel claims through headlines, apart from the text itself

I say these situations are somewhat unique to books because some of these issues arise in film and television as well as other media. For convenience and also because most film and television projects begin in the written form of a script, I have somewhat arbitrarily decided to discuss these issues in the chapter designated for publishers and writers.

10.1. Copyright Issues in Productions about Factual Events

As I discussed above in Section 3.4.1, copyright does not protect facts. If you write a book on an actual event and rely on facts presented in a previous book or film about the event, you have not committed copyright infringement. You commit copyright infringement only if you take the protectible expression from the previous works.

But what happens if you write a book that offers a summary of or serves as a resource for another fictional work? For example, suppose you write a companion guide for fans of the *Star Trek* series. Your guide defines terms such as transporter and holodeck, provides biographical information for Spock, Jean-Luc Picard and other characters, and summarizes each of the crew's adventures.

Since *Star Trek* stories are actual books, films and television programs, are you simply writing about facts and actual events? Most courts that have looked at this issue respond that you are not. If your guidebook simply aggregates fictional moments and dialogue from the *Star Trek* works, you would likely be called an infringer.

The answer is different if you use the dialogue and fictional events in a transformative manner. If your book is a commentary on *Star Trek*, the use of some dialogue and fictional moments would likely be viewed as fair use for purposes of criticism. For example, if the topic of your book is an analysis of the accuracy of scientific principles in *Star Trek*, your book would likely be safe from copyright infringement claims even though it might include a discussion of some plot lines as well as some dialogue.

Examples of producers using a fictional work as the subject matter of a book

The Seinfeld Aptitude Test. The *Seinfeld Aptitude Test* is a trivia quiz book about the television series *Seinfeld* written and published without the authorization of the *Seinfeld* copyright owners. The book draws from eighty-four of the eighty-six Seinfeld episodes that had been broadcast as of the book's publication date. Forty-one questions and/or answers contain dialogue from *Seinfeld* episodes. Although the author added new material by creating the incorrect answers to the multiple choice questions, every question and correct answer is based on a fictional moment in a *Seinfeld* episode. After the producers of *Seinfeld* filed a lawsuit, they won an injunction prohibiting further distribution of the book because the court found that the quiz book infringed the copyrights in the *Seinfeld* show. The *Seinfeld* producers also won a $403,000 damage award. (*Castle Rock Entertainment v. Carol Publishing Group*, 150 F.3d 132 (2nd Cir. 1998)).

Welcome To Twin Peaks. Scott Knickelbine wrote *Welcome to Twin Peaks: A Complete Guide to Who's Who and What's What.* The book describes and comments on the plots, characters, actors, and producers of the 1990 hit television series, *Twin Peaks.* Forty-six pages of the 128-page book contain a detailed recounting of eight *Twin Peaks* episodes with every plot twist and element of character development. The book also incorporates at least eighty-nine lines of dialogue from the television series. Finding that the book violates the copyright in the television series, the court stopped further publication of the book and assessed aggregate copyright infringement damages of nearly $150,000 against the book's author, publisher, and distributor. (*Twin Peaks Productions v. Publications International*, 996 F.2d 1366 (2nd Cir. 1993)).

Commentary on The Da Vinci Code. The *Da Vinci Code* is Dan Brown's 2003 best-selling thriller that combines art history, theology, secret codes, secret religious societies, and a resolution that claims Jesus Christ married and had children with Mary Magdalene. Brown's book has spawned dozens of books and television programs purporting either to debunk or prove Brown's portrayal of Jesus Christ and the early church some of which include *Cracking DaVinci's Code, The Truth Behind the DaVinci Code: A Challenging Response to the Bestselling Novel, The DaVinci Code: Fact or Fiction?*, and *Exposing the DaVinci Code.* These productions' primary focus is an analysis of the theories presented in The *Da Vinci Code.* They can remain squarely within the realms of commentary and fair use even if they weave some plot elements, characters and dialogue from the *Da Vinci Code* into their arguments and discussions concerning the theories.

10.2. Biographies

As discussed in Section 6.2, the more famous a person is, the fewer privacy rights he has. A person in the public eye or involved in public events does not have exclusive rights to his life story. The First Amendment allows publication of information concerning events and people who are in the public eye - even if the individuals involved object to the publication of such information. Anyone may write about those public events or public persons. It does not even matter under the law if your unauthorized biography competes with an official biography authorized by the public person.

Although the First Amendment may protect you from liability if you have not obtained permission, it does not prevent someone from trying to block your unauthorized telling of their story by filing a lawsuit if they do not like what you say. The risks of a lawsuit and the subject's chances for success on a claim increase if you weave elements of fiction into a factual story. See the discussion of fictionalization in Section 13.4. To eliminate or at least minimize these risks, many producers seek a life story rights agreement in which their subject expressly grants the right to tell his life story and waives all claims based on right of privacy, right of publicity, defamation and related actions.

Life story rights agreements frequently carry the added advantage of exclusivity. Subjects selling rights in their life story often provide background information to the producer in developing the story and script. In an exclusivity provision, your subject agrees to provide information and help only to you – and not to other producers who may be developing competing versions of the story.

I discuss life story rights agreements in more detail in Section 25.3. The Appendix also contains an example of a life story rights agreement.

10.3. Recipes and Cookbooks

In Section 3.4, I discuss that processes and procedures are not copyrightable. Certain recipes exemplify non-copyrightable procedures.

A recipe which simply lists ingredients and basic cooking directions is a list of processes and procedures and is not copyrightable.

10.3.1. A Recipe That Is Not Copyrightable

Here is a recipe for cranberry gelatin mold in a format that is not copyrightable:

Cranberry Gelatin Mold

Dissolve a 6-oz package of strawberry-flavored gelatin in 2 ½ cups of boiling water. Add 8 ounces of crushed pineapple and one 12-ounce can of whole cranberries. Allow to cool. Place gelatin mixture in bowl and chill in refrigerator until firm. If desired, garnish with whipped topping before serving.

10.3.2. A Recipe That May Be Copyrightable

If I weave expressive elements into the recipe, it stands a much better chance of being copyrightable. These elements might be suggestions for presentation, advice on wines, accompaniments, music to complete the meal, and information on the origin of the dish.

Here's a version of the recipe for cranberry gelatin mold that might be copyrightable:

Kickin' Cranberry Gelatin Mold

By adding a touch of sophistication to this well-known kids' dish, you come up with a delectable edible that will become a family favorite for years to come. Simply dissolve 6 ounces of gelatin along with 8 ounces of crushed pineapple and a can of whole cranberries in 2 ½ cups of water. After 12 hours of chillin' in the refrigerator, it emerges as a most versatile dish. It can stand on its own as a guilt-free light afternoon or late-night snack. It also fits in well as a trimming to go along with your Thanksgiving turkey dinner. With a little whipped topping, it can also grace your pound cake or vanilla ice cream when it's time for dessert.

10.3.3. Cookbooks As Copyrightable Compilations

A cookbook or a group of recipes may receive copyright protection as a compilation – even if the recipes themselves are not copyrightable. A compilation is a collection of pre-existing materials that are selected, coordinated, or arranged in such a way that the resulting work as a whole constitutes an original work of authorship. A compilation copyright protects the order and manner of the presentation of the compilation's elements, but does not necessarily protect each element individually. As a result, if a cookbook is copyrightable as a compilation, the manner and order in which the recipes are presented in the cookbook is protectible - but the individual recipes themselves are not necessarily protectible.

10.4. Collective Works and Use of Freelance Materials

Newspapers, magazines and other periodicals frequently retain freelancers to write articles and provide other materials for the publication. The publication's rights in material created by a freelancer differ from its rights in material created by employees.

If an employee of the publication creates materials, the publication owns the materials as a work made for hire. If a freelancer creates the materials, the publication has only those rights granted by the freelancer. The freelancer may grant all rights. Alternatively, the freelancer may make a more limited grant of rights. See Section 19.3.1 for a discussion of how freelancers can grant rights.

What happens if a freelancer writes an article for a publication without a written agreement or a discussion of how the publication may use the article? Normally, when there is a work from a freelancer without a written agreement, the freelancer retains all ownership rights in the commissioned material and the commissioned party has a license to use the material only for the specific project for which the freelancer created it.

Most newspapers and magazines qualify for an expanded version of this general rule. The expanded version of the rule is applicable to publications that are collective works. A collective work is one in which a number of independent contributions are assembled. Most periodicals qualify as collective works because they contain numerous articles and other materials contributed by multiple authors.

As collective works, newspapers and magazines are subject to a specific provision of the Copyright Act that expands their ability to use freelance materials. Unless there is an agreement granting broader or narrower rights, a newspaper or magazine may use freelance material in any of three ways:

- in the collective work to which the freelancer originally contributed the work

- in any revision of the collective work

- in any subsequent edition of the collective work

For example, if a freelancer writes an article for the June 2008 edition of *Life* Magazine, *Life* Magazine can publish the article in the June 2008 edition. *Life* Magazine could also publish the article in a corrected edition of the June 2008 edition, and in later editions of the magazine. On the other hand, *Life* could not reprint a copy of the article in its sister publication, *Time* Magazine.

This concept can include editions in different media such as taking a print edition and creating a multimedia compilation of a collective work. *National Geographic* created The *Complete National Geographic* on CD-ROM and DVD. The compilation contains images of every page of every *National Geographic* magazine from 1888 through 1996. *National Geographic* did not violate the copyrights of freelance writers and photographers when it did not pay them royalties for the subsequent use. The CD-ROM version qualifies as a revised version of the original collective work even though it contains materials that never appeared in the print edition of the magazine such as animated opening and closing sequences, music, article summaries and a search engine. According to the court, people purchased the *The Complete National Geographic* to see old material - and not for the newly added material.

A publication's subsequent use of a freelancer's material does have its limitations. The U.S. Supreme Court's decision in *New York Times Inc. v. Tasini*, 533 US 483 (2001) clarified that a newspaper or magazine can not distribute a freelancer's work as a stand-alone article without the explicit authorization of the freelancer. In the *Tasini* case, the *New York Times*, *Newsday*, and *Sports Illustrated* licensed freelancers' articles to online database services, which permitted the download of individual articles from these publications. The articles did not appear in the context of the original print publications for which they had been prepared. Instead, each article was presented and retrievable as a single, stand-alone article.

The intent of the *Tasini* decision was to allow a freelancer to benefit where there is a demand for the freelancer's work as a stand-alone work. In some respects, the seemingly freelancer-favorable decision has backfired on freelancers. In the aftermath of *Tasini*, many publications have become more aggressive in demanding all rights from freelancers so that the publications can use the articles in any way including online without the necessity of paying additional compensation.

10.5. Headlines As Libel

Libel is a form of defamation. Defamation is the act of making a false statement that harms a person's reputation. If the defamatory statement is communicated in a fixed form such as an image, text, or film, the defamation falls into the category of libel. I discuss defamation in depth in Chapter 8.

Normally, a court considers the headline in conjunction with the entire story when determining whether libel has occurred. However, a court may evaluate a headline independently from the story in determining the existence of libel if:

- The headline is oversized.

- The headline leads the reader to a false conclusion not supported in the full story.

- The publisher intentionally uses misleading headlines to create a false impression.

For example, one week after O.J. Simpson's acquittal for the murder of Nicole Brown Simpson and Ronald Goldman, the *Na-*

tional Examiner ran a headline that stated "COPS THINK KATO DID IT!". The article referred to Kato Kaelin, a former house guest of Simpson who had testified at Simpson's criminal trial. The actual story was located seventeen pages after the headline. "IT" referred to the police's suspicion that Kaelin had committed perjury during the trial. Kaelin sued the *National Examiner* for defamation. The court determined that the headline had the potential to convey the false and defamatory meaning that Kaelin had committed the murders of which Simpson had been accused. (*Kaelin v. Globe Communications*, 162 F.3d 1036 (9th Cir. 1998)).

CLEARANCE ISSUES FOR VISUAL ARTISTS | 11

This chapter highlights the following clearance situations which are somewhat unique to visual art:

- copyright infringement of artwork
- using a person's image in your visual art
- Visual Artists Rights Act (VARA)

11.1. Copyright Infringement of Artwork

As discussed in Section 3.4.1, it is the expression of the idea and not the idea itself that receives copyright protection. Copyright does not protect the subject matter of visual art unless the subject matter is itself copyrightable.

For example, suppose you photograph a mural. In other words, the mural is the subject of the photograph. Your photograph is protected by copyright. At the same time, the mural is also an independent artistic work which is protected by copyright in its own right.

In contrast, suppose you photograph a horse. Your photograph is protected by copyright. However, the horse is not an independent artistic work eligible for copyright protection.

Anyone may duplicate your idea of photographing a horse – even if it is the exact same horse. What another may not do is duplicate the expressive elements used by you in the photograph of the horse. Expressive elements in visual artwork include the selection of lighting, shading, camera angle (for photographs), background and perspective. In some cases the contrived positioning of a subject is also protected.

In one example from real life, a California couple commissioned Art Rogers, a professional photographer, to photograph the couple with eight German shepherd puppies. Rogers produced the photographic portrait entitled *Puppies*. Jeff Koons, a sculptor who had obtained a published notecard of *Puppies*, created *String of Puppies*, a wood sculptural version of the photograph. Koons' directions to the art studio that assisted him with the sculpture included the following instructions:

- The sculpture be just like the photo.
- The features of the humans and puppies be reproduced as per the photo.
- The puppies be painted in shades of blue with variation of light to dark as per the photo.
- The man's hair be white with shades of grey as per the black and white photo.

Koons took more than the idea of creating a piece of artwork featuring a couple holding puppies. He used elements of copyrightable expression from Rogers' *Puppies* photograph.

Koons created three editions of the sculpture, displayed them, and then sold them to collectors for a total of $367,000. In the inevitable lawsuit that followed, the court found Koons' sculpture to be a derivative work of and an infringement of Rogers' photograph. (*Rogers v. Koons*, 751 F. Supp. 474 (S.D.N.Y. 1990)).

11.2. Use of a Person's Image in Your Artwork

The right of publicity is often invoked by celebrities whose images are used in visual artwork for a commercial purpose. You are using a celebrity's image for a commercial purpose if your artwork falsely implies that the celebrity endorses the work or you are simply cashing in on the public's desire to have an image of the celebrity.

The more literal the depiction of a celebrity in your artwork, the more likely it is that your artwork violates the celebrity's right of publicity. In contrast, using a celebrity likeness in your artwork may be acceptable if you add enough creative elements to the image to qualify your use of the original image as transformative. If the image is sufficiently transformed, you have used the image to express something new and the First Amendment protects your right to use the celebrity's image.

Here's the rationale for your right to produce a transformed image. Works of parody or other distortions of the celebrity image are not good substitutes for literal depictions of the celebrity. Therefore, transformed images generally do not impact markets for celebrity memorabilia that the right of publicity is designed to protect.

Example in which use of celebrity image violates the right of publicity

Three Stooges T-Shirts.   Artist Gary Saderup drew a charcoal drawing of the Three Stooges and sold lithographs and T-shirts of his drawing. The court viewed Saderup's work as an unadorned, nearly photographic reproduction of the faces of the Three Stooges which simply capitalized on the fame of Larry, Curly and Mo (*Comedy III Productions v. Gary Saderup, Inc.,* 25 Cal.4th 387 (2001))

Examples in which use of celebrity image does not violate the right of publicity

Tiger Woods Victory at the Masters.   In 1997, Tiger Woods won the Masters Tournament, arguably the most famous golf tournament in the world. As the youngest golfer and the first golfer of African-American and Asian descent to win the Masters, Woods' victory was a historic event in the world of sports. Artist, Rick Rush, created and released a limited edition print, *The Masters of Augusta*, that features three depictions of Woods at the tournament. Woods' images appear within a collage of other images of past winners and others associated with the tournament. The collage describes, in artistic form, a historic event in sports history and conveys a message about the significance of Woods' achievement in that event.

As such, it is a transformative use of Woods' image and protected by the First Amendment. (*ETW Corp. v. Jireh Publishing*, 332 F.3d 915 (6th Cir. 2003)).

Baseball Cards. Baseball cards caricaturing and parodying well-known major league baseball players are protected by the First Amendment against a claim brought under the Oklahoma right of publicity statute. (*Cardtoons v. Major League Baseball Players*, 95 F.3d 959 (10th Cir. 1996)).

11.3. Moral Rights and the Visual Artists Rights Act

Moral rights protect the artist's reputation, honor, and integrity. European countries – especially France – provide much stronger moral rights protections to creators than the United States does. In the United States, the Visual Artists Rights Act (VARA) provides limited moral rights for visual artists. VARA became effective in June 1991, and is incorporated into the Copyright Act.

VARA offers some moral rights protections to a very small category of visual artwork: paintings, drawings, prints, sculptures. VARA also protects certain still photos. The still photos must be produced for exhibition purposes only and exist in a single copy or in a limited edition of no more than 200 consecutively numbered, signed copies. VARA does not protect posters, applied art, technical drawings, motion pictures, or artwork created as a work made for hire.

Under VARA, an artist has the following moral rights:

- the right to claim authorship of the work

- the right to prevent use of his or her name on a work the artist did not create

- the right to prevent use of his or her name on mutilated or distorted versions of the work

- the right to prevent mutilation or distortion of the work

An artist retains rights under VARA even if he sells the copyright in the artwork. While an artist can not sell or transfer his moral rights, an artist can waive moral rights through a written contract.

CLEARANCE ISSUES
FOR MUSICIANS AND MUSIC PRODUCERS

This chapter highlights the following clearance issues as they specifically relate to music:

- ownership and collaboration of music

- sampling of music

- copyright infringement of music

With respect to music clearance issues, you must first understand the distinction between a song and a sound recording. There are two distinct copyrights in every recorded song.

There is a copyright in the song which consists of the melody and any accompanying lyrics. In Copyright Act lingo songs are referred to as musical compositions.

There is a separate and distinct copyright in the recording of the song – referred to alternatively as the recording, sound recording, or master.

The copyright owner of the song is generally the songwriter or the music publishing company. The copyright owner of the sound recording is generally the record label or company that released the recording. Section 22.1 discusses in more detail the distinction between a song and a sound recording.

12.1. Ownership of and Collaboration on Music Productions

The question of "who owns the music?" crops up frequently within musical groups that perform original music. Record labels typically own the sound recordings of their artists. Sound recordings produced by bands that have no relationship with a record label are usually owned by the members of the band. Bands with no record label relationships are frequently referred to as unsigned bands.

Typically, the members of an unsigned band share ownership of their recordings. However, ownership of songs among members of an unsigned band is often more complicated than ownership of the sound recordings.

If you are in a band and you bring a song to the band that you have written completely on your own, you are clearly the owner of the copyright in the song. Even if another band member writes a new musical arrangement of the song or writes the part for his particular instrument, you are still the copyright owner of the song. However, when another band member does more than just a bit of tweaking – such as coming up with a new hook or providing lyrics – your band mate arguably becomes a co-writer, and thus a co-owner, of the song.

As discussed in Section 17.3, without a written agreement that says otherwise, each co-owner of a copyright owns an equal portion of the work. This concept applies to music. Even if one person writes the lyrics and two people write the melody, there is not necessarily a separate copyright in the lyrics and a separate copyright in the melody. Instead, there is one copyright in the entire song and each of the three people who created the song owns an equal one third portion – unless there is a written agreement that says otherwise.

Some bands decide to share the copyright in their original songs, regardless of which band member writes the songs. Before making this decision, the songwriter should consider that the copyright in the songs – and the corresponding opportunity to derive money from the songs – last for her lifetime plus seventy years. That is longer than the band is going to be together. The copyright in a song can be passed to your heirs.

You may not want to share all the revenue generated from your songs after your band is no longer together. Consider the following. Suppose you write a song, "Crystal City", while you are a member of the Jugheads. The Jugheads perform "Crystal City" at their gigs. A few years down the road after the members of the Jugheads have gone their separate ways, you record and release "Crystal City" with your new band, Lightning. Lightning's release of "Crystal City" is a run-away hit. Is it your intention to share with the members of the Jugheads all the songwriting revenue generated from Lightning's release of "Crystal City"? Maybe yes, maybe no – but that is the result you get if you share the copyright in your original songs with your former Jughead co-band members.

One alternative is for the songwriters to hold onto the copyright in their songs but allow all the band members to share in revenue generated by the song during the life of the band and perhaps for a set period thereafter. In that way, the band's songwriters preserve their interest in what could become a very valuable property while the other band members still receive some compensation for their role in the song's success.

12.2. Sampling

Sampling entails using portions of existing songs or recordings in new recordings. Music producers might also sample the audio portion of films and television programming.

12.2.1. Sampling a Song

You may decide to go into a studio and record a portion of the song and place your re-creation of the song excerpt in your newly created work. This type of sampling is sometimes referred to as an interpolation. It requires a license from the copyright owner of the song. Sometimes the copyright owner of the song to be sampled wants an ownership percentage of the newly created song – or at least a percentage participation in the income generated from the newly created song.

If you are using the song by making a new sound recording of your own performance, you do not need permission from the copyright owner of the pre-existing sound recording. The Copyright Act allows you to "duplicate" a sound recording by mimicking or imitating it – as long as you do not make an actual copy of the sound recording itself. The caveat is to exercise caution when imitating the voice and performance of a distinctive singer for any re-created sound recording used for advertising purposes. You risk violating the performer's right of publicity. See Chapter 7 for a discussion of the right of publicity.

12.2.2. Sampling a Sound Recording

You may decide to sample the sound recording. The license from the sound recording copyright owner is referred to as a master use license. The master use license can be one set fee or it can be a royalty amount based on the number of records sold.

You can not use a sound recording without using the underlying song. As a result, whenever you use an existing sound recording produced by someone other than yourself, you need a license from the copyright owner of the sound recording as well as a license from the copyright owner of the song.

If professional musicians perform on the sound recording to be sampled, you may also need to pay re-use fees to the American Federation of Musicians, an entertainment union for professional musicians.

12.2.3. Is Sampling Fair Use?

Sampling may sometimes qualify as fair use but there is no guarantee. A situation involving sampling goes through the same fair use analysis and *de minimis* analysis discussed in Sections 3.7 and 3.9.2.

Your sampling of a song stands a better chance of qualifying as a fair use or a *de minimis* use than does your sampling of a sound recording. For example, The Beastie Boy's "Pass The Mic" included three notes from jazz flutist James W. Newton's song "Choir". A California court viewed the sampling of the song as *de minimis* and not actionable as copyright infringement. (*Newton v. Michael*, 204 F. Supp.2d 1244 (C.D. Cal. 2002).

In contrast, N.W.A.'s "100 Miles And Runnin'" sampled and looped three notes from a sound recording of "Get Off Your Ass and Jam" by George Clinton and the Funkadelics.

In this case, the court said even sampling just three notes from a sound recording was not a *de minimis* use and could be actionable as copyright infringement. (*Bridgeport Music v. Dimension Films*, 383 F.3d 390 (6th Cir. 2004)).

The *100 Miles And Runnin'* case relied on a specific provision of the Copyright Act in distinguishing the sampling of a song from sampling of a sound recording. The Copyright Act allows anyone to imitate or simulate a sound recording by making a re-recording as long as no actual copy of the original sound recording is made. The *100 Miles And Runnin'* court reasoned that since you cannot pirate the whole sound recording, you cannot sample any portion of the sound recording – not even three notes. The court did not view its decision as stifling creativity because, in its words, any artist who wants to incorporate a portion of a pre-existing sound recording into a new recording can re-create the portion of that recording in a studio.

12.3. Copyright Infringement of Music

12.3.1. Infringement of Song Lyrics

For copyright infringement purposes, lyrics are analyzed similarly to literary works. If the claim is based on lyrics only, the claim may not be successful if only non-copyrightable elements have been copied. There is no infringement simply because the lyrics share the same idea or theme.

For example, two songs - "Dear Dolly" and "Dolly" - express admiration for the popular singer, Dolly Parton, and allude to her rise from humble beginnings to stardom. However, the songs express the idea differently so one does not infringe the other. "Dear Dolly" is told from the perspective of a distant admirer whose loneliness is cheered by the singing of Ms. Parton whom he calls a sweet simple girl. "Dolly" is an optimistic and upbeat composition told from the perspective of an admirer who knew Dolly Parton before she became a big star. (*Pendleton v. Acuff-Rose Publications*, 605 F. Supp. 477 (M.D.Tenn. 1984)).

Courts also recognize that certain genres of music have certain scenes-a-faire. Scenes-a-faire are incidents or settings that naturally flow from a common theme. For example, some describe the scenes-a-faire for a country and western song as references to mothers, drinking, prisons, trains, trucks, smoking, gambling, and loving. Scenes-a-faire are not copyrightable and are available for anyone to use. See Section 3.4.4 for a more detailed discussion of scenes-a-faire.

12.3.2. Infringement of Melody

Courts often use expert musicologists to determine whether the melodies of two songs are substantially similar. A court considers structure, melody, harmony and rhythm. Courts recognize that there are a limited number of ways to express oneself and that popular music shares similarities in these four elements. For example, most popular songs share the same structure in that they have an introduction, verse, chorus, and bridge.

Common phrases and chord progressions are usually not copyrightable. For example, "Take A Picture", a 1999 song that topped Billboard's Dance chart does not infringe an unpublished song by an aspiring songwriter even though both songs are in the key of A Major, have a I-IV chord progression, a guitar rhythm, and have chords in root position. (*Tisi v. Patrick*, 97 F. Supp.2d 539 (S.D.N.Y. 2000)).

Nevertheless, if several non-copyrightable elements are tied together in a unique way, there may be a sufficient basis to find copyright infringement. For example, Michael Bolton's "Love Is A Wonderful Thing" shares the following elements with the Isley Brothers 1964 song by the same title: the title hook phrase including the lyric, rhythm, and pitch; the shifted cadence; the instrumental figures; the verse/chorus relationship; and the fade ending. The combination of non-protectible elements are not in any other prior song. As a result, Bolton and related parties were found liable of copyright infringement and paid combined damages of $5.4 Million. (*Three Boys Music Corp. v. Bolton*, 212 F.3d 477 (9th Cir. 2000).

12.3.3. Infringement of Sound Recording

Copyright infringement of a sound recording must involve physical or digital copying of the sound recording. You can re-create a sound recording by recording your own performance of the underlying song. Your re-creation of the sound recording is not an infringement of the original sound recording even if you duplicate, mimic or imitate the performance rendered on the original sound recording. In other words, you are not violating the sound recording owner's rights if you go into a studio and record a re-creation of the sound recording. However, it may be infringement of the underlying song. Also, if you mimic the performance of a celebrity and use the sound recording in an advertising context, you may violate the celebrity's right of publicity. See Section 5.3.3 for a discussion of right of privacy violations triggered by such sound-a-like recordings.

It is typically obvious when someone copies a sound recording. If you copy a sound recording without a license or permission, your defense from copyright infringement is that your copying of the sound recording qualifies as a *de minimis* use or a fair use. There is a higher bar for the fair use of a sound recording compared to the fair use of a song. As discussed above in Section 12.2.3, one court has ruled that the physical copying of a sound recording never qualifies as a fair use.

CLEARANCE ISSUES FOR FILM, TV AND AUDIO-VISUAL PRODUCERS

13

This chapter highlights clearance issues unique to film, television programming, and audio-visual productions. Film and television production issues examined include the use of music, guild issues, title selection, and set decoration. The chapter also includes a discussion of clearance issues for some specific areas of audio-visual programming including news programming, documentaries, and docudramas.

13.1. Film and Television Programs In General

13.1.1. Title Protection

As discussed in Section 4.4.1, trademark law and not copyright law offers protection for titles. However, trademark protection is available only for those titles of single works that have developed secondary meaning. That means the title of a single movie, documentary, or single-episode television program generally does not have enforceable trademark rights. In contrast, the title of a series – such as a television program series or a movie series – can be protectible as a trademark.

Limited protection for a title of a single film can be secured by registering the title with the Motion Picture Association of America (MPAA). All the major movie studios belong to the MPAA. The major studios have entered into an agreement that they will respect each other's reservation of titles and not use titles that are confusingly similar. The process is administered through the MPAA Title Registration Bureau. Independent producers can participate for a fee. The Appendix has additional information on the service.

13.1.2. Consents and Releases

You should have a release for each person who appears in your audio-visual production. Section 25.4 contains a more detailed discussion of consents and releases.

13.1.3. Use of Music

There are very few audio-visual programs that do not make use of music. If you need music for your production, you have a few options. You can commission original music created specifically for your production, license existing music, or do some combination of the two.

For proper clearance, you must obtain permission to use any copyrighted music. If you are commissioning original music, the permission takes the form of a composer's agreement. If you are using pre-existing music, the permission usually takes the form of a synchronization, master use, or videogram license. I discuss music licensing in greater detail in Chapter 22.

13.1.4. Set Decoration

You must pay attention to the elements that appear on your set and in the background. Unlicensed artwork appearing in your production creates the possibility of copyright infringement claims. The producer's defense in these claims is that the appearance of the artwork is a fair use. As discussed in depth in Section 3.7, it is difficult to determine how a court will evaluate a fair use case. In the two set decoration cases discussed immediately below, even though the fact patterns are similar and the same court decided both cases within one year of each other, the rulings are strikingly different. The variation in decisions emphasizes that fair use is highly fact specific and sometimes fickle.

Faith Ringgold and Roc. Faith Ringgold is a contemporary artist who created, and owns the copyright in, a work of art entitled *Church Picnic Story Quilt.* An episode of the sitcom *Roc* used a poster of *Church Picnic* as part of the set decoration. The poster appeared in nine shots for a total of less than thirty seconds. Nothing in the dialogue, action, or camera work particularly calls the viewer's attention to the poster. Nevertheless, the court refused to dismiss Ringgold's suit and concluded that the question of fair use was a question for trial. The parties ultimately settled without a trial. (*Ringgold v. Black Entertainment Television*, 126 F.3d 70 (2nd Cir. 1997)).

Jorge Antonia Sandoval's Artwork and the movie, Seven. Jorge Antonio Sandoval created a series of fifty-two untitled and highly unusual black and white self-portrait studies. In one scene from the 1995 movie *Seven*, the police search the apartment of a photographer. On the back wall, there is a large light-box with a number of photographic transparencies attached to it including ten of Sandoval's self-portraits. The lightbox appears for a total of 35.6 seconds. The court dismissed Sandoval's lawsuit finding that the use was minimal and did not qualify as copyright infringement. (*Sandoval v. New Line Cinema, Corp.*, 147 F.3d 215 (2nd Cir. 1998)).

The same New York court decided *Ringgold* and *Sandoval*. The court justified its different results by explaining that the artwork in *Ringgold*, was "clearly visible" and "recognizable as a painting", while Sandoval's photographs as used in *Seven*, are displayed in poor lighting and at great distance so that they are unidentifiable by the average observer.

13.1.5. Public Television

There are compulsory licenses for noncommercial educational broadcast stations to use non-dramatic published musical works and published pictorial, graphic and sculptural works. A compulsory license is granted by operation of law and is available to anyone who satisfies the conditions of the license. The license terms and rates are published with the Copyright Office's regulations (37 C.F.R. §253.1) and are subject to adjustment every five years. The rates vary according to how the station wants to use the work and the type of organization (*e.g.*, tv station, radio station) making use of the work.

13.2. News Programming

13.2.1. Copyright of News Story

As discussed in Section 3.4.2, facts themselves are not copyrightable. However, the manner of presenting those facts is copyrightable. The concept applies to news stories. While the underlying facts presented in a news story are not protected by copyright, the news programming or story itself is copyrightable.

Even raw videotape footage can encompass sufficient intellectual and creative input to meet the originality requirement for copyright protection. For example, one court explained that taking footage of a news event from a helicopter requires decisions about the newsworthiness of the event and how best to tell the story, the selection of camera lenses, angles and exposures; the choices of the heights and directions from which to tape; and what portions of the event to film and for how long.

13.2.2. Acceptable and Unacceptable Newsgathering Techniques

Newsgathering techniques may generate causes of action for invasion of privacy. See Chapter 6 for an in-depth discussion of invasion of privacy. Improper newsgathering techniques may also trigger trespass, fraud, statutory wiretapping, and other legal claims. These are primarily state law claims and the results of court actions can vary widely from state to state.

News gathering techniques typically viewed as acceptable by courts include the following:

- engaging in newsgathering activities in or from a public place

- using a device such as a zoom lens to record action within public earshot or view

- photographing private property while located on public property

- entering private property with the explicit consent of the owner

Some state courts have also ruled it acceptable to make a secret recording of an event that occurs on private property, as long as the taping occurs in areas generally open to the public such as the public portion of a retail store.

Newsgathering techniques that may be viewed as unacceptable by courts include the following:

- entering private property without the owner's consent

- gaining entrance to private property through deception

- intercepting a wire or oral conversation if the people being recorded reasonably thought their conversation was private

Members of the media who gain employment with the intention of conducting an undercover investigation have been accused of fraud for failing to disclose their connection to the media and for using hidden cameras and microphones on the employers' premises. There is disparity in the manner various states view such investigative journalism techniques.

13.2.3. Fair Use of Copyrighted Material in News Programming

News broadcasts regularly incorporate references to and clips of films, television programs, music, and other images from popular culture. News broadcasts frequently use such material without obtaining permission. The unlicensed use usually - but not always - goes without challenge. Any unlicensed use by news programming is subject to the Fair Use Doctrine or other exceptions to copyright protection discussed in Section 3.7 and 3.9. While news reporting is a preferred use under the Fair Use Doctrine, it is possible for news programming to go beyond the boundaries of fair use. Here are some sample cases from real life.

News broadcast's use of material is fair use

Robert Mitchum. In the days after actor Robert Mitchum's death in July 1997, CNN, ABC and CBS each produced and broadcast separate televised obituaries. Among other achievements, Mitchum received an Academy Award nomination for his supporting role in the 1945 film *G.I. Joe*. Each of the network memorials included clips of *G.I. Joe* as well as other Mitchum films. Each memorial was less than three minutes and included from six to twenty-two seconds of *G.I. Joe* footage. In many instances, the sound of the clip was muted or inaudible as a reporter provided commentary about Mitchum's life. Inclusion of the *G. I. Joe* footage in the televised memorials was a fair use. (*Video-Cinema Films v. CNN*, 66 U.S.P.Q.2d 1473 (S.D.N.Y. 2001)).

Good Morning, America Science Fiction Segment. ABC used twenty-four seconds of footage from several 1950s science fiction movies in a *Good Morning, America* segment commenting on and criticizing alien movies. ABC's use of the clips was a fair use. (*Wade Williams Distribution v. ABC*, No. 00-5002, 2005 U.S. Dist. LEXIS 5730 (S.D.N.Y. April 5, 2005)).

News broadcast's use of material is not fair use

Good Morning, America Travel Segment. In a sixty-five second background piece, *Good Morning America* used thirty-eight seconds of footage from an eighteen-minute travelogue video. The court held that ABC's use of the footage, which included the heart or very best scenes of the video, was not a fair use. (*Hi-Tech Prod. v. Capital Cities/ABC*, 804 F. Supp. 950 (W.D. Mich. 1992), reversed on other grounds, 58 F.3d 1093 (6th Cir. 1995)).

Charlie Chaplin Obituary. In a posthumous televised retrospective of Charlie Chaplin's career, CBS used excerpts from six copyrighted Charlie Chaplin films. The use was quantitatively and qualitatively substantial as each selected scene was among Chaplin's best and each was central to the film in which it appeared. CBS's use of the footage did not qualify as a fair use. (*Roy Export Co. v. Columbia Broadcasting System*, 503 F. Supp. 1137 (S.D.N.Y. 1980)).

13.3. Documentaries and the Incidental Use of Music and Images

A documentary is a non-fiction story or series of historical events portrayed in their actual location. A documentary maintains strict fidelity to fact. Documentarians use footage, still photographs, newsreel programming, archival video, and popular cultural programming. The unlicensed usage of this material is subject to the same fair use analysis discussed in Section 3.7.

13.3.1. The Problem

Documentarians often roll film as their subjects go through their daily lives. As part of their daily routine, your subject may walk into a room with artwork on its walls, watch television, sing, or listen to the stereo or radio. Your camera picks up that copyrighted material and you may consider its inclusion essential to setting the tone and the mood of the action taking place in the documentary.

13.3.2. No Clear Answer Applicable to All Situations

Documentarians often ask whether they need to license such background music and images. The question can not be answered with a simple yes or no in all situations. In supporting the documentarian's right to use the material without obtaining a license, you would argue that the appearance of the material in the documentary is a fair use. As discussed in greater detail in Section 3.7, there is no bright line rule in determining what qualifies as fair use. Fair use is completely dependent on the circumstances in each case.

The case law is inconclusive. I am not aware of any reported decisions in which a documentarian was sued for music or images picked up in the background. There are a few cases in which news organizations were sued for copyright infringement when their reporting of a particular event picked up music in the background. As a testament to the fact-specific nature of fair use, the cases reach different results.

ESPN. The court allowed a lawsuit against ESPN to continue finding that there was a material question of fact as to whether ESPN's inadvertent inclusion of copyrighted music in a cable program was a fair use. (*Coleman v. ESPN, Inc.*, 764 F. Supp. 290 (S.D.N.Y. 1991)).

ABC's Parade. ABC's broadcast of a copyrighted song recorded during news teams' taping of a parade was a fair use. (*Italian Book Corp. v. American Broadcasting Companies*, 458 F. Supp. 65 (S.D.N.Y. 1978)).

News gathering is a good – but not a perfect analogy – for the permissibility of an unlicensed appearance of background music and images in documentaries. The Copyright Act explicitly lists news reporting as a favored use for which the Fair Use Doctrine is appropriate. A televised news program clearly falls under the category of newsgathering. A documentary most likely falls into the category of newsgathering.

13.3.3. Producer Must Evaluate Risk

Documentarians must consider the question "How much risk is there and am I willing to accept that risk?" There is always risk when you use copyrighted material without permission. In some cases, the risk may be minimal but it is never zero.

If you determine that your use is a fair use, that determination addresses the risk of whether you could win a lawsuit filed against you. The determination does not necessarily address the risk of whether the rights holder will challenge you. Many rights holders aggressively pursue the unauthorized uses of their material – even when the use qualifies as a fair use. Review the risk assessment questions in Section 16.3.

13.3.4. Real World Practices

Many documentary filmmakers decide not to take the risk of being sued for the use of background images and sounds in their documentaries. They either get permission to use the material or make sure no copyrighted sounds or images appear in the background. They turn off all televisions, radios, *etc.* prior to filming to make sure no background copyrighted elements appear in their documentaries. They may also replace any copyrighted sounds and images inadvertently picked up by the camera with material to which they have the rights.

13.3.5. Reform

The Center for Social Media and the Project on Intellectual Property and the Public Interest at American University have worked with filmmakers to develop a Statement of Best Practices. The goal is to build a well-established and well-publicized consensus about acceptable practices under the Fair Use Doctrine and remove some of the uncertainty and confusion surrounding the application of fair use. In that way, documentarians do not need to engage in self-censorship.

In addition to incorporating background sounds and images, the statement addresses other contexts in which documentaries rely on fair use including commenting critically on media, sampling popular culture to portray societal conditions, and employing archival material in historical projects.

While the statement alone will not alter the law, it serves as a benchmark to which courts can turn when evaluating the reasonableness of a particular use. You can find a complete copy of the Statement of Best Practices at www.centerforsocialmedia.org.

13.4. DocuDramas and Fictionalization

Docudramas – also referred to as fictionalizations and dramatizations - convey actual events but combine elements of fiction in the telling of those events. While docudramas present all the clearance issues of any other audio-visual work, they make the producer particularly vulnerable to claims of invasion of privacy and defamation. That's because docudramas use poetic license and present a creative interpretation of reality with invented dialogue, composite characters, composite scenes, and other dramatic embellishments.

The mere existence of fictional elements in a story line is not actionable by itself. There still must be defamation, privacy, or similar violations before anyone can make a successful claim against your docudrama.

If there are characters in your docudrama which are identifiable as real living people, you must consider the extent to which your weaving of fiction and fact produce a story that might be defamatory or violate the person's privacy rights. If your added fictional elements are innocuous, neutral, or flattering, your risk of generating a defamation claim is likely minimal. Your invented dialogue and scenes may be acceptable even if they create an unflattering image of identifiable living people provided that the fictional elements represent a fair interpretation and do not alter the substantive impression of remarks made or actions taken by the person

The privacy claims most commonly generated by docudramas are claims for false light invasion of privacy and for the public disclosure of embarrassing facts. False light is the privacy claim most similar to defamation and depends on whether actual facts are manipulated within the story to present an untruthful impression of an identifiable living person. The public disclosure of embarrassing facts depends on how the producer gathers information for the docudrama. Public disclosure of embarrassing fact claims can arise if the docudrama includes information that is truthful but to which the producer had no legitimate access. I discuss privacy claims in greater detail in Chapter 6.

An annotated script helps enormously in the clearance of a docudrama. Annotations are notes in the script that indicate information such as the following:

- the source of each scene and sensitive element and whether that source is a magazine, newspaper, or public record

- the identification of each character or entity as living, dead, real, fictional or composite

- the identification of sensitive dialogue as actual or fictional

- the identification of scenes as actual or fictional

With an annotated script, the producer and his legal advisors can properly evaluate the risk of legal actions. Your goal in creating the annotated script is to demonstrate that the truthfulness of any sensitive or negative images of a living person is supported by credible sources to which you had legitimate access.

Releases, life story rights agreements, and disclaimers may also shield the docudrama producer from claims. I discuss releases and life story rights agreements in Chapter 25 and disclaimers in Section 27.3.

CLEARANCE ISSUES FOR PRODUCERS OF WEBSITES AND SOFTWARE

This chapter highlights the following clearance issues unique to website and software developers:

- trademark protection for domain names
- copyright and trademark liability as a result of linking and other online reference techniques
- copyright and defamation immunity for online producers
- copyright infringement of computer software

The chapter also briefly highlights some of the legal issues related to the relatively new communication forms of blogging and podcasting.

14.1. Website Owners

14.1.1. Infringing Domain Names

Domain names are routing addresses used to locate a website and deliver e-mail on the internet. They are important in e-commerce and general marketing. Domain names are usually comprised of a second level domain name followed by a dot followed by a top level domain name. Top level domains include generic top level domains like .com .net .org and .edu and country code top level domains like .ca for Canada and .uk for United Kingdom.

For example, www.sashaycommunications.com is the domain name for Sashay Communications, the publisher of this book. The "com" is the top level domain name and "sashaycommunications" is the second level domain name. Second level domains are the subject of domain name disputes.

Some – but not all - domain names function as and are protectible as trademarks. A domain name is protectible as a trademark if it in fact functions as a trademark. This means the domain name must be distinctive, identify a good or service, be used in commerce, and not infringe any pre-existing trademarks. For a more detailed discussion on trademarks, see Chapter 4.

It is also possible for a domain name to infringe a trademark. Domain name registrars register domain names. There are more than eighty registrars located worldwide. They include network solutions, go-daddy, and netfirms.com. These companies register domain names on a first-come, first-served basis. As long as no one else has registered a particular domain name, you can register it. The registrars do not investigate whether your registration and use of that domain name infringes a trademark. Making such a trademark infringement determination is your responsibility.

When a domain name infringes a trademark, the trademark owner has a few options including the following:

- initiating an action under the Uniform Dispute Resolution Procedure

- filing a traditional trademark infringement lawsuit

- filing a lawsuit under the Anticybersquatting Consumer Protection Act

Uniform Dispute Resolution Procedure. The Uniform Dispute Resolution Procedure (UDRP) is an administrative procedure designed for the quick resolution of domain name disputes. The UDRP proceedings are designed to last fewer than sixty days which is faster than any lawsuit proceeding. The UDRP allows a trademark owner to challenge an existing domain name. While domain name owners must go through the UDRP proceeding if a trademark owner initiates it, the UDRP does not prevent the trademark owner nor domain name owner from pursuing traditional avenues of litigation or arbitration.

If a trademark owner wins a UDRP proceeding, the disputed domain name is cancelled or transferred to the trademark owner. Those are the only remedies a UDRP proceeding offers the trademark owner. If a trademark owner wants an award of money from the domain name owner or an injunction preventing the domain name owner from other infringing uses of the trademark, the trademark owner must use more traditional litigation options. The full UDRP policy and rules are available at www.icann.org/dndr/udrp/

Trademark Litigation. Filing a trademark infringement lawsuit is slower and more expensive than a UDRP proceeding and normally involves claims based on the Lanham Act and state statutes. Remedies offered through a lawsuit are more extensive and may include monetary damages in addition to cancellation or transfer of the domain name.

Anticybersquatting Consumer Protection Act. Cybersquatting is the registration of a domain name identical to a well-known trademark with the intention of selling the domain name back to the trademark owner at a significant profit. For example, soon after the December 1998 announcement of the merger between Mobil and Exxon, someone contacted Mobil Oil Corporation offering to sell the company the domain names exxonmobil.com and exxon-mobil.com."

The Anticybersquatting Consumer Protection Act (ACPA), adopted in November 1999 and part of the Lanham Act, provides a civil action against a person who has a bad faith intent to profit from the trademark, and registers, traffics in, or uses a domain name that is identical or confusingly similar to a distinctive or famous mark. To succeed, the trademark owner must prove that the defendant registered the domain name in bad faith.

14.1.2. Linking, Framing, and Metatags

There are some online situations that may result in copyright or trademark infringement. They involve hypertext links, framing and metatags.

Linking. Hypertext links or simply links are instructions that take you from one website to another or from one area of a website to another area. Visitors to your webpage do not see the instructions. They identify the link because it appears as highlighted text on your webpage. While some websites take a conservative approach and ask for permission prior to linking to another website, many other website owners link without asking permission. Linking generally does not subject you to any legal liability. The exceptions include deep linking and linking to infringing material.

Deep Linking. When you deep link to another website, you skip the website's home page and other opening material which the website owner wants visitors to see. A number of companies write into their website terms of service prohibitions against deep linking to any pages on their website. They argue that deep linking is deceptive and misleads consumers into thinking that you are the creator of the material to which you are linking. There have been lawsuits alleging copyright, trademark and related claims as a result of deep linking. Most of these lawsuits have settled prior to a trial with the defendant agreeing to stop deep linking to the other party's website.

Linking to Infringing Material. Linking to a website that contains material which infringes another party's copyrights can lead to claims against you for contributory copyright infringement. You are guilty of contributory copyright infringement if you encourage or make it easier for someone else to infringe copyrighted material. To minimize such claims, you might try one or more of the following methods:

- Do some investigation prior to linking to avoid linking to websites that clearly contain infringing materials.

- Rely on the safe-harbor provisions in the Digital Millennium Copyright Act (DMCA) which immunize you from copyright infringement claims as long as you remove the link to infringing material upon receiving a request from a copyright owner. See Section 14.1.3 for a discussion of the DMCA safe harbor provisions.

• Use a disclaimer on your website which can be incorporated into your terms of service such as the following:

> XYZ Website is not responsible for the content of any website that is linked to us or any website to which we are linked, whether or not we are affiliated with the operator or owner of such website. Any links from our website to any other sites are for your convenience only. XYZ Website does not give any express or implied warranties or guarantee with respect to the accuracy or usefulness of the web pages and sites accessible through such links.

Framing. Framing allows visitors to your website to view content from another website without actually leaving your website. When you frame another website, you import content from that website into a framed or windowed area within your website. Typically, the area around the frame retains the look and feel of your website. As a result, many website visitors mistakenly believe that the content within the frame is your original content. Like deep linking, framing may lead to consumer confusion and result in claims of copyright or trademark infringement.

Metatags. Metatags are index words inserted in web pages so that the page is identified when someone performs a search engine query for the word. For example, metatags for a companion webpage to *The Permission Seeker's Guide Through the Legal Jungle* might include "copyright law" "rights clearance" and "fair use".

Metatags are imbedded in the code of your website and are not visible to visitors who access a site with a normal browser. The use of a trademark as a metatag may constitute trademark infringement if it creates a likelihood of confusion as discussed in Section 4.4.2. Most liability in this area results when a company uses its competitor's trademarks as a metatag. For example, Pepsi's use of Coke as a metatag might be a problem because it would lead people searching for Coke to the site of its competitor, Pepsi.

However, using trademarks as a metatag is valid if used to describe the content and subject matter of your website. In that case, it is a fair use of the trademark. For example, it was acceptable for a former Playboy model to use "Playmate of the Year" and other Playboy trademarks as metatags because the trademarks identified her and her website was not confusingly similar with Playboy's website. (*Playboy Enterprises v. Welles*, 78 F. Supp.2d 1066 (S.D. Cal. 1999)).

14.1.3. Immunity From Defamation and Copyright Claims

If you produce a website on which visitors can post comments, images, and other materials, you might be concerned that the material your visitors post defames someone or violates copyright, trademark, or other laws. In the context of traditional media, such as newspapers and magazines, the publisher of defamatory statements or copyright infringing material might be liable. However, federal law provides immunity in these areas for online producers.

Immunity from Defamation Through Section 230 of the Communications Decency Act. Websites have special protection from defamation actions under the federal immunity created by the Communications Decency Act (CDA). Section 230 of the CDA provides that

> no provider or user of an interactive computer service shall be treated as the publisher or speaker of any information provided by another information content provider

In other words, if someone else posts a defamatory statement on your website, you, as the online producer, are not legally responsible.

The law does not actually use the term online producer. Instead, it uses the terms "providers and users of interactive computer service". Courts have treated many diverse entities as "users and providers of interactive computer service" eligible for the protection offered by Section 230 of the CDA. They include operators of electronic community bulletin boards, websites, and discussion lists

You remain immune from liability even if you take an active publishing role and make decisions about whether to publish, remove, or modify content. The CDA also provides immunity if you in good faith restrict access to or availability of material that you consider to be inappropriate or objectionable. The intent of this provision – referred to as the good Samaritan provision – is to encourage websites and other online producers to self-regulate. With the protection of the CDA, online producers can actively screen and edit online material without fear of liability.

There are a few do's and don'ts to keep in mind with respect to CDA immunity. The CDA does protect you from defamation claims, right of privacy claims, and related claims. It does not protect you from copyright and trademark claims. The CDA does protect you from legal actions stemming from comments made by others. It does not protect you from legal actions arising from comments you make yourself.

Immunity from Copyright Claims Through the Digital Millennium Copyright Act (DMCA). The Digital Millennium Copyright Act (DMCA) includes safe harbors that insulate online producers from claims of copyright infringement for material posted by their customers and online visitors. The DMCA does not use the term online media producers – but instead uses the term "interactive service provider". "Interactive service provider" covers companies such as AOL and Comcast that offer dial-up and broadband connections to the internet. The term is defined broadly enough that it arguably includes operators of websites, electronic bulletin boards, blogs, and news groups. A number of courts have applied the term to such online producers.

To qualify for the safe harbor for material posted by others, you must comply with specific DMCA requirements which include the following:

- Remove infringing material upon the request of the copyright owner. The request, referred to by the DMCA as a takedown notice, must identify the copyrighted work, describe the infringing material, and indicate the location of the infringing material on your website.

- Remove or block access to any posted material that you discover infringes someone's copyright– even if you do not receive a takedown notice from the copyright owner.

- Designate an agent to handle claims of copyright infringement, register the name of the agent with the U.S. Copyright Office, and post the agent's contact information on your website.

- Have no knowledge that infringing material is on your website and gain no financial benefit from the infringing material.

- Adopt a policy of removing or terminating the accounts of individuals who repeatedly infringe copyrighted material and make your customers and visitors aware of that policy.

The DMCA also offers remedies for the improper removal of material. A customer may submit a counter notice requesting that improperly removed material be reposted. Also, there is liability for anyone who submits a fraudulent takedown notice claiming that non-infringing material is infringing.

There are a few do's and don'ts to keep in mind with respect to the DMCA safe-harbor provisions. The DMCA protects you only from claims of copyright infringement for material posted by other people. The DMCA does not protect you from claims of copyright infringement for material you placed online yourself. The DMCA's safe harbors apply only to copyright. It does not protect you from claims of defamation, trademark, privacy, trade secret or other intellectual property claims.

A separate DMCA safe harbor provision immunizes you from copyright infringement for links to infringing material. See the discussion of liability as a result of linking to a website in Section 14.1.2. The requirements for this linking safe harbor are very similar to the requirements for the posting safe harbor provision discussed immediately above. You must remove or disable the link to infringing material upon receiving a request from the copyright owner. One distinction between this linking safe harbor and the posting safe harbor is that you do not need to designate an agent to rely on the linking safe harbor.

14.2. Software Producers

14.2.1. Infringement of Computer Programs

There are two separate levels of possible infringement for computer programs: infringement of the computer code and infringement of the audiovisual presentation.

Infringing the Computer Code. The Copyright Act defines a computer program as a set of statements or instructions to be used directly or indirectly in a computer in order to bring about a certain result. Computer games normally include a program. At code level, the infringement may be verbatim copying or copying of the structure, sequence and organization. The law recognizes that certain factors may require that a program be written in a certain manner. These factors include the operating system on which a computer must run, compatibility requirements, and accepted programming practices.

In the realm of software development, your employees and contractors may be a source of copyright infringement liability. Employees, consultants, and business partners of computer-related companies often sign non-disclosure and confidentiality agreements in which they agree neither to disclose nor use the trade secrets of the company. Working on your production or for your organization may be a violation of such an agreement. You should verify that your employees and contractors are not incorporating any elements into your production that a former employer might view as its trade secret. Non-disclosure and confidentiality agreements are not always enforceable but can carry dire consequences when they are. You should seek legal counsel if you believe your organization or production is impacted by one.

Infringing the Audiovisual Presentation. To the extent a computer program includes plot, characters, story and visual effects, it is analyzed like an audiovisual work. Like any other audiovisual presentation, computer programs can have elements that are public domain or scenes-a-faire.

For example, when the developer of one karate combat video game sued the developer of a similar program for copyright infringement, the court found several unprotectible elements common to both video games. Both video games have similar karate movements, changing background scenes, and thirty-second countdown rounds. Both also use the character of a referee whose utterances of begin, stop, white, red are depicted by a cartoon-style speech balloon.

According to the court, these elements are scenes-a-faire that one would expect to see in a karate combat video game. There was no copyright infringement. (*Data East USA v. Epyx*, 862 F.2d 204 (9th Cir. 1988)).

14.3. Bloggers

Blogs are web logs or online journals which are frequently updated. Those who write blogs are referred to as bloggers. Bloggers write on an assortment of topics and are gaining acceptance as a part of the mass media. A number of blogs are interactive and allow their visitors to post comments and other content.

There are some unsettled legal questions surrounding blogs. Bloggers most likely qualify for specific laws providing immunity to online producers. The Communications Decency Act (CDA) protects online producers from defamatory statements posted by users. The Digital Millennium Copyright Act (DMCA) protects online producers from liability for infringing material posted by visitors. A pending question is the blogger's liability when a visitor posts another company's trade secrets.

The protections offered to online producers by the CDA and the DMCA are discussed in previous sections of this chapter. I discuss trade secrets in Section 9.4.

14.4. Podcasters

Podcasts are short radio shows, audio blog, or audio-visual presentations offered through websites. They can be downloaded and played back on a computer or a portable music player like Apple's ipod. Podcasts trigger the same copyright, right of publicity, defamation, trademark, and other clearance issues discussed in this book. While many podcasts are all talk, some do include music. That brings up several online music licensing issues which I discuss in greater detail in Sections 22.7 and 22.8.2.

CLEARANCE ISSUES FOR BUSINESS 15

This chapter highlights clearance issues relevant to a business:

• clearance issues in the context of advertising

• copyright issues within the context of training

15.1. Advertising

15.1.1. Use of Music in Advertisements

The use of music in a commercial advertisement rarely qualifies as a fair use. You need a synchronization license to use a song and a master use license to use a sound recording in a commercial advertisement. Use of an existing professional recording may also require payment of re-use fees to certain entertainment unions. See Chapter 22 for a more in-depth discussion of music licensing.

15.1.2. Copyright Infringement and Advertisements

Commercials like to evoke images of popular culture. In doing so, a commercial may borrow too much from a fictional story, character, or other copyrighted work. Advertisers need to make sure they stay in compliance with copyright laws.

One example of an advertiser stepping outside the copyright fair use boundaries involves artist Brian Andreas. Andreas is the creator of a drawing called *Angels of Mercy*. The drawing depicts an angel and includes the following legend:

> Most people don't know that there are angels whose only job is to make sure you don't get too comfortable & fall asleep & miss your life.

Volkswagen, the maker of the Audi, created a commercial showing an Audi TT coupe in a garden surrounded by angelic-looking statues. A narrator says

> I think I just had a wake-up call, and it was disguised as a car, and it was screaming at me not to get too comfortable and fall asleep and miss my life.

In the copyright infringement lawsuit against Volkswagen that followed, Andreas won monetary damages in the amount of $965,000.

15.1.3. Right of Publicity and Advertisements

As discussed in Chapter 7, the right of publicity allows each individual to control and profit from the commercial value of his or her own identity. Commercial uses of a person's identity trigger right of publicity claims; non-commercial uses do not. By their very definition, product advertisements serve a commercial purpose. That means you risk a right of publicity claim if you use a celebrity's name, image, or other identifying characteristic in a product advertisement.

Producers of commercials should be aware of right of publicity claims that can spring from sound-a-like recordings. Some celebrities are recognized just by the sound of their voice. If an advertiser obtains rights in a song but cannot convince the artist who made that song famous to perform the song for the commercial, the advertiser may re-record the song in the style of the famous recording artist. If the re-recorded version imitates the celebrity singer's style and performance, there may be a violation of the celebrity's right of publicity.

15.2. Training

You may need permission to use copyrighted material as part of a training seminar, convention, or other commercial or business presentation. Depending upon the circumstances, fair use may apply.

15.2.1. Educational Uses

The Technology, Education & Copyright Harmonization (TEACH) Act of 2002 amended the Copyright Act and addressed use of copyrighted works in the context of education. The TEACH Act is designed to aid long distance education. It provides an exception to the copyright owner's public performance and exclusive rights by allowing instructors to use copyrighted material in the course of learning via the internet or other digital transmission. In other words instructors can make copyrighted materials available online or in other digital formats.

The TEACH Act is not designed to be a replacement for textbooks or other materials that would normally be purchased by the student and used for out-of-classroom review and homework. For that reason, instructors can not rely on the TEACH Act to make materials available online if those materials are specifically produced or marketed for long-distance education or are typically included in textbooks purchased by students.

The use of the material should be similar to the type of use that would take place in an actual face-to-face classroom setting. The following are the eligibility requirements for reliance on the TEACH Act:

- The organization relying on the TEACH Act must be a governmental body or an accredited nonprofit educational institution.

- The material made available must be directly related to the course curriculum.

- The material must be used at the direction of or under the supervision of an instructor – although the instructor is not required to provide real-time or constant supervision.

- The material used must be a legitimately acquired copy.

- Recipients of material must be students officially enrolled in the course. When a governmental organization relies on the TEACH Act, the recipients must be governmental officers or employees using the materials as part of their official duties.

- The organization relying on the TEACH Act must implement technological measures that prevent recipients from retaining copies of the material for longer than the class session or sharing the material with others outside the intended recipients.

There are similar exceptions to the copyright owner's exclusive public performance and display rights in face-to-face teaching situations.

PART FOUR

The Process of Clearing Rights and Seeking Permission

Part Four explains the general procedure for clearing rights. This Part begins with a discussion of the actions producers need to take in order to avoid clearance problems with their original material. Those actions include getting option agreements and documenting relationships with collaborators and contributors. Part Four then provides guidance on locating rights holders, requesting permission, and negotiating rights agreements.

Chapters in Part Four:

GETTING ORGANIZED 16

16.1. Listing Materials

Clearing rights often involves lots of paper. The more rights you have to clear, the more organized you need to be. This chapter includes organizational tips to help you approach a rights clearance project.

Some producers prepare rights bibles. A rights bible is a per-second (for audio-visual or audio productions) or per page (for printed productions) listing of each item in the production obtained from a third party. The items include images, music, and footage. Sometimes distributors require that the producer deliver a rights bible with the completed production.

Your production may not require the full detail of a rights bible. Nevertheless, for each item provided by a third party, you should track the following information:

- name and contact information of the rights owner
- how the rights were obtained
- terms of the license agreement
- when the rights were cleared
- duration of the license

16.2. Determining If You Need Permission

For each item incorporated into your production, you should determine with which category of right you are dealing. It might be copyright, trademark, privacy, or other right. Often the same material triggers rights in several areas. The Clearance Checklist in Chapter 2 along with its references to applicable sections of this book provides initial guidance to help you identify the rights issues you must address.

Next, assess whether your contemplated use of the item requires permission. Several chapters of Part Two include a discussion of the circumstances in which permission may not be required for certain types of uses. However, remember that rights clearance issues are fact specific. No reference book can address the nuances of every rights situation you may encounter. If you are in doubt about the need for permission, consult an attorney experienced in rights clearance issues.

16.3. Evaluating Risks of Not Having Permission

There may be legal justification for using someone's material without permission. Realize that there is always some level of risk when you use someone's proprietary material without permission. While the risk may sometimes be minimal, it is never zero. It is up to you to decide whether or not you can and want to accept the risk.

An attorney who reviews your production can offer an assessment of whether your use requires permission. However, in many cases, the lawyer's opinion is only a risk analysis. It is not a guarantee. No attorney can assure you that an unauthorized use of material will not trigger legal action from the rights owner. An attorney can only evaluate the likelihood of a lawsuit and the likelihood of your winning the case in the event a rights owner sues you.

Before proceeding without permission, ask yourself some common sense questions:

Would your use upset the typical rights owner? This is a reality check. Put yourself into the shoes of the rights owner. Would you be angry and want to take legal action if someone used your material without your permission in the way you want to use the rights owner's material? If your answer is yes, it is likely the rights owner whose material you wish to use will respond in the same way.

Has the rights owner previously objected to similar uses of material? It is a good bet that rights owners who have been aggressive in protecting their rights in the past will continue to be aggressive in protecting their rights in the future.

Does the rights owner have the resources and knowledge to pursue an action against you - even if the action would be without merit? A well-established company with an in-house legal department can more easily make a fuss about your production than can an individual with more limited resources. Nevertheless, do not completely dismiss the cash-strapped smaller rights owner. If his claim is legitimate and offers the possibility of having the losing side pay attorneys' fees, he can probably find an attorney to assist him on a contingency basis. See Section 3.1.3 for a discussion of right to attorneys' fees in a copyright infringement lawsuit.

How much exposure will your production receive? Is your production a newsletter going to a hundred club members, is it a CD distributed to a few thousand, or is it a television program to be nationally televised? It makes a difference. The more exposure your production receives, the more likely it is that your unauthorized use of material will come to the attention of and spark an objection from the rights owner.

Will your unauthorized use of material expose other people to risk? Rights owners filing lawsuits typically sue not only the producer but also the people and organizations involved in distributing the production to the public. Potential targets include authors, publishers, record labels, advertising companies, broadcasters, and distributors. Some of these people and organizations may be your clients or people with whom you wish to develop extended business relationships. Dragging others into your rights clearance problems is not good for business. It can also be expensive. Distribution and other agreements include indemnification clauses in which you agree to reimburse the distributor for any losses it may suffer as a result of any rights violations in your production.

Is there anyone involved in your production who has ample re-sources? People or organizations who have – or who are perceived to have – significant amounts of money make attractive targets for lawsuits. Even if you are cash poor, your distributor may not be.

Will you ever need anything from this rights owner? Relation-ships are important in the media industry. Will you need to return to the same rights owner to request rights for a future production? If yes, using the rights owner's work without authorization – even if he takes no formal action against you – can sour your future nego-tiations for rights you may need from that owner at a later date.

16.4. Determining Your Budget

Determine how much your production can afford to spend for the purchase of rights. Be realistic. The Appendix includes a compila-tion of price ranges for obtaining different categories of rights. If you have a very limited budget, consider some of the options out-lined below in Section 16.7 for minimizing your clearance costs.

16.5. Understanding the Impact of Rights Decisions on Your Production

The items you want to put into your production may carry high li-cense fees. If you have a limited budget, and you pursue expensive music, photos and film clips, you may not be able to purchase rights sufficient for the full exploitation of your project.

License fees increase proportionately with the length of time, the number of media platforms, and the geographic scope in which you wish to exercise those rights. You may be tempted to settle for more limited time-frames, media platforms, and territories just to lower costs to an amount you can afford. This strategy can endanger your ability to exploit your production.

Suppose you license a song for your television program and the license allows you to use the song within your production on free television within North America. Before you can show your production on home video or on a cable television network or on foreign television, you must expand your license agreement to include permission for the additional uses. It may or may not be feasible for you to pay the money to upgrade the required licenses.

It may be preferable to have a production that you can fully distribute and exploit as you please – even if it means placing in your production some of your second choices in music, images, and other licensed material.

Here are the license terms with the greatest impact on your ability to exploit your production:

Duration of License. A one-year license is less expensive than a ten-year license and a ten-year license is less expensive than a license that runs in perpetuity. You may not be able to afford a license for an extended period of time. Sometimes a rights owner refuses to grant licenses over a certain number of years. After the expiration of the license, you are not able to distribute, sell or exhibit your production without first renewing the expired license.

Media Platforms. Sometimes rights owners sell rights for different media separately. For example, a music publisher might charge you $5,000 to use a song in your film to be released theatrically. The music publisher may require additional fees if you release your film on television and additional fees if you release the film onto video. Your budget may not allow you to purchase all rights at one time.

Geographic Territories. Sometimes rights owners sell rights for different regions separately. For example, an image bank might charge you $500 to use an illustration in your magazine to be distributed in North America. If you decide to distribute your magazine in Asia, you will need an additional license to cover that region.

If you are unable to purchase all rights you need at one time, you should try to negotiate and include in your license agreement the option to purchase expanded rights in the material. See Section 19.3.3 for further discussion.

16.6. Deciding Whether to Work with a Rights Clearance Company

Rights clearance companies specialize in the hands-on aspect of clearing rights. They come in all different sizes from single-person operations to larger firms. Some work in only one area such as music, print or film. Others work in a number of areas. You can retain them to assist you in obtaining the rights you need.

The decision to work with a rights clearance company depends on your budget, time constraints, and the complexity of your rights clearance issues. Since agencies clear rights full-time, they tend to do the work with great efficiency. Of course, there is no guarantee that a rights clearance company will be able to obtain the rights you need. If a rights owner is vehemently opposed to his material in your production, he is going to say no whether it is you or a rights clearance company making the request.

However, with their experience and proprietary sources of information, rights clearance companies can often identify rights owner in much less time than it would take you. They can also often tell you immediately whether the rights you want are going to be impossible, or nearly impossible, to get. They can then suggest more promising alternatives.

The potential downside to working with a rights clearance company is that it may not take a vested interest in your project and may not necessarily appeal to the good will of the rights owner. For example, you may be so passionate about having a certain celebrity's name attached to your pro-environment advertising campaign that you research every cause in which the celebrity has participated and use your findings to draft a plea guaranteed to tug at the celebrity's heart strings and then get the plea personally delivered to the celebrity through your connection with the best friend of the hair stylist of the celebrity's Mom. Most rights clearance companies are not going to adopt such measures.

When seeking rights clearance companies, ask how they bill and what additional services they provide. Most bill at a flat rate, by the hour, or through some combination of the two.

16.7. Minimizing Clearance Costs

If you have a limited budget to devote to obtaining rights, here are some techniques for minimizing your costs.

Remain Creative. You are in the entertainment and media business so you are a creative person by nature. Even if you are on the business side, you are probably drawn to the field by an internal creative energy. Do not set aside your creative nature just because you have put on your rights clearance hat. Creativity benefits the rights clearance process just as it benefits other aspects of media production. If one element or item proves impossible to license, you need to seek imaginative alternatives.

Start the Process Early. If you are clearing rights for a production with many rights, allow yourself several months. It is not unusual for a rights owner to take a month or longer to respond to a request for permission. You are in the worst possible position if you have incorporated items requiring licenses into a completed production without first obtaining the necessary permissions.

Stay Flexible. Staying flexible is easy or difficult depending upon your specific project. You are in a much better position with the attitude that "I need a piece of contemporary art work for this scene" over the attitude "I need rights to Roy Lichtenstein's *Spray*, and that's all that will be acceptable".

Use Works by Local, Independent and Upcoming Artists. Use original music, art, poetry, and other content by independent artists. There are thousands of talented and just-about-to-be-famous writers, filmmakers, visual artists, and musicians who welcome the exposure offered by inclusion in your production and will license rights for a fair but comparatively modest fee. Some independent artists will license their material to certain productions for a credit or other non-monetary compensation.

Use Library Music. Library music, also called production music, is written specifically for use in audio and audio-visual productions. Libraries charge in a variety of ways including by needle-drop, bulk rate and through annual subscriptions. The use of library music is discussed in greater depth in Section 22.5.3.

Use Stock Footage and Stock Images. Stock footage and stock images are libraries of video material and photographs offered to producers for incorporation into their productions. See Section 21.2 for a discussion of stock footage and Section 23.2 for a discussion of stock images. The licensing process is becoming easier as more companies computerize the process, offer online catalogs, and issue licenses online. A downside to using stock footage and images is that they may have been in many other projects and may have been seen many times before.

Try One-Stop Shopping. You may be able to negotiate discounts if you obtain rights in several items from the same rights holder. Production music libraries and stock houses often offer such bulk discounts.

16.8. Licensing Through Collective Rights Organizations

Copyright owners frequently form relationships with companies or organizations that administer the licensing of their works. They are called collective rights organizations. Collective rights organizations frequently specialize in one category of material – print, music, artwork, etc. Some of the collective rights organizations discussed in detail in this book are the performing rights organizations which issue public performance licenses for songs, and stock image companies which issue licenses for images. The Appendix includes a more complete list of collective rights organizations.

Many of these collective rights organizations have online stores that allow you to browse their catalogs of material and acquire licenses immediately online. Some offer discounts for multiple purchases. If there is an applicable collective rights organizations for the rights you seek, that's a good place to start your request for permission.

PUTTING YOUR OWN HOUSE IN ORDER 17

17.1. Looking In Versus Looking Out

Most of this book concerns clearing rights in and licensing third party material. Another crucial part of the clearance process is making sure that the material you create internally has no clearance problems. I address that issue in this chapter.

17.2. Production Based on Underlying Work

If the basis of your production is another work such as a book, movie, television show, or board game, you need to obtain the rights in the underlying work before making your production. For example, a filmmaker might base a film on a book, a musician might base a song on a poem, and a software developer might base a computer game on a comic strip. They need permission from the owners of the book, the poem, or the comic strip. The book, the poem, and the comic strip are the underlying works for each of these productions.

17.2.1. Option Agreement

Acquisition of the rights in an underlying work typically begins with an option. By analogy, acquiring an option is like placing a hold on an item you wish to purchase or putting the item on lay-away. During the option period, no one else can purchase the rights. If you do not complete your purchase of the rights within a negotiated time period, the rights become available for purchase by someone else.

The producer optioning an underlying work pays an option price equal to a small percentage of the purchase price. The amount of the option price depends on a number of factors such as the popularity of the underlying work, the length of the option period, and the media in which the producer intends to use the rights. Similar factors determine the ultimate purchase price you pay in the event you exercise the option and license the rights.

An option period typically runs from six months to two years. One year is most common. If the production costs are to be significant, the producer may use the option period to pitch the project and determine its marketability. Having an option to the rights gives the producer credibility when approaching potential financial backers, distributors, and talent.

If the producer determines the project has a chance for success, the producer will purchase the rights by exercising the option. The option agreement between the rights holder and the producer should specify what action is required to exercise the option. Exercising the option normally requires the producer to send the rights holder a written note that the producer wants to exercise the option. Usually, the producer must include payment of the pre-negotiated purchase price along with the written note.

If the producer decides that a project based on the underlying work is a "no-go", the producer can simply allow the option to lapse. Once the option lapses, the producer has no more financial obligation to the rights holder, and all rights in the underlying work are returned to the rights holder who can then make those rights available for purchase by other potential producers.

A producer can skip the option agreement and just purchase the rights in the underlying work. Taking this approach and avoiding the costs and time associated with entering an option agreement may make sense if the rights in the underlying work are moderately priced or if the producer is positive the production will go forward. The more expensive the rights in the underlying work, the more likely it is the producer will take the intermediate step of first obtaining an option.

17.3. Collaborators, Contributors, and Joint Ownership

There are probably a number of people you enlist to work on your production. Contributors might include actors, models, musicians and other talent. You should obtain a written agreement from every person you hire to be a part of your production. In addition to specifying the services to be provided by the talent, the talent agreement should include the talent's waiver of right of publicity and other claims. The talent should also grant the right to use the talent's performance, appearance or contribution in the producer's production.

Contributors and collaborators can also take the form of illustrators, editors, indexers, consultants, researchers, background musicians, recording engineers, and others. In many situations, it never occurs to the producer or to the collaborator that the collaborator might be entitled to claim joint ownership in the production.

Yet, there are cases in which a collaborator works on a production and later claims partial ownership of the production. If you do not intend your collaborators and contributors to share in the ownership of the production, you can eliminate this problem by clearly communicating your intentions and, most importantly, putting your intentions into a written agreement signed by both you and the collaborator. If you plan to share copyright ownership, you and your collaborators should still have a written agreement in the form of a collaboration agreement which addresses ownership, creative control, division of costs and profits, and other issues.

17.3.1. Who Can Claim Joint Ownership?

In copyright jargon, a creative work with multiple creators or authors is a joint work. You do not need a contract for the creation of a joint work so it is possible to take on a joint author without the explicit intention of doing so. The following default rules from the Copyright Act apply to a joint work unless the authors agree in writing to an alternative arrangement:

- Each author is an equal owner of the work.

- Each author has the right to grant a non-exclusive license in the work without permission from the other authors; however, he must give all other owners a proportionate share of any licensing revenue.

- The outright sale of the work or the grant of an exclusive license of the work requires the authorization of all authors.

The Copyright Act does not define the terms joint author, co-author, or joint ownership. It does define the term joint work as "a work prepared by two or more authors with the intention that their contributions be merged into inseparable parts or interdependent parts of a unitary whole". In plain English, that definition means that before a collaborator or contributor can claim joint ownership of a production, the following must occur:

- Each author must make a contribution to the production.

- Each author's contribution must be more than minimal.

- Each author's contribution must be copyrightable on its own merit.

- The authors must intend that their contributions form one production.

As you might guess, the validity of a joint authorship claim is highly fact specific. The individual claiming to be a joint author must show independent copyrightable contributions and intent.

Independent Copyrightable Contributions. The joint author must have made independent copyrightable contributions to the work. This means that each author's contribution be copyrightable on its own merit. Recall from the discussion of copyright in Section 3.4, certain things are not copyrightable. These include facts, ideas, concepts, names, stock characters, and scenes-a-faire. A contributor who contributes only such elements has not contributed independently copyrightable material and, thus, does not have a claim of joint authorship.

Intent. The authors must intend that their contributions be combined into one production. If one person is the dominant author, the intent of that author becomes increasingly more important. When deciding intent, a court examines who had decision-making authority, how the work was credited, and how the role of each contributor is presented to others.

How Problems Arise Even When There's No Joint Authorship. A collaborator who fails at an attempt to claim joint authorship may still have some recourse. For example, Lynn Thomson, a dramaturge for the hit Broadway musical, *Rent*, lost her claim for co-authorship. However, the court determined that the lyrics and dialogue Thomson contributed to *Rent* are independently copyrightable. Thomson filed a supplemental lawsuit to prohibit use in *Rent* of the copyrightable elements she had contributed. The case settled with the *Rent* producers paying Thomson an undisclosed amount. (*Thomson v. Larson*, 147 F.3d 195 (2nd Cir. 1998)).

Sample Cases Involving Contributors and Collaborators. Here are some real-life examples of contributors and collaborators who claimed joint authorship:

A Play about Jackie "Moms" Mabley. (*Childress v. Taylor*, 945 F.2d 500 (2nd Cir. 1991)).

Situation: Clarice Taylor, an actress, started assembling material about the comedienne Jackie "Moms" Mabley. Taylor interviewed Moms Mabley's friends and family, collected Moms Mabley jokes, and did other library research of the comedienne's life. Taylor passed the research to her playwright friend, Alice Childress, whom she asked to write a play about Moms Mabley. Childress wrote the play by developing the structure and writing the dialogue. In addition to providing the research, Taylor contributed to the playwriting process by discussing characters and scenes with

Childress and speaking with Childress on a regular basis about the play's progress. The two worked with no written agreement and eventually ended up in a lawsuit where Childress claimed to be the sole author of the play and Taylor claimed to be a joint author of the play.

Court Ruling: The court sided with Childress finding her to be the sole author because (i) there was no evidence that Childress, the dominant author, considered Taylor a co-author and, thus, there was no intent to create a joint work and (ii) Taylor, who provided only facts and research to the writing process, contributed no independently, copyrightable elements to the play.

Spawn Comic Book Characters. (*Gaiman v. McFarlane*, 360 F.3d 644 (7th Cir. 2004)).

Situation: Todd McFarlane, the creator of the *Spawn* comic-book series, retained Neil Gaiman as a writer. The two had no written contract. There was only an oral agreement in which McFarlane assured Gaiman that he would treat Gaiman better than the big guys. After retaining Gaiman, McFarlane introduced three new characters into the *Spawn* comic book series. Gaiman described the characters and wrote their dialogue. McFarlane illustrated the characters. Gaiman claimed joint ownership in the copyright to the characters. McFarlane claimed that Gaiman had contributed only ideas and should not be deemed a co-creator and joint author of the three characters.

Court Ruling: Gaiman is a joint author of the work. Gaiman provided details for the characters including name, age, facial features, title, manner of speech, costume, and what each character knows and says. Those details are what made them distinct characters. According to the court, Gaiman's contribution had expressive content without which the three new *Spawn* characters would not have been characters at all, but merely drawings.

Malcolm X, a Spike Lee Film. (Aalmuhammed v. Lee , 202 F.3d 1227 (9th Cir. 2000)).

Situation: Jefri Aalmuhammed worked as a consultant for the motion picture *Malcolm X.* The film was directed and co-produced by Spike Lee, distributed by Warner Brothers, and starred Denzel Washington. Aalmuhammed had no written contract with Warner Brothers or Lee, but he did expect and he did receive compensation. Aalmuhammed claimed joint copyright ownership in the film and presented evidence that his involvement in making the movie was extensive and included the following contributions:

- reviewing and suggesting extensive script revisions, most of which dealt with the religious and historical accuracy of scenes depicting Malcolm X's religious conversion and pilgrimage to Mecca

- creating at least two entire scenes with new characters

- translating Arabic into English for subtitles

- supplying his own voice for voice-overs

- selecting the proper prayers and religious practices for the characters

- editing parts of the movie during post production

- meeting with numerous Islamic organizations to persuade them that the movie was an accurate depiction of Malcolm X's life

Court Ruling: Despite his valuable contribution, Aalmuhammed is not a co-author of the film. Aalmuhammad made suggestions but had no control over whether the suggestions were incorporated into the film. Instead, Warner Brothers and Spike Lee controlled the film. Although the court rejected Aalmuhammad's joint work claim, the case continued on other issues.

The Songs of Better Than Ezra. (*BTE v. Bonnecaze*, 43 F. Supp.2d 619 (E.D. La. 1999)).

Situation: Better Than Ezra is an alternative rock band that has been on the national music scene since the early 1990's. In 1996, Cary Bonnecaze, the band's drummer, left the group. He later filed a lawsuit claiming to be a joint author of the songs released by the band and demanding his share of the revenue generated by those songs. Kevin Griffin, the group's lead vocalist and guitarist, claimed to be the sole author of the songs.

Court Ruling: While Bonnecaze did have a copyright interest in the recordings of the band, he did not have an interest in the underlying songs. Griffin introduced songs to his band members who would aid in refining them into the version recorded by the band. Bonnecaze claims that he contributed inseparable and interdependent parts of certain songs including harmony, lyrics, percussion, song rhythms, melody, and musical structure. However, Bonnecaze never fixed his contributions into a tangible form of expression prior to the band's albums which is a requisite in showing independent copyrightability.

SUBMITTING THE REQUEST FOR PERMISSION

18.1. Identifying the Rights Owner

Finding the appropriate person to ask for permission is often the most difficult part of clearing rights. Sometimes, you do get lucky and finding the proper rights owner simply requires reading the CD cover, the book title page, or the film credits. At other times, the search for the rights owner leads you smack into a brick wall.

Making the process more difficult is the fact that use of some material may require permission from multiple parties. I refer to those as items with stacked rights. Here are some examples:

- If you use a recording of a song, you need permission from the owner of the recording and from the owner of the song.

- If you use a photograph of artwork, you need permission from the artist who created the artwork as well as permission from the photographer who took the photographs of the artwork.

- If you use a film clip, you need permission from the film producer as well as actors, directors, writers and other creative people whose work appears in the clip.

This chapter includes general guidance for identifying rights owners for all categories of media. Part Five provides more detailed guidance specific to the category of material for which you seek to identify the rights owner.

To be most efficient in the rights clearance process, you need basic internet search skills. If you are not comfortable with searching the world wide web, run – do not walk – to your nearest public library or community college for basic lessons. Many larger rights owners post on their websites directions and forms for requesting permission. Also, there are many databases with rights information available online, some of which are free for use.

If you use the techniques discussed in this book and still are unable to identify the rights owner, you may want to give the project to a rights clearance company or enlist the aid of a copyright search company. If it is impossible to locate the rights owner, here are the alternatives to which producers commonly turn. Starting with the least risky option, your alternatives include the following:.

- Use something else. Hopefully, you give yourself enough time for the rights clearance process so that this option is available.

- Rely on fair use. If the material is crucial for your project, try to re-format your use so it is a fair use of the material. Of course, this is not possible for all productions. Consider working with an attorney in re-formatting your use of the material. As discussed in Section 3.7, application of the Fair Use Doctrine is subjective and fact-specific. There is no guarantee a court will view your use as a fair use. Also, if there are other entities involved with your project – like distributors – they may not be comfortable with reliance on fair use.

- Use it anyway. Some people use the material anyway and set aside an amount for a license fee in the event the rights owner shows up. Currently, there is no good faith exception to the Copyright Act. There is nothing to say that if the rights owner materializes, he has to accept the amount of money you have set aside as a license fee or that he accepts your use and will not sue for copyright infringement.

Note that being unable to locate the rights holder is a different situation from the case in which a producer locates the rights owner, submits a request, and simply does not receive a response from the rights owner.

18.1.1. Orphan Copyright Works

Change may be on the horizon. The Copyright Office is examining the issues raised by orphan works. Orphan works are copyrighted works whose owners are difficult or even impossible to locate. The Copyright Office is examining possible legislative, regulatory or other solutions to address these concerns.

For example, the United States might model its policy on the policy currently used in Canada. Canadian copyright law has a specific provision permitting anyone who seeks permission to make a copyright use of a work and cannot locate the copyright owner to petition the Canadian Copyright Board for a license. The Copyright Board makes a determination as to whether sufficient effort has been made to locate the owner. If so, the Copyright Board may grant a license for the proposed use. It sets terms and fees for the proposed use of the work in its discretion and holds collected fees in a fund from which the copyright owner, if he or she ever surfaces and makes a claim, may be paid.

18.2. Preparing the Request

There are no absolute rules for a permission request. Many large organizations offer instructions or even a form - sometimes online - for your submission of permission requests. Follow those instructions and use the forms when they are available. If you need permission from an organization or individual that offers no such guidelines, you can prepare your own form of request. At a minimum, your permission request should include the following:

- a description of your production (title, producer, short synopsis, *etc.*)

- identification of the material you want to use

- a description of the scope of rights you need (formats, territories, languages)

The Appendix includes samples of letters requesting permission.

18.3. Describing Your Production

Rights owners often want to know how you plan to use their material. Sometimes it is sufficient to provide a summary of how the material is to be used in your production. There are some rights owners who ask to see the entire script or the entire book or entire production before granting permission. It is up to you as the producer to determine if your need for the material warrants compliance with such a request.

In extreme situations, the rights owner may even ask for the right to review and approve the final incorporation of his material in your production. You should grant such approval rights with extreme caution and consider how crucial the particular material is for your production. It may not be worth the headache.

18.4. Identifying the Material You Want to Use

Provide as much information as possible to help the recipient of your permission request identify the material you want to use. If the recipient has to figure out what material you want from a sketchy description, it slows down the process.

Example of a not-so-good description:

I would like to use an excerpt from *Meet the Press*.

Example of a better description:

I would like to use a ten-second excerpt of Tim Russert's interview with White House Chief of Staff Joshua Bolton from the *Meet the Press* episode that aired on July 23, 2006. It is the portion of the interview in which Mr. Russert asks and Mr. Bolton responds to questions concerning the 2006 mid-term elections.

18.5. *Determining the Scope of Rights You Need*

Give some thought to the scope of rights you request. The broader your request, the higher the license fee. You do not want to ask (and pay) for broader rights than you need. At the same time, it is preferable to get all the rights you need (or options to acquire those rights) upfront. When determining which rights you need, ask yourself the following questions:

- In what media will you use the rights?

- Do you plan to make edits or adaptations?

- For what period of time do you need the rights?

- In which markets and territories will the production be distributed?

18.6. *Setting the License Fee*

There is no uniform way of negotiating the license fee. Here are some possible strategies you might use in your permission request letter:

- Don't mention a specific amount for a license fee. Let the other side indicate the amount it wants.

- Make an offer and see if the rights owner either accepts your offer or makes a counter offer.

- If there is one particular item in which you want rights, negotiate that license first if time permits. If the negotiated license includes a most favored nations clause, you can then submit requests for material less crucial to your project offering an amount that does not trigger the most favored nations clause. Most favored nations clauses are discussed in Section 19.3.8.

ΠEGOTIATING THE RIGHTS AGREEMENT | 19

19.1. Contract Basics

The purpose of a contract is to show that two or more people have reached a mutual understanding. All contracts do not have to be in writing. Many oral agreements can be binding. However, there are certain contracts that by law must be in writing in order to be effective. They include contracts for the following:

- the transfer of a copyright
- the grant of an exclusive license in a copyright
- the creation of a freelance work as a work made for hire

Many collaboration agreements, freelance agreements, consulting agreements, and agreements for original music involve a copyright assignment, exclusive license, or a work made for hire and, therefore, must be in writing to be effective.

Note that while the grant of an exclusive license must be in writing, there is no requirement that the grant of a non-exclusive license be in writing. When you seek permission to incorporate third party music, text, artwork or other material into your production you are usually – but not always – seeking a non-exclusive license. Such permission could be conveyed by oral agreement. However, even when circumstances do not legally require a written contract, it is a good idea to have a written contract as a record of the terms to which the parties agreed.

19.2. Format of Rights Agreement

An exchange of letters or emails can sometimes serve as a contract for a non-exclusive license. For those contracts that must be in writing, you need a more formal agreement. There is at least one court that has ruled that an exchange of emails does not satisfy the requirement that the transfer of a copyright must be in writing. You probably also want to get permission in the format of a formal license agreement with signatures by both parties if

- you are putting significant money into your production,
- you plan wide distribution of your production, or
- you are answerable to third parties such as distributors and insurers.

A formal agreement does not mean that the license need be long or have dense, hard to understand language. It can be brief and in plain language. The Appendix includes examples of rights and license agreements.

19.3. Parts of a Rights Agreement

19.3.1. Grant of Rights

All rights agreements grant you authority to use the material. The rights owner may grant the authority as a license, as an assignment, or as a work made for hire.

Grant as a License. A license grants permission to use material for a specific purpose. Media producers usually obtain licenses for copyrighted material. Licenses can also cover the right to use a person's name or image or a trademark. The license can be exclusive or non-exclusive. An exclusive license for the use of copyrighted material must be in writing. I discuss the concept of exclusivity further in Section 19.3.4.

Grant as an Assignment. An assignment transfers all or substantially all of the rights in a copyrighted work. An assignment of a copyright must be in writing. For the purposes of rights clearance, the concepts of assignment as well as the concept of work made for hire, discussed immediately below, refer only to copyrighted works and usually only to those copyrighted works which the producer has specifically commissioned for her production.

While there are circumstances in which a trademark owner can assign a trademark, those circumstances do not include any of the ways in which a producer is likely to incorporate a trademark into her production. Hence, for the matters discussed in this reference book, a producer would always obtain permission to use a trademark through a license agreement.

Grant as a Work Made For Hire. For our purposes, the term work made for hire is relevant only to copyrighted works. When a work qualifies as a work made for hire, copyright law views the employer or person who commissioned the work as the author of the work. As the recognized author, the employer – and not the person who actually created the work – has the authority to exercise all the exclusive rights in the work. See Section 3.2 for a discussion of the exclusive rights in a copyrighted work. There are only two ways in which a copyrighted work becomes a work made for hire:

Work Created by an Employee. If an employee creates a copyrighted work within the scope of his employment, the resulting work is a work made for hire. Copyright law recognizes the employer as the copyright owner. For example, a newspaper owns the copyright in all the articles written for the paper by an employee of the newspaper. The newspaper may or may not be the copyright owner of an article written by a freelance writer.

Work Created by a Freelancer. If a person who is not an employee creates a copyrighted work at the request of a producer, the resulting work is a work made for hire only if two conditions are met:

- The freelancer signs a written agreement stating that the result-ing work will be a work made for hire.

- The copyrighted work belongs to one of the categories of com-missioned works listed in the Copyright Act as eligible to be a work made for hire. Eligible works include a contribution to a collective work, any work created specifically for an audio-visual production, a translation, a supplementary work, or a work created as part of a compilation. Supplementary works include maps, editorial notes, illustrations, a musical arrange-ment, and an index.

Many contracts refer to works as works made for hire even if the work does not qualify under one of the tests discussed above. Those contracts typically include assignment language as a back-up grant of rights in case there is a challenge to the status of the work as a work made for hire.

Who's an Employee and Who's a Freelancer? Sometimes there is a dispute regarding an individual's status as an employee or free-lancer. The distinction is important. In an employee-employer re-lationship, a copyrighted work is a work made for hire and owned by the employer whether or not the employee and employer have a written agreement. A copyrighted work created by a freelancer is owned by the freelancer unless there is a written agreement signed by the freelancer indicating otherwise.

There is no bright-line test to determine who's an employee and who's a freelancer. A court evaluates whether the relationship has elements that are more like an employer-employee relationship or more like a freelance relationship. How the parties act within the relationship carries much more weight than the name by which the parties refer to the relationship. Just because you refer to a contributor as an employee does not necessarily mean a court will agree with your characterization of the relationship.

Conditions Suggesting an Employee-Employer Relationship. The more of the following conditions exist, the more likely it is that you are an employer, the worker is an employee, and you own the work as a work made for hire:

- You control the manner and means by which the work is created.

- You contribute to the aesthetic decisions in completing the work. Simply providing general ideas of what you want and approving the work to make sure the worker is going in the right direction is not sufficient.

- You provide the materials and tools required for the project.

- The worker performs the work at your site.

- Your relationship with the worker extends beyond one specific project.

- You assign multiple projects to the worker.

- You set the worker's schedule.

- You dictate the method of payment.

- You hire (or exercise influence over who is hired) and pay any assistants or additional contributors retained to work on the project.

- The project is part of your regular business.

- Your compensation to the worker includes employee benefits such as health care and a 401k plan.

- You make state and federal withholdings from the compensation paid to the worker and pay the employer's portion of social security.

Conditions Suggesting a Freelance Relationship. The more of the following conditions exist, the more likely it is that the worker is a freelancer and you control only those rights which the freelancer has granted to you:

- The worker supplies his own tools and materials.

- The worker completes the project at his own work site.

- The worker completes the project with no or little direct supervision from you.

- You retain the worker for only one particular project or for a short period of time.

- The worker completes the project according to his own schedule.

- The worker is in complete control of hiring and paying any assistants he may have.

- You pay no employee benefits or social security taxes as part of the worker's compensation.

19.3.2. Scope of Distribution

Make sure the agreement covers the methods in which you plan to distribute the production. The important components are media, geographic territory, and duration. The following language grants a license to use the material in your production forever, throughout the world, and in any type of media:

Rights Owner grants Producer an irrevocable, non-exclusive, perpetual, worldwide right and license to incorporate the Material into the Production and to distribute the Production (with the Material therein) in any form, media, language or technology, now known or later developed.

Media and Market. A license agreement may allow distribution in one, some or all media. For example, if you license the right to include a song in your film production, you may initially license only theatrical rights. Theatrical rights give you permission to show your film in theatres. Before you can distribute your film on television or home video, you must obtain television and home video rights in the song.

Common categories for the breakdown of media are theatrical, videocassette recordings intended for home viewing, DVD intended for home viewing, television (which is further divided into free television, cable television, pay television, satellite television, *etc.*), and the internet. Some license agreements specify a particular market such as the educational market.

Term. The term is the duration for which you have rights in the material. Common terms are one year, five years, ten years, the duration of the copyright, and perpetuity. Perpetuity means forever.

Territory. The territory specifies the geographic region in which you may use the material. Common breakdowns for territories are local, regional, the United States, North America, Europe, international, worldwide, and the universe.

19.3.3. Upgrades

The broader the rights you need, the more expensive the license fee will be. You may not have the resources to purchase at one time all the rights you envision needing. Suppose you license a song for your production and the license allows you to use the song within your production on free television within North America. Before you can show your production on home video or on a cable television network or on foreign television, you must upgrade your rights to include permission for the additional uses. If you are unable to purchase all the rights you may need at one time, you should try to negotiate and include in your license agreement the option to expand your use of the material. The contract provision with your option to expand your use of the material should also include the cost of purchasing the additional rights. In that way, you do not have to go through a new negotiation when and if you need additional rights.

19.3.4. Exclusivity

The majority of license agreements are non-exclusive but some are exclusive. Exclusivity means that the rights owner will not grant the same rights to anyone else. There are varying degrees of exclusivity. Sometimes exclusivity is absolute meaning that the rights owner will not allow anyone other than you to use the material. Alternatively, the exclusivity may be defined by industry or product type. For example, if you are a film producer, you might ask that a song not be licensed for use in any other film. A producer of an automobile television commercial might ask that the song not be licensed for use in any other automobile advertisements. Often there is a time limit placed on the period of exclusivity.

19.3.5. Fee

Licensing fees vary tremendously and depend on a number of factors including the scope of your use and the popularity of the material to be licensed. Section 18.6 includes suggestions on negotiating the license fee.

19.3.6. Representations and Warranties

In essence, representations and warranties are guaranties. In the representations and warranties section of the rights agreement, the rights owner makes a number of statements such as the rights owner has the authority to grant you a license in the material and the material is the original creation of the rights owner.

The purpose of the representations and warranties is to assure you that the license you are purchasing is valid. Many rights owners refuse to give representations and warranties and in fact include a disclaimer in the license agreement. Your ability to obtain representations and warranties from the rights owner depends on your bargaining power.

19.3.7. Indemnification

An indemnification provision becomes important if any of the representations and warranties made by the rights owner turn out to be false. By agreeing to indemnify you, the rights owner agrees to pay or reimburse you for any monetary loss you suffer as a result of relying on the representation that ultimately turned out to be false.

Indemnification may not be possible to get. Many rights owners refuse to provide indemnification. Some even turn it around and insist that you indemnify them for any use of the material that goes beyond what the rights agreement allows.

19.3.8. Most Favored Nations Status

In a most favored nations status clause, a rights owner granting permission requires that you treat him as well as any other rights owners with whom you enter an agreement. Most favored nations status is commonly applicable to the license fee.

For example, suppose you want to license a recording for inclusion in your computer game. As discussed in Section 22.5.2, you need a license in the sound recording and a license in the underlying song. Suppose you approach the copyright owner of the sound recording first. The sound recording copyright owner grants you a license for a license fee of $2,000 and insists on most favored nations status with the copyright owner of the song.

You subsequently negotiate a license agreement with the copyright owner of the song for $3,000. Through the most favored nations clause, you agreed to treat the sound recording owner as well as you treat the song owner. You must now pay the sound recording copyright owner an additional $1,000 so the license fee he receives matches the license fee you are paying to the song copyright owner.

19.4. Follow-up

Do not exceed the scope of your rights agreement. If the rights agreement says that you may use the material for television only or in North America only, that is the extent of your license. If you use the material for a home DVD or in European countries, you must first upgrade your license to cover those uses. If you do not first obtain such permission, you are most likely violating the rights of the rights owner.

Also, be sure to obtain signed copies of the rights agreement and to keep copies of your signed rights agreement. If another company purchases ownership of the material you license, all the licensing agreements issued by the previous owner may not make it to the new owner. Your copy of the signed rights agreement may be the only proof of your legal right to use the material.

PART FIVE

Seeking Permission to Use Specific Materials

Part Five builds on Part Four. Part Four offered general guidance on how to approach the rights clearance process. Part Five provides more detailed instructions for seeking permission to use specific categories of materials.

Chapters in Part Five:

CLEARING RIGHTS AND SEEKING PERMISSION TO USE BOOKS AND OTHER PRINTED MATERIALS

20.1. Books

You may want to base your production on a book or you may want to use an excerpt of a book in a way that does not qualify as fair use. Before doing so, you need permission from the publisher or author depending on which one controls the rights you need.

20.1.1. Who Controls the Rights in a Book

For most published books, the author holds the copyright. The author may then license certain rights to a publisher. The grant of rights to a publisher can vary significantly from one publishing contract to the next. While the rights held by the publisher for print uses of the book are generally extensive and exclusive, authors may retain some rights in their books. The most common rights retained by authors include the rights

- to make a film or television production based on the book,
- to format the book as an audiobook or a book-on-tape or CD, and
- to sell the book in foreign markets.

An author may divide rights among different publishers. For example, an author may license paperback rights to publishing company A and hardcover rights to publishing company B.

20.1.2. Contacting the Author or Publisher

If you want rights in a book, start by contacting the publishing company which should be noted on the book's title page.

Most large publishing companies have a rights and permissions department. The publishing company can tell you if it controls the rights you desire to license.

If you do not have a copy of the book, you may be able to find basic publishing information by searching for the book title or author's name on an online bookseller's site or in the catalog of your local public library.

Once you have the publishing company's name, enter it into a search engine to determine if the publisher has an internet presence that includes instructions for requesting permission. If it does not, get the telephone number from information and call. If the publisher does not control the rights you seek, it should be able to give you the name and contact information for the person or organization that does.

You can also contact the author either directly or through her agent. Some authors maintain their own websites which usually include information on who represents them and how to contact them. The Appendix includes resources for locating authors and their agents.

20.2. Magazines and Newspapers

20.2.1. Who Controls Rights in Magazine and Newspaper Materials

Recall from Section 10.4 that most magazines and newspapers are collective works containing material from a number of writers, photographers, and other contributors. When seeking permission to use material from a collective work, a relevant question is whether the person who authored the material in which you seek permission contributed to the periodical as an employee or as a freelancer of the publication.

If the contributor is an employee of the publication, the publication owns all rights in the material and has authorization to grant you a license in the material. If the contributor is a freelancer, the publication might own all rights if the freelancer assigned all rights or the freelancer sold the material as a work made for hire.

Otherwise, the freelancer may have only licensed the publication the right to publish the material one time. In that case, it is the freelance contributor who controls the rights that you want to license. A 2001 Supreme Court decision, *New York Times v. Tasini*, 533 U.S. 483 (2001), has altered the dynamics of relationships between publishing companies and freelancers. In *Tasini*, the Supreme Court ruled that a periodical may not subsequently distribute a freelancer's work as a stand-alone article without the explicit authorization of the freelancer. In the aftermath of the *Tasini* decision, many publications are becoming more aggressive in acquiring all rights in materials contributed by freelancers. See Section 19.3.1 for a more comprehensive discussion of a commissioning party's rights in a freelancer's work.

Writers and photographers of magazines and newspapers often receive bylines. You can sometimes tell who is an employee and who is a freelancer by reading the masthead or noting the format of the byline. For example, the *Washington Post* designates employee writers as follows:

By Jane Writer, Washington Post Staff Writer

The *Washington Post* uses the following style to designate freelance writers:

By Jane Writer, Special to the Washington Post

20.2.2. Locating the Rights Owners of Magazine and Newspaper Articles

Contacting the Publication. If you want permission to use an article or other material in a magazine, newspaper or other periodical, start with the publication in which you saw the material. Many magazines and newspapers have an online presence which sometimes allows you to request permission online. Generally, these online permission forms are for reprint rights so it may not be applicable to the use you seek. However, the form should offer a contact email address or telephone number to which you can direct an inquiry regarding permission for other uses. If the publication has no online presence or offers no instructions on seeking permission, check with the collective rights organizations to determine if one of them licenses rights for the publication. See Section 16.8 for a discussion of obtaining permission through collective rights organizations.

Contacting Individual Authors. If you determine that the writer wrote the article as a freelancer and retained rights in the article, you must obtain rights directly from the writer. Again, the collective rights organizations are a good place to start your search. Most writers who specialize in magazine and newspaper articles do not have agents but many do have online websites which include their contact information.

Seeking Permission from Syndication Companies. Magazines and newspapers often use syndicated materials. Syndicated materials are articles and other content that are published simultaneously in a number of periodicals. Many columns and most comic strips appearing in newspapers are syndicated. For example, Ann Landers and Miss Manners are both syndicated columns. The periodicals that publish the syndicated material normally have only limited rights. Those limited rights generally do not include authorization to grant you or any other third parties permission to use the material.

Typically, syndication companies handle the rights in syndicated material. Syndication companies are in the business of licensing rights so their online information usually contains instructions on requesting permission. Syndicated materials appearing in newspapers frequently include the syndication company's name and website address.

20.3. Unpublished Printed Materials

Copyright law extends protection to unpublished materials so you need permission to use material even if it is unpublished. An example of unpublished material you might want to use is a letter or a speech.

You may have a difficult time locating the copyright owner of unpublished materials. If you cannot locate the copyright owner of an unpublished work, you have to consider the alternatives and the risks associated with those alternatives. For more guidance in deciding whether to include that material in your production, see Section 18.1 on Identifying the Rights Owner and 16.3 on Evaluating Risks of Not Having Permission.

CLEARING RIGHTS AND
SEEKING PERMISSION TO USE VISUAL ART

21.1. Finding and Obtaining Images

21.1.1. If You Have Identified the Photograph You Want to Use

If you have seen the photograph in which you want rights, start with an examination of the publication or location where you saw it. If the photograph appears in a newspaper, magazine, or other periodical, note that many periodicals include materials that the publication does not own. If the publication possesses only limited rights to use a photograph, the publication probably does not have authorization to grant you a license to use that photograph in your production.

Photographs in periodicals frequently include the source in very small type at the bottom or along the side. For example, the type may indicate "First Run Features" or "Associated Press" or "Reuters" – which are all companies that produce and own various types of content. If you see such a reference, that is the source with which you should start your quest for permission. If you cannot find the contact information for the source through an internet search engine, the publication in which you saw the material might be able to provide the information.

21.1.2. If You Are Seeking Photographs to Use

Perhaps you know the type of image you want but you are unsure of where to find such an image. There are a few resources available to you.

Internet Portals. One option is to use the internet to search for photos. Internet portals like Yahoo and Google index images that are displayed on the world wide web. Using these search engines, you can search for images using a location, event or name as the keyword. Most of the images identified by the search service are protected by copyright. The search engines do not have authorization to grant rights to use these images. You can click on the images to view the page and the context in which they are displayed. You can then investigate or contact the site owner and use the other methods discussed in this book to obtain any necessary permissions to use the photograph.

Photo Researcher. There are individuals and companies that specialize in finding images. In addition to locating images for producers, many photo researchers also request permissions and negotiate license arrangements similar to the rights clearance companies discussed in Section 16.6. Photo researchers may charge by the hour or by the project.

21.2. Stock Images

Stock image companies – or stock houses - control and license catalogs of images. Stock houses come in a variety of sizes:

- Large publicly-traded companies that have millions of images from thousands of artists in their collections. Examples include Getty Images, Corbis, and Jupiter Images.

- Individual photographers who license images from their portfolios.

- Media publications and organizations that offer images that have appeared in their publications as stock image. Examples include the Associated Press, the *New York Times*, and *National Geographic*.

Increasingly, stock image companies offer online stores that allow you to preview, license, and obtain delivery of an image for your production within minutes.

21.2.1. Pricing and Licensing of Stock Images

Most stock houses license their images on a per image basis. If you need numerous images or images on a regular basis, you should investigate the monthly or annual subscription services offered by some stock houses.

Stock houses may categorize the images in their catalogs as royalty free images, and as per license use images. I offer some generalizations for the meaning behind these terms. However, there is not one consistent definition and these terms really mean whatever the particular stock house's license agreement defines them to mean.

Royalty Free. Although some royalty-free images may be in the public domain, many royalty-free images are in fact protected by copyright. Royalty-free does not mean you may use the image without paying a license fee. The royalty-free language means that once you license the image, you may use it multiple times for multiple projects without paying additional fees.

While royalty-free images are sometimes sold as part of a collection, most stock houses sell each royalty-free image individually. When sold on a per image basis, the price is determined by the size and resolution of the image. The stock house may limit the manner in which you may use the image. For example, the stock house may prohibit the use of the image on certain products offered for retail sale such as calendars, T-shirts and photo mugs. The licensing agreement should explain all such limitations.

Per Use License. With images licensed on a per use basis, you receive permission to use the image for one specific use. Per use licensed images are also referred to as rights-managed or rights-protected images. As a broad generalization, per use license images are higher-quality than royalty-free images. The per use license images normally come with a corresponding premium fee which is calculated according to several factors such as

- the size of the image you use,
- where the image is to be placed in your production,
- the length of time during which you want to use the image, and
- how widely you plan to distribute the image.

Some stock houses offer an online price calculator that generates a quote and processes the license sale after you provide specific information concerning your intended use of the image.

Exclusivity. One potential downside to using stock images is the inability to control other uses of the image. Unless you purchase exclusive rights, the stock house may license the same image to other people and allow them to use it on productions that are similar to yours and within the same time period in which you plan to use the image. It may be possible to purchase exclusivity for some per-use licensed images which, in turn, makes the licensing fee higher. Exclusive rights are typically not available for royalty free images.

21.2.2. Additional Rights Needed When Using Stock Images

Using a stock image may require you to do more than obtain a license from the stock house. The license granted by the stock house frequently includes only rights related to the copyright of the image. However, the use of an image may trigger privacy, publicity, defamation, trademark and other issues – depending upon who appears in the images and how you intend to use the image.

Stock houses sometimes leave you on your own to clear these additional rights. Some licensing agreements may even have you indemnify the stock house which means you reimburse the stock house for any monetary loss it suffers due to your failure to obtain the necessary additional rights.

To determine what additional rights you need, read the license agreement issued by the stock house. For additional clarification, have a conversation with a representative from the stock image house. A well-run stock house should be able to tell you what rights the stock house controls in the image. While responsibility for determining and acquiring additional rights is normally up to you, the stock house may be able to provide general guidance. The stock house can sometimes provide contact information for obtaining many of the additional rights you need.

See Section 21.5 for more discussion of the additional rights you should consider when using images and other visual art.

21.3. Fine Art

If you seek permission to use fine art, start with where you saw the artwork. Note that the person who possesses the physical copy of the art does not necessarily own the copyright in the art. For example, a museum or gallery may own the physical artwork while the artist retains the copyright. If you want rights in artwork which you see in a museum or gallery, the museum or gallery staff should be able to identify the artist and/or the copyright owner. If you want rights in fine art which you see in printed material such as a book, calendar, magazine, or postcard, the printed material may identify the artist. If not, contact the publisher of the printed material to request the name of the copyright owner.

Many museums and galleries have websites that include specific instructions on how to obtain permission and the actual slides or digital images you need.

21.4. Visual Characters

Visual characters can be protected by copyright or by trademark. The process for seeking permission often depends on the category of visual character.

Visual Characters from Comic Strips. Visual characters may be associated with syndicated comic strips. Typically, syndication companies handle the rights in syndicated material. For permission to use this material, contact the syndicate. Syndicates are in the business of licensing rights so their online information frequently contains instructions on how to request permission. For comic strips check in between the frames for copyright notices, website addresses, and other contact information.

Visual Characters from Film and Television. If it is a visual character associated with a film or television program, use the suggestions for seeking permission in film, television and other audio-visual productions in Chapter 23.

Visual Characters Associated with Products and Services. If it is a visual character associated with a service or product, the visual character probably also qualifies as a trademark. Use the suggestions for seeking permission to use trademarks and names in Chapter 26. Owners of characters associated with a product or service are likely to be more selective about licensing their characters. For these owners, licensing is not their primary business, and they will not want any uses that might negatively impact the reputation of the product.

21.5. Other Necessary Rights for the use of Visual Art

The use of visual art sometimes requires permission in addition to that of the visual artist. This is especially true with images you may obtain from a stock image house. Read Section 21.2.2 for more information on additional rights needed when using stock images.

The issues with which you need to be concerned include the following:

Images that Depict People. You may need a release from people depicted in the image. Potential claims include right of privacy, right of publicity, and defamation. Refer to Chapter 25 for additional guidance on obtaining consents from people.

If you obtain the image from a stock image house, the stock house may have obtained a release from persons appearing in images designed specifically for use in advertising and other promotional purposes. In contrast, stock houses often do not have releases for images obtained through news gathering and reporting activities.

Even if the visual artist who supplies the image has a release, the release may not be sufficient for your intended use. For example, it may not cover a use dealing with sensitive material. You may need to obtain additional permissions from the person and/or use a disclaimer with the image. Sensitive areas include uses related to contraception, sexual matters, substance abuse, domestic abuse, alcohol, tobacco, AIDS, cancer and other serious physical or mental ailments.

Images that Depict Copyrighted Works.   Recall from our discussion in Section 18.1 that rights may be stacked. The copyright in the image is separate from any copyright in the subject of the image. For example, if the image displays copyrighted artwork, you may need permission from the artist of the artwork in addition to permission from the copyright owner of the image.

Images that Depict Trademarks.   Depending on your use, it is possible you could be accused of infringing the trademark appearing in the image. This is the same product appearance analysis discussed in Section 4.4.3.   There is trademark infringement only if there is a likelihood of consumer confusion.

CLEARING RIGHTS AND SEEKING PERMISSION TO USE MUSIC

22.1. Are You Using the Song, the Sound Recording or Both?

When you want to use music, you must first determine whether you want to use the song, the sound recording or both. Your answer determines from whom you must seek permission.

Copyright law protects music. Every recorded song has two distinct copyrights. There is a copyright in the song which is comprised of the melody and any accompanying lyrics. There is a separate copyright in the sound recording. The sound recording is the recorded performance of the song.

22.1.1. A Single Song Can Spawn Multiple Sound Recordings

A single song may have several different sound recordings. For example, a number of artists have recorded the song *Amazing Grace*. They include Aretha Franklin, Elvis Presley, and Leontyne Price. The familiar melody and lyrics make up the song. Aretha Franklin's recorded performance of *Amazing Grace* is one sound recording; Elvis Presley's recorded performance of the song is a separate sound recording; and Leontyne Price's recorded rendition of *Amazing Grace* is still a third and distinct sound recording. That's three separate sound recordings for the same song.

22.1.2. Ownership of the Song and Sound Recording

While the copyright owner of the song and of the sound recording can be the same person, that is typically not the case. Also, the artist you may associate with the song does not necessarily have an ownership interest in the song or in the sound recording.

Who Owns the Song? The songwriter is typically the initial copyright owner of the song. A songwriter may later transfer the copyrights in her songs to a music publishing company. As you might have guessed, music publishing companies are in the business of music publishing. Music publishing is the commercial exploitation of songs through the issuance of licenses authorizing various uses of the songs. The music publisher's primary job is to license songs. For that reason, it is likely that a music publishing company will respond more quickly to your permission request than a record company will.

Who Owns the Sound Recording? With very few exceptions, artist recording contracts provide that the record company owns the copyright in sound recordings made under the contract. As a result, if the recording artist works with an established record label, the record label probably owns the copyright in the sound recording.

It is not always easy to get the attention of a major label for a response to your permission request. Major record labels are not in the business of licensing sound recordings. Their primary focus is selling records. Licenses that do not have the potential of generating substantial revenue are often not of great interest to them.

Independent Bands and Musicians. Recording artists and bands who release recordings independently without the assistance of an established label are frequently referred to as unsigned or independent. Independent recording artists and bands usually own the copyrights in their sound recordings. Likewise, independent musicians who perform songs they have composed themselves usually own the copyright in the songs.

Band members often collaborate on songs without having an agreement addressing ownership of those songs. The situation sometimes leads to disputes among the band members. The likelihood that an independent band has no band agreement (*i.e.*, an agreement among band members) is higher than the likelihood that a band working with a major record label has no band agreement. If you are licensing music from a band, you do not want to get in the middle of a dispute concerning ownership of the music. Methods of minimizing this risk include having all band members sign the license agreement although this option may not always be practical. You can also address the issue in the representations, warranties, and indemnification sections of your license agreement with the band.

22.2. Identifying the Copyright Owner of Music

Here are resources for identifying the copyright owner of music. The Appendix includes additional details and resources.

Physical Copy of Recording. If you have a physical recording of the music, look at the packaging. The packaging should tell you which record label released the CD. The liner notes should identify the writer of each song, the music publishing company of the song, and with which performing rights society the songwriter and music publisher are associated. If you have older physical copies, note that ownership of songs and sound recordings often change. Hence, the ownership may be different than what is reflected in the physical copy you have. The same applies to sheet music discussed below.

Sheet Music. Printed sheet music should identify relevant information related to the song including the songwriters, their music publishing companies, and the names of their performing rights organization.

Online Catalogs of Performing Rights Organizations and of Harry Fox. ASCAP, BMI, and SESAC are the three United States performing rights organizations for songs. Harry Fox is a rights organization that issues mechanical licenses on behalf of music publishers. Each offers an online, searchable catalog of the songs it administers which you can access for free.

268 The Permission Seeker's Guide Through The Legal Jungle

Online Music Stores. Websites that sell sheet music, music downloads and physical CDs such as amazon.com and CDBaby can provide helpful information for your search.

Artist and Label Websites. Check the website of the label, publishing company or artist. You can frequently locate the website through the use of an internet search engine.

22.3. Types of Music Licenses

The music industry gives specific names to many licenses according to whether it is the song or sound recording you are using and according to how you are using it.

22.3.1. Licenses for Songs

Public Performance License. Each time there is a public performance of a song, the songwriter and music publishing company are entitled to receive royalty income. The public performance of a song results from numerous situations including the radio broadcast of the song, the inclusion of the song in a televised program, and the live performance of the song at a nightclub. To comply with copyright law, the radio station, television network, and night club must have a performing rights license authorizing the public performance.

Synchronization License. A synchronization license gives you authorization to use a song in an audio-visual production like a commercial, film, video, or television show. Synchronization, or synch for short, refers to the fact that the song is synchronized with the visual images of the audio-visual production.

Mechanical License. A mechanical license gives you the right to make and distribute a recording of a song. Record labels and recording artists who distribute recordings of songs written by other people must obtain a mechanical license for each song.

22.3.2. Licenses for Sound Recordings

Master Use License. When you obtain a master use license, you have authorization to use a sound recording in an audio-visual production. The master use license is completely distinct from the synchronization license which authorizes you to use only the song in an audio-visual production. For example, if you obtain permission to use a particular song in your video commercial and decide to make and use your own recorded rendition of the song, you need a synchronization license but not a master use license.

On the other hand, there are also situations in which you may need a master use license but not a synchronization license. Suppose you use the Boston Symphony Orchestra's 1998 recording of an 18th century classical piece as background music in your television commercial. The 18th century classical piece is in the public domain so you do not need a synchronization license to use it. However, the Boston Symphony's 1998 recording of the piece is still protected by copyright. You need a master use license to place it in your commercial.

License to Perform via Digital Audio Transmission. The Digital Performance Right and Sound Recordings Act of 1995 and the Digital Millennium Copyright Act of 1998 give sound recording owners the rights to control and receive royalty compensation for the public performance of their recordings online and in other digital formats. See Section 22.7 for further discussion.

22.4. Performing Music In Public

The writer and music publisher of a song are entitled to receive payment for each public performance of the song.

22.4.1. Sound Recording Copyright Owners Have Limited Public Performance Rights

General public performance rights apply only to the song and not to the sound recording. Hence, if you publicly perform recordings of a song, you need a public performance license from the copyright owner of the song but not from the copyright owner of the sound recording. Think of a d.j. playing records at a crowded nightclub. When the d.j. plays the record, there is a public performance of the song and a public performance of the sound recording. However, only the copyright owner of the song is entitled to receive royalties from the public performance. That's because there is no general public performance right for sound recordings.

There is an exception to the pubic performance license requirement for sound recordings. You do need a license if you are performing the sound recordings via the internet or via other means of digital audio transmission. Of course, this exception is becoming more significant as the internet and digital media become more prevalent in our lives. I discuss the public performance license requirement for sound recordings played over the internet further in Section 22.7.

22.4.2. Seeking Permission for the Public Performance of Songs Through ASCAP, BMI and SESAC

Each time a song is played in a club, on the radio, on television, on an internet site, or other public forum, a public performance of the song takes place. To eliminate the need to negotiate a separate license with each venue that wants to perform their songs, songwriters and music publishers affiliate with performing rights organizations.

There are three performing rights organizations (PROs) for songs in the United States. They are ASCAP, BMI, and SESAC. Each of the PROs represents a separate roster of songwriters and music publishers. BMI is the largest with over 250,000 affiliated songwriters and music publishers, followed by ASCAP with over 100,000, and then SESAC with approximately 6,000.

The PROs negotiate performing rights licenses and collect performing rights revenues for songs. The PROs often negotiate blanket licenses with venues to perform any song in the catalog of the performing rights society issuing the blanket license.

It is generally the venue owner – and not the producer of the production - who must obtain and pay for the public performance license. That means each television station, website, concert hall, or nightclub has the responsibility of acquiring and paying for the public performance license.

If you are the venue, you are the responsible party. For example, if a website you control offers performances of copyrighted songs, you are responsible for obtaining a public performance license.

Public performance license fees vary according to the circumstances in which the song is to be performed, the size and/or audience capacity of the venue, and other factors. Each of the PROs offers detailed information on the categories of public performance licenses as well as online applications to obtain those licenses.

22.4.3. Dramatic and Non-Dramatic Public Performance Rights

The music industry recognizes two different types of public performance rights:

- non-dramatic performance rights
- dramatic performance rights

The first category grants permission to present non-dramatic public performances of a song. The non-dramatic performance of a song includes playing the song on the radio, in a nightclub, or as the background music in a film. If you wish to make a theatrical presentation of a song or act out a song by using character interaction, props, and costumes to tell the "plot" of the song, you need to obtain dramatic performance rights in the song.

The PROs deal exclusively with non-dramatic performance rights. To obtain dramatic performance rights, you must contact the song's copyright owner or music publishing company directly.

22.5. Using Music in Films and Other Audio-Visual Productions

If you need music for your film, television program, software program, internet website, CD-ROM, or other audio-visual production, you have at least two choices. You can either commission original music or license existing music.

22.5.1. Commissioning Original Music

The agreements for original music between the songwriter and the producer often look very similar to single song agreements between songwriters and music publishing companies. The songwriter frequently delivers the song as a work made for hire which means that the producer owns the copyright in the song.

With some negotiating power, the songwriter may retain a portion or all of the copyright in the song. This is especially true if the production is low-budget and does not compensate the songwriter enough to justify the songwriter relinquishing the copyright in the song. If you commission songs in which you will not own the copyright, you need to obtain from the songwriter a license that addresses all your uses of the song.

Producers normally compensate the songwriter with a fixed fee plus a negotiated royalty for any use of the song outside of the production. The royalty split between the producer and the composer for uses outside the production is generally fifty-fifty.

If you commission original songs, you also need to produce a recording. Sometimes the songwriter composing the music also delivers a recording of the music as part of the composer agreement. The Appendix includes a sample composer agreement for original music.

22.5.2. Licensing Existing Music

The Song. To incorporate an existing song into your production, you need a synchronization license or synch license for short. You obtain a synch license from the song's copyright owner which is typically the songwriter or a music publishing company.

Synchronization fees are subject to negotiation and vary according to the popularity of the song and the importance of the song in your production. Factors a music publisher might consider when setting a synchronization license fee include the following:

- geographic territories and media (*e.g.*, theatrical, home video, internet, *etc.*) in which the production is to be distributed
- the amount of the song to be used in the production
- the number of times the production uses the song
- the relevance of the song in the production

For example, using the song as the theme is more expensive than a character performing the song on-camera which is more expensive than the song being used as background.

The owner of the song is sometimes willing to take a lower synch license fee if the use has the potential of generating money at the back end in the form of public performance and mechanical license revenue. Back end public performance revenue might be generated by the broadcast of the production on television.

For example, the use of a song in a national television commercial can generate significant public performance revenue for the songwriter and music publishing company. Mechanical license revenue is generated with the release of a soundtrack album of the production.

Once you license an existing song, you still need a recording of the song. You have two choices. You can use an existing recording of that song. If you take this route, you must obtain a master use license from the copyright owner of the sound recording. Your other choice is to record your own rendition of the song for use in your production. With this option, you need no master use license because you are the copyright owner of the new recording.

The Recording. To incorporate an existing sound recording into your production, you need a master use license from the sound recording's copyright owner which is typically the record label that released the recording. Like synchronization fees, master use license fees are subject to negotiation and vary according to the popularity of the recording and the importance of the recording in the production.

Use of a recording always includes use of the underlying song. Hence, when you use a recording, you must obtain the appropriate licenses for both the recording and the song. Producers sometimes choose to create a new recording of a song rather than use an existing recording of the song. Creating a new recording negates the need to obtain a master use license.

22.5.3. Using Library Music

To simplify the music licensing process, you can choose to use music from a production music library. Production music libraries offer music that has been written especially for use in audio and audio-visual productions.

With one stop, you get a synchronization license for rights in the song and a master use license for rights in the sound recording. You can use production music for all of your production's musical needs or use a combination of production music along with music you commission or license from other sources.

Production music libraries typically offer large selections of music and styles. You can obtain music on a compact disc or obtain it online. Many production music libraries offer online websites that allow you to preview, license, and download the tracks you want.

When distributed on CD, each CD typically contains eight to fifteen compositions, each one offered in several different versions or lengths. For example, each selection might come as a full length version, an underscore or rhythm track version, and several different broadcast lengths.

Production music libraries are also a good place to start if you are seeking original music for your production. Some production houses offer music composition and recording services for projects in need of original music.

You can also use their online directories to search for individual composers whom you can then contact directly.

Production Library Pricing and Licensing Mechanisms. Most music libraries license their music on a royalty-free, needle-drop, or subscription basis.

Royalty-Free or Buy-Out Music. Royalty-free does not mean that you can use the music free of charge or that the music is not protected by copyright. Although some songs from a production library are in the public domain, most of the songs are composed specifically for use as background music and are protected by copyright.

In general, royalty-free signifies that after paying a one-time license fee for the music, you may use the music as many times as you like in as many productions as you like without paying an additional royalty. However, royalty-free can mean whatever the licensing agreement says it means so you need to read the licensing agreements carefully. Terms offered by different production music companies do vary.

For example, one production library's standard license fee for single-tracks falls in the range of $55.00 and includes a license for local broadcasts (defined as a broadcast that is within a 300 mile radius of the producer's business address). Nationwide broadcast rights cost an additional $145 and worldwide broadcast rights cost an additional $225.

Other uses that might require an additional fee for production music include the following:

- use in a theatrical motion picture
- certain types of broadcast content (*e.g.*, made for TV movies; network television prime time programming; and national television commercials on ABC, CBS, NBC, FOX)
- inclusion in mass-market retail products.

A single production music CD might cost anywhere from $10 to $150 or more. For example, one production music library sells royalty-free collections ranging from single CDs starting at $59 to a 289 CD-collection for $4,840.

Needle-Drop or Per-Use License. The term needle-drop is a hold-over from the days when music libraries were distributed on vinyl records. Each time you use any portion of a song (*e.g.,* each time you drop the needle onto the vinyl record), you pay a license fee. Needle-drop music is now sometimes referred to as laser-drop music in recognition of the more common use of CDs over vinyl records.

Here is an example of how needle-drop licensing works. If you create a video game and use Music Selection-A four times within the video game and Music Selection-B two times, you would pay six needle-drop fees. Sometimes you can obtain a production blanket license to cover one production or series of productions. Hence, if you had a production blanket license for your video game, you would pay one license fee and be able to use music from the chosen collection as many times as you want.

Needle-drop libraries with this type of license structure usually charge more per track than royalty-free music libraries. Typical fees range from $65 to several hundred dollars per needle-drop, depending upon the type of media and geographic territory in which you use the music.

Subscription Production Blanket or Annual Blanket. You can buy a "blanket license" that covers a single project. You can also get a contract that covers projects you produce during a period of time. You typically get to choose a fixed number of CDs to create your library. Some production libraries issuing blanket licenses require you to submit reports that detail which songs you use and how long the cue is for each project that includes music from the library.

Subscription licenses have many variations. For example, one particular subscription service allows unlimited access to its production library. In each annual subscription period, you can opt for a specified number of tracks or you can choose the unlimited track option. The subscription allows you to use tracks for one specific default media platform or market. The default might be for film productions, television productions, radio productions, games, corporate productions, or other categories. Using the music for other markets or platforms would require an additional license.

22.5.4. Filing Cue Sheets

If you use music in a production to be broadcast or distributed publicly you must file a cue sheet with both the production music company and with the appropriate performing rights organizations. While the producer is not responsible for paying the performance license fees, most license agreements obligate the producer to prepare and file a cue sheet with the songwriter's performing rights organization.

The cue sheet is a listing of the music used in a production and includes the title, composer, publisher, timing and type of usage for each musical piece. The performing rights organizations use cue sheets to calculate the amount of public performance licensing royalties to be paid to songwriters and music publishing companies

The Appendix includes a sample cue sheet. There is no cost to you as the producer for filing a cue sheet.

22.6. Making Recordings of Existing Songs

To make and distribute a recording of an existing song, you need a mechanical license from the copyright owner of the song. You need a mechanical license whether you are making and distributing physical copies (*e.g.*, CDs, tapes) of the song or downloads of the song. Record labels and recording artists who record songs written by other people regularly obtain mechanical licenses for the material they produce.

22.6.1. Compulsory Mechanical License

If you want to record a song that has already been commercially released, you can obtain a compulsory mechanical license. A compulsory mechanical license is a statutory license. That means the license is automatically granted by operation of law to anyone who satisfies the conditions of the license. You do not need the express permission of the song's copyright owner. You are entitled to a compulsory mechanical license in a song if all the following conditions apply:

- The copyright owner authorized the initial commercial release of the song.

- The song is non-dramatic. While the Copyright Act does not provide a specific definition for the term "non-dramatic song", most people think of it as a song that is not from a musical or an opera.

- You provide certain notices and accounting statements to the copyright owner.

- You pay the copyright owner the license fee set by law. The compulsory mechanical license fee - also called the statutory rate - is listed in the Appendix.

22.6.2. Seeking a Mechanical License through the Copyright Office

Obtaining a compulsory mechanical license requires sending certain notices and accountings to the song's copyright owner including the following:

- a Notice of Intention to Obtain a Compulsory License

- a monthly royalty fee payment accompanied by a Monthly Statement of Account

- an Annual Statement of Account which must be certified by a certified public accountant

You must file the Notice Of Intention prior to any distribution of the recording. Otherwise, you risk losing the right to the compulsory license. For example, in one case, distribution of a recording nine days before proper notice was sent led to denial of the compulsory mechanical license. (*24/7 Records v. Sony Music Entertainment*, 429 F.3d 39 (2nd Cir. 2005)). The Appendix contains sample forms for obtaining a compulsory mechanical license.

22.6.3. Seeking a Mechanical License through Harry Fox

To avoid the paperwork required by the Copyright Act, many people seeking a mechanical license choose to work through the Harry Fox Agency or directly with the copyright owner. The Harry Fox Agency, the wholly-owned licensing subsidiary of the National Music Publishers' Association, issues mechanical licenses on behalf of more than 30,000 music publishers. Harry Fox issues a standard mechanical license which, other than relaxing notice and statement requirements, substantially mirrors the compulsory mechanical license available through the Copyright Office.

You can get and submit the Harry Fox mechanical license request form online. If you want to obtain a mechanical license for physical recordings (CDs, cassettes, vinyl), you must obtain a license for a minimum quantity of 500 copies. If you want to create and distribute downloads of a song, you must obtain a license for a minimum of 150 permanent downloads

22.6.4. What a Compulsory Mechanical License Does Not Cover

If you want to take any of the following actions, you need to negotiate a mechanical license directly with the copyright owner of the song. Neither a compulsory mechanical license nor a license issued by Harry Fox covers these actions:

Making Major Changes to the Song. While the compulsory mechanical license allows you to make a new musical arrangement as necessary to conform the song to your style and interpretation, you cannot change the basic melody, the lyrics or the fundamental character of the song. For these types of changes, you need permission to make an adaptation or derivative work of the song. Recall from the discussion in Section 3.2.2 that making a derivative work is one of the exclusive rights held by the copyright owner. There is no compulsory license for a derivative work. Hence, you need direct permission from the copyright owner of the song who may freely say yes or no to the request.

Reducing the Statutory Rate. A reduction in the mechanical statutory rate requires the permission of the copyright owner. Generally, only a party with some bargaining power - such as a record label or artist who can sell a significant number of copies of the resulting recording - is able to negotiate a reduced rate.

First Commercial Release. You must negotiate a license with the copyright owner to be the first to release a song commercially.

Other Actions. Other actions that are not covered by a compulsory mechanical license or a mechanical license issued through Harry Fox, and require the direct permission of the copyright owner include reprinting lyrics, distributing sheet music, placing the song in an audio-visual program, and sampling the song.

22.7. Using Music on the Internet

The license required for the use of music on the internet depends on (i) whether you are using the song, the sound recording or both and (ii) how you are using them.

Streaming and downloading are common uses of music on the internet. Both uses require a license. Streamed music, also referred to as internet radio or webcasting, can be accessed in real time or live. For example, some radio stations stream programs on the internet at the same time the program is being broadcast over the air. With downloaded or compressed music, a copy of the music must be placed on the listener's computer hard drive or digital music device before the user can listen to it.

22.7.1. Seeking Permission to Use a Song on the Internet

Downloading the Song. Offering a song for downloading on the internet requires a mechanical license. If the song has already been commercially released, you can obtain a compulsory mechanical license. See Section 22.6.1 for a discussion of compulsory mechanical licenses. For example, an independent band that records an existing song and wants to offer those recordings as downloads needs a mechanical license in the song.

Streaming the Song. Streaming a song on the internet requires a public performance license from one of the performing rights organizations (PROs) for songs or directly from the copyright owner. In the United States, there are three PROs for songs. They are ASCAP, BMI, and SESAC. See Section 22.4.2 for a more detailed discussion of PROs. Most producers that stream music on the internet obtain a blanket license from one or more of the PROs. The blanket license covers all the songs in the catalog of the PRO that issued the license. The fee for the blanket license usually depends on the internet site's estimated gross revenue for uses related to music.

22.7.2. Seeking Permission to Use a Sound Recording on the Internet

When you use a sound recording, you also use the underlying song. Hence, whenever you license rights in a sound recording, you must also clear rights in the underlying song.

Downloading the Sound Recording. Offering a recording on the internet for downloading requires a license to reproduce and distribute the recording. There is no central administrator that issues these licenses and a compulsory license is available only in the limited circumstances of ephemeral recordings. Ephemeral recordings are copies temporarily placed on a computer hard drive or server so the music can be streamed. As a result, you must negotiate reproduction and distribution licenses directly with the record label.

The major record labels control about eighty percent of commercial sound recordings and have granted licenses for downloading their recordings only in a handful of cases to digital music stores like iTunes, Yahoo, and Napster.

Streaming the Sound Recording. Streaming a sound recording on the internet requires a license for a public performance by digital audio transmission. There is a statutory license available for websites that offer music through non-interactive programs. In essence, non-interactive status requires that listeners are not able to choose the sound recordings played on the program. There is a laundry list of requirements to qualify as non-interactive including the following:

- Any archived programs must be at least five hours in duration and may be posted on a website for no more than two weeks.

- Any looped programs ((*i.e.*, continuous programs that repeat automatically when finished) must be at least three hours long.

- Programs that are less than one hour long that are performed at scheduled times may be performed only three times in a two-week period. Programs that are more than one hour long that are performed at scheduled times may be performed only four times within a two-week period.

- You may not play more than three songs from a particular album or more than four songs by a particular artist during any three-hour period.

- You may not publish a playlist of songs or artists in advance.

Many webcasters and internet radio stations qualify as non-interactive and can take advantage of the statutory license. A statutory license means that the license fee and other terms are set by law. As long as webcasters and internet radio stations comply with the provisions of the statutory license, they do not need the express permission of the sound recording copyright owner. In contrast, website owners whose music programming does not qualify as non-interactive must negotiate a license directly with the record label.

Getting a Statutory License from SoundExchange to Stream a Sound Recording. SoundExchange, a performing rights organization for sound recordings, issues the statutory licenses that are available for the non-interactive streaming of sound recordings on the internet, collects the corresponding fees, and distributes those fees to artists and record labels. Note that SoundExchange issues licenses only for the non-interactive streaming of recordings. To offer a sound recording as a download or as a stream in which the listener is able to choose the music played, you must obtain a license directly from the owner of the sound recording.

To obtain a statutory license, you must first file with the Copyright Office a Notice of Use of Sound Recordings under Statutory License. You can find the notice form and instructions for its completion on the Copyright Office's website. After filing the notice, you can begin streaming sound recordings. You must comply with all of the terms and conditions of the statutory license which are set out in sections 112 and 114 of the Copyright Act and the relevant regulations. Full compliance requires making all payments and filing all statements of account and reports of use when due.

Payment of Sound Recording Public Performance License Fees. Statutory rates are set through a proceeding at the Copyright Office. At the time of this writing, the proceeding to determine license rates for non-interactive streaming of sound recordings for 2006 through 2010 is ongoing. Once established, rates will be retroactive to January 1, 2006.

There are nine categories and sub-categories of digital audio transmission services, each of which may have different royalty rates and terms. The rates applicable in 2005 gave license-holders three options for calculating rates - Per Performance,   Per Aggregate Tuning Hour, or as a Percentage of Revenues.

- Per Performance. A single performance is comprised of one listener listening to one recording of a song. Hence, one listener listening to one song is one performance. Two listeners listening to the same recording of a song is two performances. A listener is a player or a receiving device receiving streamed music, regardless of the number of individuals present to hear the transmission. Hence, if four people are listening to music being streamed over one receiving device, those four people count as one person. The minimum annual fee is $500 per channel but no more than $2,500.

- Per Aggregate Tuning Hour. An aggregate tuning hour measures the number of hours each person listens to the programming. If one listener listens for one hour, that is one aggregate tuning hour. An aggregate tuning hour would also result if two people listened for thirty minutes each, three people listened for twenty minutes each, or four people listened for fifteen minutes each. The minimum annual fee is $500 per channel but no more than $2,500.

- Percentage of Revenues. 10.9% of subscription service revenues, but in no event less then 27¢ per month for each person who subscribes to the subscription service. The minimum fee is $5,000 per year.

All streaming services pay a minimum rate. The minimum rate was $500 under the rates applicable through 2006. There are discounted rates and terms available for small commercial webcasters and noncommercial webcasters.

Report of Use. If you receive a statutory license for a public performance via digital audio transmission, you must provide detailed information to SoundExchange regarding your use of each sound recording. The required information includes the name of the service, name of the featured artist, sound recording title, and the album title. At the time of this writing, the Copyright Office is still determining final rules for the collection of this information.

There are vendors who offer software to track the required information. The industry anticipates additional tracking programs to become available as the area evolves and regulations concerning reports of use are finalized. You can contact SoundExchange for a listing of some of the vendors currently offering tracking solutions.

22.8. Using Music in New Media

There are many emerging uses of music. They include offering music as ringtones, over cellular phones, and through other portable digital music devices. The same music law principles already discussed in this chapter apply to such emerging uses.

Same Question: Song, Sound Recording or Both? As with all music licensing questions, you must begin with the question of whether you are using the song, the sound recording, or both.

Use of the Song. If you are using the song, you need a license from the copyright owner of the song. The process of obtaining the license depends on how you plan to use the song:

Public Performance of the Song. If your use involves a public performance of the song, you can probably obtain the license through one of the PROs. Each PRO offers on its website a list of all the uses that - at least in the PRO's opinion - qualify as a public performance and require a license and the payment of royalties. There are disputes between the PROs and other music industry groups regarding whether certain emerging uses are public performance or private performances. Refer to Section 22.4 for additional details on the public performance of songs.

Reproduction and/or Distribution of the Song. If you are creating or distributing copies of the song, you need a mechanical license. You can often obtain a mechanical license through Harry Fox. Refer to Section 22.6 for additional details.

Other Uses. For any other uses such as changing the song, you will likely need permission directly from the copyright owner of the song which is the songwriter or the songwriter's music publishing company.

Use of the Sound Recording. If you are using the sound recording, you need a license from the copyright owner of the sound recording. As discussed in Section 22.7.2, there is a compulsory license available through SoundExchange for the non-interactive streaming of sound recordings via the internet or via other digital means. All other uses of sound recordings require direct negotiation with the copyright owner which is normally the record company.

22.8.1. Ringtones

Ringtones replace the ringing sound on cellular telephone calls. When someone calls you on your cellular phone, instead of hearing a normal telephone ring, you may hear an excerpt from a popular song. While ringtones are most frequently music, they can also be an audio clip from a film or television program or a quote from a celebrity voice.

A ringback is a variation of a ringtone. You hear a ringback when you place a call to a telephone while you are waiting for the person at the other end to answer.

When first introduced, ringtones were original reproductions of popular songs. First generation ringtones were produced monophonically or polyphonically and had a toy-like quality in the sound. Ringtones that are clips of actual sound recordings are now being offered. For example, your ringtone might be five seconds of Frank Sinatra's recorded performance of *New York, New York*. Ringtones excerpted from actual sound recordings go by a number of names including master ringtones, truetones, songtones, and pre-recorded tones.

Licenses for Use of the Song. To clear ringtones, you potentially need public performance licenses and mechanical licenses. These licenses are described in more detail in Sections 22.4 and 22.6.

Public Performance License for Use of the Song. There is debate concerning whether the playing of a ringtone on a consumer's mobile phone is a public performance. Music publishers and performing rights organizations have taken the stance that a license is required. If required, it is the ringtone provider, not the owner of the mobile telephone, who is responsible for obtaining the public performance license. There is no debate that a public performance license is required for a consumer to preview ringtones through an internet site. Public performance licenses for both purposes are covered in the PROs' ringtone blanket licenses.

Mechanical License for Use of the Song. You need a mechanical license for reproduction and distribution of the ringtone. If you are licensing master ringtone rights from the sound recording copyright owner, the mechanical license may be included with the license you obtain from the sound recording owner. Otherwise, you must secure the mechanical license yourself.

Music publishers assert that ringtones do not qualify for the compulsory mechanical license that governs CD and digital download royalties paid to music publishers. Both ringtone companies and the record labels have objected to this position.

In late 2006, the Copyright Office issued an opinion agreeing with the ringtone providers and record labels that the compulsory mechanical license is available for ringtones. In its opinion, the Copyright Office also said it is appropriate for a compulsory mechanical royalty rate for ringtones to be established in an upcoming copyright proceeding. This suggests that the compulsory mechanical license rate for ringtones may ultimately differ from the compulsory mechanical license rate for physical records and digital downloads.

The issue is not completely resolved. Music publishers are unhappy with the Copyright Office's opinion and are evaluating their responsive options. In the meantime, Harry Fox does not issue mechanical licenses for ringtones. Harry Fox does offer a service in which it facilitates ringtone manufacturers obtaining ringtone licenses directly from multiple music publishers.

The ultimate outcome could significantly impact the royalty revenue received by music publishers. For monophonic and polyphonic ringtones, music publishers demand and receive between ten percent and fifteen percent of the retail price of every ringtone sold. Monophonic and polyphonic ringtones sell for $1 to $2. Master ringtones cost about $3. Ten to fifteen percent of $1 to $3 is significantly more than music publishers receive under the current statutory mechanical license rate.

License for Use of the Sound Recording. If the ringtone is a master ringtone or an actual clip from a sound recording, you need a license to reproduce the sound recording. You obtain this license directly from the copyright owner of the sound recording which is normally the record label that released the sound recording. Major record companies are demanding royalties of fifty percent or more of the retail price of the ringtone. The major record company then pays the mechanical license fee to the music publisher. Hence, the ringtone agreement with the record label normally includes authorization for the reproduction of the song.

22.8.2. Podcasts

Podcasts are audio or audio-visual programs offered through online websites. They can be downloaded and played back on a computer or a portable music player like Apple's iPod. Podcasts trigger the same copyright, right of publicity, defamation, trademark, and other clearance issues discussed in this reference book.

The use of music in podcasts does bring up several online music licensing issues that deserve special attention. The music licensing requirements for an audio-only podcast depend on whether the podcast is offered as a stream or as a download. See Section 22.7 for more information about streaming and downloading music on the internet. Unfortunately, for podcasters it is not always clear whether the podcast should be categorized as a download or as a stream.

There is also no industry-wide consensus as to whether podcasts result in a public performance. The public rights organizations (PROs) take the stand that any music included in a podcast is being publicly performed. Each of the PROs issue licenses that cover podcasts. See Section 3.2.4 for a discussion of what constitutes a public performance and Section 22.4 for a discussion of the PROs and public performance licenses.

If you produce an audio-visual podcast, your use of music is similar to the use of music by a film or television program. You need synchronization and/or master use licenses. See Section 22.5 for a discussion of using music in audio-visual productions.

23.1. Use of Footage in General

Footage is a clip or a short segment of an audio-visual production. Sources of footage include government agencies, local and network news agencies, movie studios, production companies, foreign broadcasters, commercial stock houses, independent filmmakers, and private individuals. This chapter focuses on licensing audio-visual clips or footage of audio-visual programs to incorporate into a production. If you want to license the right to screen an entire film at a school, church, or other organization, contact the Motion Picture Licensing Corporation, the production company, or the distributor.

23.1.1. Stacked Rights in Audio-Visual Productions

Because audio-visual programs often incorporate music, people, and images, they present the challenge of stacked rights. In other words, you may need to seek permission from several sources in order to clear one audio-visual clip. Depending on your intended use and the rights held by the entity licensing the clip, you may also need permission from the owners of the music featured in the clip, from the actors appearing in the clip, and from the program's writers and directors. In this regard, commercial film and television clips made with union talent present the greatest challenges with respect to stacked rights. I discuss clearing rights in film and television clips in greater detail below in Section 23.4.

23.1.2. Identifying the Copyright Owner of an Audio-Visual Production

Copyright owners of audio-visual programming tend to be easier to identify than copyright owners of print materials and music. If you have access to a copy of the program, watch the credits. The caveat for older programs is that ownership may have changed hands. The Appendix lists several sources of contact information for movie studios and production companies. Once you identify the production company, check to see if the company has a website that offers information on requesting permission. Many cable networks that produce original programming offer such information online.

23.2. Stock Footage

Stock footage houses maintain libraries of video material and offer it to producers for incorporation into their productions. Some specialize in a particular genre or period. Stock footage houses generally do not have access to popular films and television programming. They are similar in operation to the stock image houses discussed in Section 21.2. In fact, some companies offer both stock images and stock footage. Like stock image houses, stock footage houses come in different sizes including the following:

- Large companies that are exclusively in the business of licensing stock footage (and other types of stock materials such as stock images) and have thousands of hours of footage in their collections.

- Small production companies and individual filmmakers who license footage from audio-visual programming that they have shot for other purposes.

- Networks and production companies with a side business of offering excerpts from their programming as stock footage. Examples include the HBO Sports Archive and the BBC.

23.2.1. Pricing and Licensing of Stock Footage

Stock footage houses license material on a per use basis or on a royalty-free basis. Over the last several years, commercial stock footage houses have consolidated and many producers claim that prices are rising. Licensing as much stock footage as possible from one source may offer producers opportunities to negotiate a less expensive package deal.

Increasingly, stock footage companies offer online stores that make it possible to preview and order much of the footage offered by the stock house. Alternatively, you can sometimes screen footage at the stock footage house's office. If the footage is not available and the stock footage office location is not convenient for you, you can often obtain a time-coded screening. Most stock houses prepare screening tapes at a fixed rate of $75 to $150 or for an hourly rate of about $50.

Additional fees charged by stock footage houses may include an hourly rate to cover staff time. Services provided to you by the stock house staff include searching the catalog, previewing tapes, locating production records, investigating rights, and placing your ordered footage on a master tape.

Once you place an order, stock houses typically deliver footage within one to five days. Once they provide master materials, stock houses expect you to pay for the ordered footage whether you use it in your production or not. Depending on your specific project, some footage houses request that you submit a footage report indicating how you have used the footage in your production.

Per Use License.   Most stock houses license footage on a per use basis. With footage licensed on a per use basis, you receive permission to use the footage in one production for one specific use and for a specified period of time. The fee is calculated per second or per minute of footage used. The exact amount you pay per second or per minute depends on the subject matter of the footage and your intended use.

Stock houses frequently impose a minimum amount for an order. The stock footage house may calculate the seconds for each cut of footage separately rather than totaling the seconds for all the cuts you license. Each cut of footage generates an additional fee.

Royalty-Free Footage. Some footage houses do offer royalty-free footage. Royalty-free does not mean the footage is free. The royalty-free language generally means that once you license the footage, you may use it multiple times for multiple projects without paying additional fees. The one restriction is that you cannot re-sell it as footage. Although some royalty-free footage may be in the public domain, much royalty-free footage is in fact protected by copyright. As a very broad generalization, royalty-free footage is more generic in content and of lower aesthetic quality than footage licensed on a per use basis.

Exclusivity. One potential downside to using stock footage is the inability to control other uses of the footage. Unless your license includes exclusive rights, the stock house can license the same footage to any other producer. Most stock footage is licensed on a non-exclusive basis.

23.2.2. Additional Rights Needed When Using Stock Footage

Using stock footage may require you to do more than obtain a license from the stock house. The license granted by the stock house frequently includes only rights related to the copyright of the footage. However, the footage may trigger privacy, publicity, defamation, trademark and other issues – depending upon who appears in the footage and how you intend to use it. Like stock image houses discussed in Section 21.2, stock footage houses often leave you on your own to clear these additional rights and sometimes even require that you indemnify the stock house for use of footage in which you did not obtain the necessary additional rights.

Refer to Section 21.2 where I discuss these additional rights to clear in the context of stock image houses. There is one additional right for stock footage that does not come up for stock images. That is the clearance of any music that may be in the footage. See Section 23.4 for a discussion of clearing music in the context of film and television clips. See Section 22.5 for a more general discussion of what is involved in clearing music for use in audio-visual productions.

You may also want to refer to Section 13.3 for a discussion of the incidental use of music. Although Section 13.3 focuses on documentary productions, it is relevant to other productions where music may creep into the production.

23.3. News Footage

Even though news footage typically focuses on public events, the footage is copyrightable and requires a license for use unless your use qualifies for one of the exceptions to copyright protection. See Section 3.9 for a discussion of when permission may not be required to use copyrighted works.

News programs obtain their footage from a variety of services and sources so it is possible that the station or network on which you saw the footage does not own the footage. The station should be able to tell you who does own it. If the news item concerns a widely covered current event, you may be able to find similar footage easily from another stock footage house.

If you have seen specific news footage you want to use, you can begin by contacting the station that aired the footage. A national office or central library may administer and license the footage of all its affiliates. For example, most of ABC's news footage is licensed through ABC Videosource. These central libraries operate like other large stock footage companies.

National and international news organizations license footage on a per second basis. The per second fee depends on the specific rights you wish to obtain. News footage that includes on air talent appearances is more expensive and more difficult to obtain than footage that does not. For example, one network requires a detailed description of the project in which the requested footage with the on-air talent will be used, as well as script pages showing the context in which the footage will be used.

23.4. Film and TV Clips

Production companies and movie studios own popular films and television programs. Licensing footage is not the primary business of production companies and studios. Your use may not be important to major studios. Studios may be more concerned over how the footage is to be used in your production than a stock footage company would be. The Appendix includes resources to locate film and television producers.

It is often difficult to use clips from popular films and television programs if you are a producer with limited resources.

Pricing for film and television clips is per second or per minute. Exact pricing depends upon the rights you want to obtain. Prices are often in the thousands of dollars per minute. To use clips of popular films and television programs, you need to obtain permission from and to make payment to multiple rights holders including the following:

- actors appearing in the clips
- directors and writers who worked on the program
- owners of music included in the clip
- owners of other copyrights and trademarks appearing in the clip such as artwork, special effects, animation, and choreography

Music in film and television clips can be problematic. If it is background music or part of the score, it is probable that the production company commissioned it as a work made for hire and is able to grant rights in that music. On the other hand, if it is music for which the production company obtained a license itself, it is probable that the production company's license will not cover your use of the clip in your production.

Many music copyright owners take the position that use in a separate production of a clip containing their music requires a separate license. You will need to obtain your own license for the song and/or sound recording. Refer to Section 22.5 on clearing music for use in audio-visual productions.

23.5. Permission from Talent and Entertainment Guilds to Use Film and TV Clips

Entertainment guilds are labor unions designed to protect creative people. They negotiate and enforce collective bargaining agreements that establish minimum levels of compensation, benefits, and working conditions for their members. Many are affiliated with the American Federation of Labor-Congress of Industrial Organizations (AFL-CIO). The unions most relevant to rights clearance include the following:

- Screen Actors Guild (SAG)
- American Federation of Television and Radio Artists (AFTRA)
- Directors Guild of America (DGA)
- Writers Guild of America (WGA)
- American Federation of Musicians (AFM)

Entertainment guilds are significant if you are using an audio-visual clip to which union talent contributed. Most popular film and television programming falls into this category. In that case, you must obtain clearance from and make payment to the applicable guild or guild member.

23.5.1. Screen Actors Guild (SAG)

The Screen Actors Guild, or SAG, is the union for actors. Its jurisdiction covers prime-time television programs, theatrical features and television films, television commercials, public television, non-broadcast industrial and educational films, animation, interactive programs, and music videos.

If your clip includes SAG actors, you must clear the clip for each SAG member appearing in the clip. This includes current SAG members, deceased performers (for whom permission is granted by their estate), and stunt people. You do not need to seek permission from or pay extras.

SAG Members. You must obtain the consent of and pay a fee to each SAG performer who appears in the clip. If the SAG performer is deceased, you must obtain consent from and make payment to the estate of the SAG performer. You must pay the SAG performer a minimum rate equal to the minimum SAG wage for the medium in which you plan to use the clip. For example, if you plan to use the clip in a motion picture, you must pay the SAG performer the day performer rate. This is just the minimum you must pay. A SAG performer can demand a payment that is higher than the SAG minimum.

An additional fee is due to the SAG actor for each subsequent use the production containing the clip. For example, if you use the clip in your film to be released in theatres, you pay the negotiated fee to the SAG actor. If you later distribute your film on television or on dvd, you must pay the SAG actor an additional fee.

The additional fee depends on the subsequent use of the production containing the clip. If the use is covered by one of the SAG collective bargaining agreements, you would pay an additional fee based on the residual formula specified in that collective bargaining agreement. If the use is not covered by one of the SAG collective bargaining agreement, your subsequent payment would be equal to 100% of the initial bargained-for rate.

There are some exceptions to the consent and payment requirements. A star performer may waive the payment. If you have difficulty determining whether a certain performer qualifies as a "star" performer, you can ask SAG prior to seeking the waiver.

The SAG rules provide that a producer may exhibit on television any motion picture which began principal photography prior to February 1, 1960. Some producers and rights clearance professionals have interpreted this provision to mean that the use of clips from pre-1960 films do not require consent of or payment to SAG members. SAG does not interpret this provision as being applicable to the use of clips and says that the requirement to obtain consent and pay for the use of clips has no date limitation except for clips involving stunt people, as discussed below.

Stunt People. If the clip includes stunts, you must pay all stunt people who can be identified as performing in the clip. However, you do not have to negotiate with or obtain the consent of the stunt people – unless you are using the clip in a music video or compilation stunt program. The required payment for most uses is SAG's current minimum day performer rate.

There are exceptions to the requirement that payment be made to stunt people appearing in clips. You do not have to make payments to stunt people for use of a clip from a motion picture on which production started prior to February 1956 provided that you are using the clip in a theatrical movie. Similarly, you do not have to pay stunt people for use of a clip from a motion picture in which production started prior to August 1948 if you are using the clip in a made-for-television movie.

Extras. You do not need to obtain permission from or pay extras who appear in the clip. Extras are the actors who appear in the background and add atmosphere to a film or television program scene. For example, extras are the people marching in the parade or the patrons dining at the restaurant. Extras have no speaking lines and are rarely recognizable. Parts that speak are categorized as principals. However, a non-speaking part may be a principal part requiring consent and payment if the part is distinct and recognizable.

Failure to Obtain Consent. SAG imposes a penalty if you use a clip without the performer's consent. The penalty is equal to three times the amount originally paid the performer for the number of days of work covered by the clip used. The penalty is a contractual provision so SAG can apply it only to producers who have agreed to accept SAG's minimum standards and who are signatories to a SAG collective bargaining agreement.

Many independent producers are not SAG signatories. However, that is not necessarily a clean escape from the penalty and other SAG provisions related to clips featuring SAG talent. The producer of the program from which the clip comes will be a SAG signatory. SAG can enforce compliance with its clip requirements through its contracts with the SAG producer. In turn, the SAG producer who holds the copyright in the film or television program and from whom you license the right to use the clip in your production will likely place a requirement in the license agreement that you adhere to any guild requirements. Finally, it is SAG's opinion that the SAG performer may have a right of publicity claim against any producer who uses a clip without consent and payment.

Locating SAG Members. The Appendix lists some resources for locating actors and other people. SAG can provide assistance if a producer is unable to find the SAG member. Here's how that process works, according to SAG.

The producer should send SAG a letter, which SAG will then forward to the SAG member. If the letter is returned, SAG considers that member unlocatable and the producer does not have to pay for use of the clip at that time. However, if the performer comes forward at a later date, the producer is required to negotiate a payment at that time. Fortunately, if the SAG member does later surface, the producer is not responsible for the penalty discussed above, meaning that the producer does not have to pay the performer three times the amount originally paid the performer for his work on the clip.

If the letter does not come back, SAG presumes that the member has been located but has chosen not to respond. In such cases, SAG will offer to send another letter. However, the producer cannot use the clip until the SAG member responds with a grant of consent.

23.5.2. American Federation of Television and Radio Artists (AFTRA)

The American Federation of Television and Radio Artists, or AF-TRA, is the union for performers that appear in television and radio programs, sound recordings, interactive programs, animation, music videos, and non-broadcast industrial and educational programs.

Both SAG and AFTRA cover television programming. The SAG rules cover television programming that meets one or more of the following criteria:

- The programming is dramatic. A dramatic program is one with a story line so situation comedies are considered dramatic.

- The program is offered during prime-time. Prime-time is normally considered between 8 p.m. and 11 p.m.

- The programming is offered on a network. Networks include ABC, CBS, NBC, and FOX, but may also include some pay television networks.

AFTRA rules cover television programming that falls outside the SAG rules so the AFTRA rules cover programming such as the following:

- non-dramatic programs, such as talk shows, variety shows, game shows and reality shows

- entertainment/news shows, such as *Entertainment Tonight* and *Access Hollywood*

- soap operas

- non-prime time sitcoms, like those seen on Saturday morning,

- syndicated or non-network sitcoms (including many of the sitcoms seen on Fox, UPN and WB)

AFTRA Members. As a general rule, you should assume that you must obtain the consent of and pay a fee to each AFTRA member appearing in the clip. However, there are many exceptions to this general rule. The requirements to obtain consent and make payment depend upon:

- the length of the clip,
- whether a "star" appears in the clip,
- the percentage of clips in your production,
- the type of production using the clips, and
- other factors.

For example, you do not need to obtain consent from or make payment to AFTRA members for use of a brief excerpt from a news program in another news program. You do not need to obtain consent from or pay extras or background actors appearing in the clips. The AFTRA rules also allow you to use without payment or consent an excerpt of up to two minutes from any AFTRA program in a news program. On the other hand, you must obtain consent and make payment if more than seventy-five percent of your production consists of clips.

With respect to required payments for clip use, the AFTRA compensation structure is more complicated than that of SAG. AFTRA bases its pricing around program fees. There is a different fee payable to an AFTRA member for a thirty-minute program, for a sixty-minute program, and so on. When there is a fee for clip use, the minimum fee is generally an amount equal to:

- the minimum program fee for the program from which the clip is taken or
- the minimum program fee of the production in which the clip is used.

You pay whichever program fee is greater. Again, there are numerous exceptions to this general rule. For example, the fees are higher if you are using clips in a production consisting of seventy-five percent of more of clips. There are additional payments required for subsequent uses of the production in which the clips are used.

The AFTRA rules and exceptions for clip use are too numerous and complex for this book to cover in depth. Once you have information concerning the clips you want to use and the production in which you want to use those clips, you should consult with AFTRA to confirm what consents and payments are required. For those situations in which you do need to obtain consent, AFTRA can offer assistance in locating hard-to-find AFTRA members.

23.5.3. Directors Guild of America (DGA)

The Directors Guild of America, or DGA, is the union for those professionals who work in motion pictures and television as directors, associate or assistant directors, control room production assistants, and stage managers. To use a clip on which a DGA member has worked, you do not need the consent of the individual DGA members. You just need to pay.

You make the payment directly to DGA which then submits the payments to their members. The payments are one-time only with no need to pay again for subsequent uses of the production containing the clip. You are not required to make any DGA payments for the use of clips from motion pictures produced prior to May 1960. This pre-1960 rule does not apply to television clips and you must pay for those regardless of when the television program was produced.

DGA has a schedule of payments for clip usage posted on its website. The rate depends upon the type of production the clip comes from, the length of the clip, and the type of production in which you will use the clip.

For example, as this book goes to press, the DGA fee to use up to ten seconds of a television clip in a television program is $353. The DGA fee to use forty seconds of a feature film in a television program or film is $689. DGA charges an additional 12.5% for pension and welfare payments. DGA gives a six percent discount for usage of film clips in documentaries and magazine programs. Productions comprised of more than fifty percent television clips are compilation shows which are subject to different rates. Producers must keep track of the directors and submit the payment to DGA.

23.5.4. Writers Guild of America (WGA)

The Writer's Guild of America, or WGA, is the union for writers of motion pictures, television, and radio. You can obtain from WGA a schedule of payments due to writers upon the use of a clip from a production in which WGA members participated.

To use a clip on which a WGA member has worked, you do not need the consent of the individual WGA members. You just need to make payment. The rates vary depending upon whether the clip comes from television or film, the length of the clip, and in what type of production you will use the clip. The payments are one-time only with no need to pay again for a subsequent use of the production containing the clip. There is no pension and health payment due. Like the DGA, the WGA charges a higher compilation rate if more than fifty percent of your production is comprised of clips.

Producers are to keep track of the writers and submit the payment to WGA. WGA then submits the payments to their members.

23.5.5. American Federation of Musicians (AFM)

The American Federation of Musicians, or AFM, represents instrumentalists. The feature film or television program from which the clip comes may include music performed by AFM members. The AFM requires payment in those circumstances.

23.6. *Alternatives to Commercial Film Clips*

23.6.1. Movie Trailers

Is it possible to avoid the hassle of clearing a film clip by using the trailer? A trailer consists of excerpts from a motion picture used as a pre-release promotional tool for a motion picture. Those excerpts are frequently combined with additional graphics and voice-over narration. Some claim that a number of these trailers are in the public domain.

Here is the argument. These trailers did not adhere to the copyright formalities that existed prior to 1989. As discussed in Section 3.9, there were a number of formalities with which older works had to comply in order to retain copyright protection. These formalities include filing a renewal application after twenty-eight years for works published prior to 1964 and using a copyright notice on works published prior to 1989. The overwhelming majority of copyright owners of movie trailers did not file renewal applications. Likewise many trailers released prior to 1989 did not include a copyright notice. Some argue that such trailers have fallen into the public domain even if the films from which they were excerpted are still protected by copyright.

There is no direct legal support for this position. There are copyright infringement lawsuits against producers who have used excerpts from film trailers. Courts have based their analysis on the concepts of fair use and copyright infringement without making a distinction between the trailer and the full film.

When A&E used a twenty-second clip from the trailer for the film, *It Conquered The World*, the court acknowledged that the trailer itself was not subject to copyright protection. Nevertheless, the court still viewed those clips as subject to copyright because the film from which they were drawn was protected by copyright. Ultimately, the court decided A&E's use of the twenty-second film clip qualified as a fair use because of the way in which A&E used the clip. The fact that A&E obtained the clip from a trailer had no impact on the court's decision.

The cases show that a court will conduct its analysis based on the copyright status of the film. No court has viewed the trailer as a separate work that is distinct from the film. The same public domain and fair use standards discussed in Sections 3.7 through 3.9 apply.

23.6.2. Film Posters

Another option is showing still images from the film. They are much easier and less expensive to clear. Start with the production company to obtain the permission you need. You do not need to obtain permission from or make payments to any of the guilds for use of still images. You do have to consider whether your use sparks any right of publicity issues. The right of publicity is discussed in Chapter 7.

24.1. Websites and Software In General

A number of legal theories apply to the clearance of websites and software. For the purposes of most of the media producers reading this book, copyright law and trademark law are the most significant. Those are the areas on which I focus in this chapter.

24.2. Websites and Other Online Materials

With very few exceptions, the same copyright and trademark laws that apply to the offline world are applicable to material posted online. You cannot assume that because material is posted online, you are free to use such material in any way that you please.

If you are interested in using an article or other material you see online, you can start your search for permission by exploring the website on which the material appears. Some websites specify in their Terms of Service section how you may use the material. The Terms of Service often prohibits your use of the website's material without the website owner's permission. The common exception is the printing of one copy for personal use.

However, there are many websites offering clip art, templates, and other creative material that are free and available for others to use. The permission may come with limitations such as a restriction on commercial use or a requirement that the creator receive an acknowledgement. It is important to read any information about permission included on the website.

The website owner may not own all the material posted and have only a limited license to use the material. That limited license probably does not include the right to authorize others to use it.

With the ease of copying digital material, there are also many websites that use material without authorization.

The website may identify the contributor who owns the material and provide an email address or other contact information. If you can identify the owner of the material, use the techniques discussed in the relevant sections of Part Five to obtain permission.

If the website does not provide any such information regarding ownership of the content, try contacting the website operator whose contact information is hopefully included on one of the web pages. There are of course millions of websites. They range from professional websites to hobby websites and from the well-maintained to the abandoned. The possibility of not receiving a response to your permission request is a stark reality.

24.3. Software Materials

In many ways, producers of computer games and entertainment software are similar to television and movie producers. Like audiovisual programming, entertainment software tends to incorporate many different elements including music, artwork, video, and text.

The software producer may own these elements outright or it may have only limited rights in the elements. Many software products are actually derivative works or adaptations of other creative productions such as a movie, a comic strip, a book, or a toy. Depending on how you want to use the material, you may need to direct your permission request to the owner of the underlying work rather than to the software producer.

If you have the computer program that contains the material you want to use, you should be able to locate and identify the software producer through the licensing agreement, through the credits embedded in the program, or through an internet search. If you determine that it is an underlying rights holder from whom you need permission, use the techniques discussed in the relevant sections of Part Five to obtain permission.

24.3.1. Using Computer Screen Shots

One of the trickier issues of rights clearance and computer software is the need for permission to use a computer screen shot. A computer screen shot is a small image depicting the computer in a frozen moment during the use of a computer program. It is the software equivalent to a still shot from a motion picture. Computer magazines and instructional books routinely include computer screen shots to illustrate the software programs they discuss. The requirement to have a license to use a computer screen shot is not clear. Use of a screen shot potentially invokes several areas of law:

Copyright. Copyright protects the audio-visual display of a computer program. Applying the four-factor fair use test discussed in Section 3.7, there is a good argument that the use of a screen shot in a review or instructional guide is a fair use:

- Factor One. Purpose of the Use. The use is criticism or educational, both of which are favored uses under the Fair Use Doctrine.

- Factor Two. Nature of the Work. At least one court opinion has said that while the software program itself is creative, a single screen shot is an inanimate sliver of the program and is not necessarily creative. (*Sony v. Bleem*, 214 F.3d 934 (9th Cir. 2000)).

- Factor Three. Amount of the Work Used. Normally, it is undisputed that a single screen shot is a small portion of the entire computer program. To the extent the computer program is a game with a plot controlled interactively by the player, a single screen shot is of little substance to the overall copyrighted work.

- Factor Four. Effect on the Market. At least one court has found that there is no market for single screen shots.

Using screen shots has been found to be okay for comparative advertising purposes. It was fair use for a company to use screen shots of a Sony Playstation video game in an advertisement that compared the look of the game when played with a Sony PlayStation console versus the look when played on a personal computer. (*Sony v. Bleem*, 214 F.3d 934 (9th Cir. 2000)).

Trademark. Trademark is an issue if the software manufacturer's name or other identifying marks appear in the screen shot. Trademark infringement comes into play only when there is a likelihood of confusion. If your use of the trademark is only for illustrative purposes and does not mislead as to source or sponsorship, your use of the trademark is a nominative and non-infringing use. See Chapter 4 for further discussion of trademark infringement.

Privacy or Defamation. To the extent images of people appear in the screen shot, there could be a privacy or defamation claim. However, if you are using the screen shot for a review or a how-to guide, such claims seem remote.

Contract. Computer software programs are sold to consumers with licensing agreements. Purchasers agree to the terms of the license agreement by opening or installing the software (frequently referred to as a shrink-wrap agreement) or by checking off a box when downloading a program (frequently referred to as a click-wrap agreement).

Some software companies use licensing agreements to enforce rights which are not protected by copyright law. There are outstanding questions regarding the enforceability of click-wrap and shrink-wrap agreements – especially if their terms appear over-reaching. For example, at one time, Network Associates, the developer of McAfee anti-virus and other popular computer utility software programs, included the following restriction in its packaging material:

> The customer will not publish reviews of this product without prior consent from Network Associates, Inc.

Network Associates relied on the language when demanding the retraction of a negative review of its Gauntlet firewall program published in an online magazine. When the incident came to the attention of the State of New York, a New York court ruled the language unenforceable and fined Network Associates for fraudulent, deceptive and illegal acts and practices. *(State of New York v Network Associates Inc.,* 195 Misc.2d 384 *(NY Sup. Ct. 2003)).*

Industry Practice and the Bottom Line with Respect to Screen Shots. Publishers of computer related books and magazines have divergent policies concerning computer screen shot licenses. Some book and magazine publishers require authors to obtain licenses for screen shots. Others do not. Some software developers do include their policies about use of screen shots in their licensing material and on their websites.

I am not aware of any court opinions that directly address the use of computer screen shots in reviews and instructional materials. The fact that there are few court decisions in which software developers sued a publisher for the unauthorized use of a computer screen shot may suggest that software developers accept such uses. While you can factor developers' lack of legal action into your risk analysis, it is not an absolute guarantee. The broader your intended distribution and the more screen shots of any particular program you intend to use, the more likely it is that your production will attract the attention of the software developer.

All else being equal, it is better to have a license - if you can get one on reasonable terms. License agreements have been known to contain language preventing the accompanying text from saying anything critical about the software. Such language certainly limits your ability to give an honest review of the software and is arguably unenforceable.

The bottom line is you must evaluate the risk. There is always some level of risk – even though the risk may be minimal – when you use proprietary material without permission. As discussed in Section 1.5.4, keep in mind that being sued is a separate risk from losing the lawsuit.

CLEARING RIGHTS AND SEEKING PERMISSION WITH RESPECT TO PEOPLE

25.1. Dealing with People in Your Production

This chapter focuses on obtaining consents and releases from the following two categories of people:

- people on whom you base your production and
- people making brief appearances in your production.

This chapter does not focus on the actors, performers, models and other talent you hire for your production. You should have talent or other appropriate agreements for those individuals as part of putting your own house in order.

For those people in the first category on whom you base your production, you probably want a life story rights agreement or an interview agreement. For those people in the second category who briefly appear in your production, you can probably use a simpler consent, release, or a posted notice.

25.2. Locating People

Whenever possible get the person's consent before you incorporate the person into your production. If the person is a celebrity whom you wish to incorporate into or make the subject of your production, you can attempt to reach the person through his representative. This representative might be a manager, agent, or publicist. For famous, deceased personalities, the representative might be an agency, the estate, a lawyer, or the family foundation. The Appendix includes resources for locating people.

25.3. Life Story Rights Agreement

The chances of adverse claims increase if your production includes private personal facts about a person or make statements about a person that might be objectionable. To eliminate or at least minimize these risks, many producers seek a life story rights agreement in which the subject expressly grants to the producer rights in the person's life story. The person granting the life story rights also agrees not to sue the producer for violation of the right of privacy, right of publicity, defamation or related claims as a result of how the production ultimately portrays the person.

Producers of films, theatrical productions, and literary materials are the producers most likely to use life story rights agreements. Life story rights agreements sometimes are broken into two parts. In the first part, the producer obtains an option to purchase the life story rights. See Section 17.2 for a discussion of optioning rights. The producer then has a period of time – typically six months to two years – to determine if he wants to exercise the option and purchase the life story rights.

There is no set fee for the purchase of life story rights. It depends on the value the producer attaches to having the rights. Rights granted through a life story rights agreement tend to be very broad. They extend to all media and they are exclusive rights. Often they allow the producer to fictionalize elements of the person's life story. The Appendix contains an example of a life story rights agreement.

Life story rights agreements frequently carry the added advantage of access to the subject as a consultant. Subjects often provide background information to the producer for story and script development. If the agreement is exclusive – which most life story rights agreements are - the subject agrees to provide information and help only to you, and not to other producers who may be developing competing versions of the story.

The exclusivity does not necessarily stop other producers from telling the subject's story. The exclusivity does give you the advantage of access to details that may not be publicly available, comfort that your subject is not going to sue you for the final production, and the credibility of having the subject endorse your version of his story.

25.4. Consents and Releases

Consents and releases are similar to life story rights agreements in that a person is consenting to his appearance in your production and releasing you from any claims associated with his appearance in the production. They are normally narrower in scope than life story rights agreements.

Unlike life story rights agreements, releases and consents do not grant exclusivity to the producer. They are straightforward agreements but there are right and wrong ways to prepare and obtain them.

Someone who signs a consent or a release is usually not the focus or the primary subject of your production. It is usually someone who appears briefly in your production such as a member of the audience captured briefly by the camera, a pedestrian responding to a few questions in a sidewalk interview that is part of a longer documentary or television program, or a model authorizing the use of her photograph. In general, the industry accepts that releases are not necessary if the person is part of a crowd or background shot and his image is shown for only a few seconds and does not receive special emphasis.

25.4.1. Consideration

In the above discussion of life story rights, an individual gave the producer the right to tell the individual's story in the producer's production along with the individual's assurance that the individual would not sue the producer. In exchange for those rights and promises, the producer normally pays a monetary sum to the individual.

The money is consideration. Consideration is a legal term and refers to the benefit each person derives from a contract. Consideration can be money but it can be other items or promises as well.

A valid contract requires that each party to the contract receive and give consideration.

Frequently, a producer pays no monetary sum in return for receiving a simple consent or release. This creates the problem of lack of consideration. One solution is to indicate that appearing in the production is a benefit, and that the producer is relying on the individual's consent in incorporating him into the production. For example, the following language might appear in an interview release:

> I am signing this release to encourage the Producer to conduct and use the interview. I understand that the Producer will incur substantial expense in reliance on the representations and agreements I make in this release.

25.4.2. Clear Understanding Required

The person giving the consent should have a clear understanding of your production and his role in it. For example, suppose you obtain a consent for an interview from someone after telling him your production is about the beauty of fall foliage. It turns out your production is about a more controversial topic like the effects of environmental pollution on trees and plants. The person granting the interview has an argument that the consent you obtained from him is invalid.

Consents are not necessarily transferable from one media producer to the next. Just because a person consents to an appearance in one production does not mean he consents to an appearance in your production. Your ability to rely on a consent given for another production depends on how the consent is worded and the similarities and differences between your production and the production to which the person consented. The more outrageous or potentially objectionable your production and the person's appearance in it, the more important it is that the person understands to what he is consenting in order for the consent to withstand scrutiny.

Here is where a good dose of common sense helps. Suppose a woman consents to the use of her photo for advertising purposes in all media and she gives that consent to the producer of a television commercial for grapes. It might be reasonable for you to rely on the consent in using the photograph for a print advertisement for a kitchen blender. For most people, grapes have the same level of outrageousness (or lack thereof) as a kitchen blender. On the other hand, if you want to use the woman's picture on a billboard for contraception or for a drug rehabilitation center, you should consider getting her explicit consent beforehand.

In one real-world example, a woman's consent to the use of her photo in one nude magazine was not consent to the use of the same photo in another nude magazine where she was represented as a lesbian. (*Douglas v. Hustler Magazine*, 769 F.2d 1128, (7th Cir. 1985)).

25.4.3. Capacity to Give Consent

In order for the release or consent to be valid, the person giving the consent must have the capacity to do so. Minors do not have the capacity to give consent. Any consent from a minor requires the consent of the minor's parent or guardian. Other people who lack the capacity to give consent include the following:

- those who are under the influence of drugs or alcohol
- those who are in shock as the result of an injury or accident
- those who are mentally incompetent

Once again, common sense helps. If you need a consent from someone you suspect is legally incapable of providing it, get the consent at another time when the person is "himself". When dealing with minors or the mentally incompetent, obtain the consent from the person's guardian.

25.4.4. Consents Acquired by Stock Houses and Other Licensors

I briefly discussed this issue in Sections 21.2.2 and 23.2.2 on additional rights needed when using stock images and stock footage.

When you obtain material from stock houses, you may need clearances in addition to your license from the stock house. To make this determination, start with the license issued by the stock house. Stock houses sometimes disclaim all responsibility with respect to individuals or other elements in their material. In those cases, figuring out and getting any additional permissions for your use is your responsibility.

Professional news organizations generally get signed releases from the individuals who appear in their material. This does not necessarily apply to coverage of breaking news in which many passersby and onlookers may be on the scene. Whether or not you can rely on that consent depends on a number of factors including whether the original consent is written to cover subsequent uses and whether your subsequent use is consistent with the release.

25.4.5. Implement and Follow Proper Procedures

You should implement and follow procedures to verify that consents are legitimate. If you or your production team has no face-to-face or personal contact with the person giving the release, you should take steps to make sure it is a valid release – especially if use of the material may be objectionable. You could be liable if the release is fraudulent.

For example, a housewife had a privacy action against *Hustler* when the magazine published a stolen nude photo of her submitted with a forged consent form. (*Wood v. Hustler Magazine*, 736 F.2d 1084 (5th Cir. 1984)). *Hustler* ended up paying the woman $150,000 in damages. According to the court, there were numerous deficiencies in how *Hustler* magazine verified the validity of the consent including the following:

- *Hustler* had no written verification procedure and failed to follow adequately its informal policy.

- After calling the number listed on the forged consent form, a *Hustler* staff member completed the verification procedure by asking a few leading questions of the same person who submitted the forged consent form.

- The *Hustler* staff did not question the accuracy of the woman's name on the consent form even when staff members suspected the name was fake.

- *Hustler* did not require the submission of a social security number or a driver's license number with the consent form.

- *Hustler* did not require notarization of the consent form.

- *Hustler* asked no follow-up questions when directed to send a $50 check in payment for use of the photo to a person other than the woman in the photo.

25.4.6. Review Your Consent Form for Completeness

Verify that your consent covers all intended uses. Read your release and evaluate it against how you intend to use the footage, information or material of the person granting the release. Preferably you can make your release as broad as possible so that all uses are permissible. The Appendix includes a sample of a broad release.

Unfortunately, even when you seemingly do everything right, things can sometimes still go wrong. For example, when doing a documentary on a mental health facility, CBS producers took all the right steps in acquiring the consent. They obtained permission from the facility's director, from the unit supervisor, and from the individual patients. During two meetings with potential participants, the director and producers explained to the patients the nature of the documentary, the viewpoint that the documentary would espouse, that participation was optional, and the nature of the patients' participation. However, one patient's consent was still invalid because the patient signed a consent for an interview which did not include a consent for a television appearance. Ultimately the lack of consent was not relevant because the patient appeared in the documentary for only four seconds and the court categorized the short appearance as fleeting, incidental, and, thus, non-actionable. (*Delan by Delan v. CBS*, 458 N.Y.S.2d (1983)).

25.4.7. Express Consent Versus Implied Consent

Express Consent. Express consent is better than implied consent. In this sense, express means clear, direct, explicit, and unambiguous. Express consent can be oral or written. Oral agreements are valid in many circumstances. If you are working with a camera, the person can give oral consent on camera.

Personally, I prefer that consent always be written. It is easier to produce a written agreement as evidence of the consent. The more prominent the person's role in your production, the more you want to record the person's consent in the form of a written release.

If you need to acquire consent from a number of people and do not want the hassle of individual agreements, you can do the consent in the format of a sign-up list. The Appendix includes a sample of a consent sign-up list.

Implied Consent. A person can give implied consent through his conduct. For example, if the person realizes he is being filmed for a television production and makes no objection, he has arguably provided implied consent to his appearance on the television program. If you use a notice for the audience or for a crowd scene, participants may be viewed as giving implied consent. Here is a sample notice:

THE EVENT YOU HAVE ENTERED IS BEING FILMED BY A VIDEO PRODUCTION COMPANY. BY ENTERING THE STAGE BEYOND THIS SIGN, YOU ARE HEREBY CONSENTING AND AGREEING TO YOUR PICTURE AND IMAGE BEING USED FOR ANY REPRODUCTION OF ANY TYPE AND SALE WITHOUT FURTHER COMPENSATION.

When using posted notices, you should once again apply common sense. For the consent to be enforceable, people should have a reasonable opportunity to decline participation. If the person has paid $200 for a ticket to a show and declining to enter beyond your posted notice means not seeing the show and forfeiting the $200, the person has an argument that the consent is not valid.

A posted notice might work for a street crowd scene in which people could walk on the opposite side of the street if they do not want to be filmed. It might also work for break-away shots of members of an audience. However, the more featured the person is, the more you want to obtain express consent.

In one real-life example in which implicit consent was insufficient, a production company used a posted notice at a nightclub during a wet T-shirt contest. Written notices informing contestants of the future commercial use of their images were placed around the dressing room, stage, entrances, and exits. The production company claimed that the contest emcee announced over the loudspeaker that the event was being filmed for a future production.

A television news anchor who participated in the contest obtained an injunction forbidding the production company's use of her image. She claimed not to have seen the posted notices, the video cameras, or any other indication that the contest was being filmed. The court ruled that under Florida law, the production company needed at a minimum explicit oral consent from the news anchor in order for the consent to be valid. (*Bosley v. WildWetT.com*, 310 F. Supp.2d 914 (N.D. Oh. 2004)).

CLEARING RIGHTS AND SEEKING PERMISSION TO USE TRADEMARKS, PRODUCTS, AND LOCATIONS

26.1. Seeking Permission to Use Buildings and Locations

If the building or location is non-distinctive, you do not need permission to include its image in your production. You can consider a building non-distinctive if most people would not associate it with a specific person, organization, or product.

26.1.1. Trademarked Buildings

Some buildings and structures may be trademarked. Examples of trademarked buildings and structures include McDonald's Golden Arches, the Golden Gate Bridge in San Francisco, the Empire State Building in New York City, the Guggenheim Museum in New York, and Sears Towers in Chicago.

You can include them in your production as long as your use does not constitute a likelihood of confusion or draw on the fame of the trademark. See Chapter 4 for a discussion of trademark infringement and the likelihood of confusion.

26.1.2. Copyrighted Buildings

Buildings and structures built after 1990 are eligible for copyright protection – but only if the building is designed in a manner that is original and not wholly functional. One such original building is the Rock and Roll Hall of Fame & Museum in Cleveland, Ohio. The front of the building is dominated by a large, reclining, triangular facade of steel and glass. The rear of the building extends out over Lake Erie, and is a combination of interconnected and unusually shaped, white buildings.

Exclusive rights for copyrighted buildings are more limited than for other copyrighted works. Anyone may make and distribute a two-dimensional reproduction of a building. That means you can distribute or display pictures, paintings, photographs, films, or other pictorial representations of the building.

You may photograph or film the building as long as you can do so from a public place. If the building is not visible from a public place and you must enter private property to film or photograph it, you need permission. Otherwise, you are trespassing.

26.1.3. Location Releases

If you determine that the building is distinctive or you need to enter private property for your use of the building, you probably need a location release. Location releases have some similarities to the releases for people discussed in Chapter 25. They give producers permission to include images of a particular building or home in their productions. The location release also specifies when the producer will have access to the location.

Do not confuse location releases with film permits. Municipalities issue film permits for filming in a public location such as on a street or in a park. Owners of private property issue location releases for private homes and buildings.

The location release does not necessarily cover all the items that are inside the building. You must be aware of any copyrighted works or trademarks at the location. Artwork is a special concern. Even though the property owner possesses a physical copy of the artwork – even if it is the sole existing copy of the particular artwork – he may not own the copyright in the artwork. Depending on how that artwork is included in your production, you may need permission from the copyright owner of the artwork.

26.2. Seeking Permission to Use Products

Brand name products trigger the issue of trademarks. Several court rulings say the unauthorized appearance of a brand-name product in a production is okay as long as the appearance does not tarnish the product's reputation, draw on the goodwill associated with the product, or mislead people to believe that the product manufacturer has endorsed or sponsored the production. See Chapter 4 for a more detailed discussion on the use of trademarks.

If you are featuring a product or otherwise determine that it is advisable to have permission, you can obtain permission for an appearance of a product through a prop release. The Appendix includes a sample form that can be used as a prop release.

The good news for rights clearance purposes is that many trademark and product owners want a favorable appearance of their product in your production. They view it as good advertising. Some product owners will grant permission for free and in some cases will pay for the privilege of having their product featured in a production.

26.3. Locating Trademark and Product Owners

26.3.1. Trademarks and Products

If you want to confirm whether a name you are using in your production is a trademark, you can start by checking with the United States Patent and Trademark Office (PTO). The PTO offers a searchable database of pending and registered trademarks which you can search for free on the PTO's website. The database includes the owner name and contact information for each listed trademark.

There is one caveat to use of the PTO's database. Recall from the discussion in Chapter 4 that registration with the PTO is not required to establish trademark rights. As a result, there are many valid trademarks that are not in the PTO database.

You might also determine the existence of trademark rights by checking products for trademark notices. Owners of trademarks that have been registered with the PTO are supposed to include a trademark notice whenever they use the trademark. The trademark notice is usually the capital letter "R" in a circle which is usually written in small type and placed to the right of and slightly above the trademark.

If you find a federal trademark notice, you can find contact information for the trademark owner by searching the PTO's database.

Notice is optional for trademarks that are not registered with the PTO. The proper notice for an unregistered trademark is the capital letters "TM" for a product or "SM" for a service.

There are also services that will check your production against databases to make sure you are not using any real names of people, companies, or products.

PART SIX

Minimizing Your Risks and Protecting Yourself

Unfortunately, even when you take all prudent rights clearance steps, something may still go wrong. Part Six includes liability-minimizing techniques such as obtaining errors and omissions insurance, using disclaimers, and implementing common sense operational procedures. It also outlines what you can expect in the event you are sued.

Chapters in Part Six:

METHODS OF MINIMIZING RISK 27

27.1. Obtaining Errors and Omissions Insurance

Even producers who take all reasonable clearance precautions occasionally miss something. There are also cases in which a rights owner makes a meritless claim against a producer. Errors and omissions insurance, or E&O insurance, protects you in those circumstances. E&O insurance is called by a number of other names including media liability insurance, media peril insurance, and producer's liability insurance.

E&O insurance is a distinct type of insurance in the entertainment industry. It differs from cast insurance, workers compensation, and general liability insurance. The types of suits covered by the E&O insurance vary by policy and can include issues like copyright infringement, idea misappropriation, trademark infringement, defamation, invasion of the right of privacy, and improper newsgathering techniques.

E&O insurance is designed to cover the liabilities of those producers who have a clearance claim even though they take all advisable clearance actions. E&O insurance is not a substitute for proper clearance of your production. Like any other insurer, E&O insurers want to minimize the amount of money they pay in claims. The policy does not cover you for knowingly violating copyright, trademark, and related laws.

27.1.1. Application Procedure

An E&O insurer will not issue you a policy if it perceives there is a high risk of someone filing a lawsuit against your production. In order to obtain the insurance, you complete a detailed application in which you confirm:

- You have written agreements with all the creative people who contributed to the production.

- You have written releases from all recognizable people and distinctive locations in the production.

- You have appropriate licenses for all music, film clips, artwork, quotes, and third party material appearing in your production.

If you are using material without a license, the E&O insurance company will want an explanation as to why such use is permissible and why the use will not result in a legal claim. They often require that producers work with an attorney and sometimes require that the attorney certify that all necessary steps have been taken to clear all rights. E&O insurers also require that you submit copyright reports and title opinions, discussed below, as part of the application.

Insurance brokers recommend that producers complete and submit an E&O insurance application prior to production or prior to the start date of principal photography. Even if you believe that you can do without E&O insurance, many distributors require that you obtain an E&O insurance policy. This is especially true for distributors of film and television programs.

Liability limits are expressed with two separate maximums. There is a maximum that the insurer will pay for any individual claim. There is also an overall maximum that the insurer will pay under the policy. For example, a policy with $1 Million/$3 Million limits would pay a maximum of $1 Million for any individual claim and an aggregate total of $3 Million for all claims made under the policy.

Like most insurance policies, E&O insurance policies include deductibles – which is the amount of a claim you must pay before the insurance company will make any payments. Higher risk leads to higher deductibles.

When shopping for E&O insurance, you may want to work with an insurance broker who will help you shop for the best deal, ensure that the policy is consistent with your business needs, and act as a liaison between you and the insurance company during the application process and later in the event any claims are filed against you.

27.1.2. Duty to Defend Versus Duty to Indemnify

Insurance companies may have a duty to indemnify you, a duty to defend you, or both. Under a duty to indemnify, the insurance company pays any monetary damages a court orders you to pay as a result of losing a lawsuit. Under a duty to defend, the insurer pays the cost for attorneys, investigators and expert consultants retained to defend you from the lawsuit filed against you. If the policy offers a duty to indemnify without a duty to defend, you may be responsible for paying your own legal costs for responding to the lawsuit.

27.1.3. Claims-Made Policy Versus Occurrence-Based Policy

Insurance companies issue policies on a claims-made basis or an occurrence basis. The distinction between the two types of policies is significant.

A claims-made policy covers only those claims which you report during the policy period. An occurrence policy covers those claims resulting from events or incidents which occurred during the policy period. Thus, in a claims-made policy, coverage does not continue after expiration of the policy.

For example, suppose you have an E&O insurance claims-based policy that runs from January 2007 through December 31, 2008 for your production. Someone files a copyright infringement action against you related to your production on February 5, 2009. Your receipt of the lawsuit is your first indication that such a claim exists.

The E&O claims-based insurance policy will not cover you for the copyright infringement because the claim came after expiration of the policy. By contrast, if your policy were an occurrence-based policy, you would be covered for the copyright infringement claim because the claim is based on an event that happened during the policy period.

27.2. Copyright and Title Reports

If your production is an audio-visual production, most errors and omissions insurers and most distributors require that you provide a copyright report and a title report. Producers may sometimes be interested in these reports – outside of the requirements of insurers and distributors– as a way to track down the proper owners of materials they want to license and to verify for the producer's own purposes that rights are properly cleared.

Copyright Report. A copyright report traces the ownership of the underlying material – such as a book - on which your production is based as well as the ownership of the completed production. Insurers and distributors do not require copyright reports if you wrote the material yourself and the material is previously unpublished.

Title Report. A title report lists productions with similar titles to your proposed title as well as trademarks similar to your proposed title. With the help of a title report you and your attorney can determine whether your proposed title will generate any problems. Section 4.4.1 discusses legal issues generated by title selection.

Title reports are very similar to a trademark clearance report that a business obtains prior to choosing a name for its company or product. Most title reports cover a search of the Copyright Office's records, the Trademark Office's records, and other entertainment databases.

A title report is distinct from a title opinion. A title opinion is a letter normally prepared by your attorney which indicates, in the attorney's opinion, whether the title is available for use on your production. Your attorney bases her title opinion on the results of the title report.

The Appendix includes a listing of companies that prepare copyright and title reports.

27.3. Disclaimers

Disclaimers may shield producers from claims. To be effective, your disclaimer must be noticeable, clearly stated, and command the average viewer's attention.

Examples of disclaimers that did not work

Godzilla Trivia Book. (*Toho v. William Morrow*, 33 F. Supp. 1206 (C.D. Cal. 1998)) William Morrow and Co. produced a trivia book about Godzilla without the permission of the copyright owner of the Godzilla character. The book included disclaimers on both the front and back covers. On the front cover, the word "UNAUTHORIZED" appeared at the very top of the page, in relatively small lettering, surrounded by an orange bordering. On the back cover the following disclaimer appeared:

> THIS BOOK WAS NOT PREPARED, APPROVED, LICENSED OR EN-
> DORSED BY ANY ENTITY INVOLVED IN CREATING OR PRODUCING
> ANY GODZILLA MOVIE, INCLUDING COLUMBIA/TRISTAR AND TOHO
> CO. LTD

The Godzilla producers sued for trademark and copyright in-fringement. The court found the disclaimers to be ineffective in alleviating the potential for consumer confusion for the following reasons:

- The word "UNAUTHORIZED" on the front cover only con-veys a limited amount of information.

- The more complete disclaimer on the back cover is insufficient because most consumers focus on the front cover of a book prior to purchase.

- The color of the disclaimer on the front cover does not effec-tively attract the attention of the average consumer because its bordering is in the same shade as the title.

- The word "UNAUTHORIZED" is located at the top of the page where most consumers' eyes are not likely to dwell.

- The disclaimer is not on the spine, a place most consumers are likely to view before seeing the cover.

Twin Peaks Trivia Book. Scott Knickelbine wrote *Welcome to Twin Peaks: A Complete Guide to Who's Who and What's What*, a trivia book about the 1990 hit television series, *Twin Peaks.* The cover of the book contains the following disclaimer:

> Publications International, Ltd, the publisher of the book, is not affiliated with Lynch/Frost Productions (producer of Twin Peaks), ABC, and various other entities.

The producers of *Twin Peaks* sued for copyright and trademark infringement. The court found the disclaimer to be ineffective. It is uncertain whether an adequate disclaimer would have saved the *Welcome to Twin Peaks* author from losing the lawsuit; however, according to the court, a disclaimer similar to the following would have been clearer and more effective:

> This publication has not been prepared, approved, or licensed by any entity that created or produced the well-known TV program Twin Peaks.

Disclaimers that may work

Disclaimers are a way of showing your good faith of not violating anyone else's rights. If you do everything wrong, a disclaimer is not going to save you. You can invalidate your disclaimer by your conduct. For example, suppose your book contains a disclaimer on the title page that it is completely fictional and any similarities to actual people and events are completely coincidental. If you then release advertisements that explicitly say the book is factual, no court is going to give your disclaimer serious consideration.

The Appendix includes sample disclaimers for different types of productions that may be effective when combined with appropriate behavior on the part of the producer.

DEALING WITH LAWSUITS | 28

28.1. Steps in a Rights Clearance Legal Action

Even when you take all prudent rights clearance steps, you may still be confronted by a lawsuit. A rights owner may voice an initial objection by filing a lawsuit or by sending you a cease and desist letter. Even when a lawsuit is initiated, many cases do not make it to trial. The lawsuit may be dismissed, or the parties may settle prior to a trial.

Here are some of the steps that could be included in a legal proceeding over a rights clearance issue:

Cease and Desist Letter. A cease and desist letter is a letter that a rights holder or her attorney sends to someone who is allegedly violating the rights holder's rights. In the letter, the rights holder explains how your actions are violating his rights and demands that you stop such activities.

For example, the rights owner may claim that the title of your production infringes his trademark, that your book defames him, or that your poster infringes the copyright in his original artwork. The rights owner might also demand that you pay him a licensing fee as compensation for your unauthorized use.

Cease and desist letters usually carry the threat of additional legal action, usually a lawsuit, if you do not stop your activity. Some cease and desist letters are the equivalent of the rights owner huffing and puffing with insufficient power to blow your house down. The rights owner may have a weak or no valid legal argument against your activities and hopes that the cease and desist letter will scare you into compliance. In other cases, the rights owner means business and has the intention and the resources to follow through with a lawsuit if you fail to comply.

If you receive a cease and desist letter, negotiation of a solution other than full compliance might be a possibility. Your attorney can help you evaluate your options and choose the best course of action.

Complaint and Answer. Lawsuits begin with someone filing a complaint with the court. It is normally the rights holder who files the complaint. However, sometimes after becoming frustrated by the actions of a particular rights holder, the producer may initiate a proceeding by filing a complaint with the court. The person initiating the lawsuit is the plaintiff. The person being sued is the defendant.

In the complaint, the plaintiff explains how the defendant has violated his rights and the relief he wants. The requested relief is normally a sum of money to be paid by the defendant to the plaintiff or an injunction ordering the defendant to cease his activities, or both. A producer who files a complaint against a rights holder usually asks the court to issue a declaratory ruling that the producer's use of the rights holder's material is allowable under the law.

If someone initiates a lawsuit by filing a complaint against you, you want to consult an attorney and notify your insurer if you have a policy that potentially covers the plaintiff's claim. Failure to notify your insurer can result in a denial of coverage even in cases where the insurer would have otherwise been required to pay for costs associated with the lawsuit. As the defendant, you have a specified period of time in which to respond to the complaint. The deadline depends on the specific court and ranges from approximately twenty to thirty days. If you do not file a timely answer, you risk losing the lawsuit by default.

Preliminary Injunction. The rights owner may attempt to obtain a preliminary injunction prior to a trial. The injunction prohibits the defendant from engaging in a particular activity. For a rights clearance case, the prohibited activity might be releasing a book or film. Courts grant preliminary injunctions if the plaintiff can show the following:

• The plaintiff is likely to win the lawsuit on the issue.

- The plaintiff would suffer an irreparable injury without the injunction.

- The plaintiff's injury without the injunction would outweigh any injury suffered by the defendant as a result of the injunction being issued.

- Granting the injunction is not inconsistent with the public interest.

Motion to Dismiss. The defendant may file papers, called a motion to dismiss, asking the court to dismiss the plaintiff's complaint. In the motion, the defendant argues that the plaintiff has no valid legal case even if all the events alleged in the complaint actually did occur.

Discovery. The term discovery refers to the time period during which the parties in the lawsuits request information and documents from each other in an attempt to uncover information relevant to their cases. Methods of discovery most common in rights clearance lawsuits include the following:

- *Deposition.* One party responds verbally under oath to questions asked by the other party's attorney. A transcript is made simultaneously of the responses given during the deposition and attorneys may quote from that transcript during a trial.

- *Interrogatories.* One party submits written responses to written questions posed by the other party.

- *Request for Documents.* One party supplies copies of documents requested by the other party.

Motion for Summary Judgment. The plaintiff, the defendant, or both may file a motion for summary judgment. It is a request that the court decide the outcome of the case without a trial (or at least without a complete trial) and based solely on the parties arguments and the documents provided during the discovery process.

Trial. If the action reaches the trial stage, each party presents evidence and witnesses that support its side of the case. In a jury trial, a group of everyday citizens listen to and decide the outcome of the dispute. In a bench trial, a single judge hears the evidence and decides the outcome.

Appeal. If either party is displeased with the outcome of the trial, he can request an appeal. If the appeal is granted, a higher court reviews the case. Appeals are normally heard by a panel of judges rather than by a jury.

28.2. Where Can You Be Sued?

If you are a producer residing in Connecticut, can you be sued in New York or Ohio or Kansas? It depends. When a court agrees to preside over a lawsuit filed against you, the court is exercising personal jurisdiction over you. Not all courts have personal jurisdiction over all producers.

If you are a resident of the state in which the court is located, the court has personal jurisdiction over you. It is a different story if you live outside of the state in which the court is located. The United States Constitution limits a state's right to exert personal jurisdiction over a person or company that is located outside the state.

In order for another state to exercise personal jurisdiction over you, you must have some relationship or engage in some type of activity within the state. If you engage in sufficient activities within a state to justify your being sued in that state, you are said to have minimum contacts with that state. When determining whether you have sufficient minimum contacts to be sued in a particular state, courts often consider the following questions:

- How substantial are your activities in the state?

- Is the plaintiff's claim related to your activities in the state?

- Is it reasonable for the state to exercise personal jurisdiction over you. In other words, should you have reasonably expected that you might be sued in the state?

Whether a court has personal jurisdiction is very fact specific and depends on the particular circumstances in each situation. The cases discussed below provide examples of how a court might approach a personal jurisdiction question.

Cases in which the producer could be sued out-of-state

Magazine with National Distribution. A New Hampshire court had jurisdiction over *Hustler* magazine, an Ohio corporation. *Hustler's* sale of up to 15,000 copies of the magazine in New Hampshire each month established minimum contacts with New Hampshire. (*Keeton v. Hustler Magazine, Inc.*, 465 U.S. 770 (1984)).

Publisher with National Distribution. South Carolina had personal jurisdiction over Norton, a New York company. Norton regularly sells books to approximately 315 book stores located in South Carolina, regularly sends sales representatives to the state, and holds small book fairs in the state. (*Moosally v. W.W. Norton*, 594 S.E.2d 878 (S.C. Ct. App. 2004)).

Cases in which the producer could not be sued out-of-state

Individual Television Producer. South Carolina could not exercise jurisdiction over a producer who resides in Virginia. The producer had produced a television program which aired in South Carolina; covered a funeral in South Carolina as a reporter for CBS; authored a book which copies of which were sold in South Carolina; had the movie version of his book aired in South Carolina on the FX Network; and made at least one business call to South Carolina research. Those activities by themselves were not sufficient minimum contacts for personal jurisdiction. (*Moosally v. W.W. Norton*, 594 S.E.2d 878 (S.C. Ct. App. 2004)).

Out-of-State Advertising. California had no personal jurisdiction in a right of publicity action in which Arnold Schwarzenegger as the Terminator was used in an automobile advertisement circulated in an Ohio newspaper. There was no evidence that the defendant auto dealership had any operations or employees in California, had ever advertised in California, or had ever sold a car to anyone in California. (*Schwarzenegger v. Martin*, 374 F.3d 797 (9th Cir. 2004)).

APPENDICES

Resources and Forms

The appendices include resources and forms to assist you in the process of clearing rights.

Appendices:

Appendix A   Resources
Appendix B   Forms

A.1. Resources for Protecting Your Work

United States Copyright Office, 101 Independence Avenue, SE, Washington, DC 20559, (202) 707-3000 (information specialists available on weekdays from 8:30 a.m. to 5:00 p.m., EST; recorded information available 24 hours per day), (202) 707-9100 (forms and publication hotline). Forms and publications are also available online at www.copyright.gov.

United States Patent and Trademark Office, 2900 Crystal Drive, Arlington, VA 22202, general information: (703) 308-HELP, www.uspto.gov.

Motion Picture Association of America (MPAA) Title Registration Bureau, 15503 Venture Boulevard, Encino, CA 91436, (818) 995-6600. There is a $300 annual subscription fee and a $200 title registration fee which entitles producers to register up to ten titles for United States theatrical motion pictures.

WGA Script Registry Service, 7000 West Third Street, Los Angeles, CA 90048, (323) 782-4500, www.wga.org, email: ipr@wga.org.

A.2. Sample Licensing Fees

Use these sample license fees for guidance on what your cost for obtaining rights may be. The purchase of rights can cost significantly more or, in some cases, significantly less than the sample fees listed here. License fees are dependent on contract terms including the territory, media, and duration covered by the license.

A.2.1. Sample License Fees for Books and Printed Materials

Use of a Quote. $25 to $200+, depending on popularity of the source of the quote and your particular use.

Reprint of an Article. $50 to $400+, depending on popularity of article and your particular use. For example, reprinting of a *Wall Street Journal* article is quoted by the Copyright Clearance Center as $300 for reprinting in a magazine with a circulation of 20,000, $335 for reprinting in a CD-ROM with distribution of 1,000 copies, and $1,082 for reprinting in a book with distribution of 100,000 copies.

A.2.2. Sample License Fees for Visual Art

Reprint of a Comic. $20 to $500+, depending on popularity of comic and your particular use. For example, one of the more moderately priced cartoon banks charges a license fee of $20 for use on a commercial website, $50 for use in a publication with circulation of 20,000, and $100 for use on a cable or television program. Another cartoon bank charges a license fee of $500 or $600 for reprint of a cartoon in a book or magazine with distribution of 500,000 copies.

Use of Stock Images. Varies depending upon use. $200 to $700+ for rights-managed images. $50 to $200+ for royalty-free images. Here are some examples:

- $265 license fee for a photograph of Senator Barak Obama for use in interior of book with distribution of 10,000 copies. This is a rights-managed image from Corbis.

- $600 license fee for image of 2005 London bombing for use on magazine cover with circulation of 50,000. This is a rights-managed image from Getty Images.

- $430 license fee for photograph of Julius and Ethel Rosenberg for use in U.S. television documentary. This is a rights-managed image from Getty Images.

- $79 to $329 license fee for image of a kite in flight. Final license fee depends on image size. This is a royalty-free image from Jupiter Media.

A.2.3. Sample License Fees for Music

Mechanical License. Although the statutory rate is applicable only to compulsory mechanical licenses, the statutory (or compulsory) rate is also the basis for most negotiated mechanical licenses. The statutory rate changes periodically. The statutory rate effective from January 1, 2006 through December 31, 2007 is 9.1¢ for each copy if your recording of the song is five minutes or shorter. If your recording of the song is longer than five minutes, the rate is 1.75¢ per minute. For historical and future rates, see the licensing section of the Copyright Office's website (www.copyright.gov).

Synchronization License. Synchronization (or synch) licenses are very negotiable and depend upon the popularity of the music and your intended use. The sample prices below are for commercially popular music. License fees for songs that are considered "classics" can be significantly more expensive. License fees for music by artists who are less well-known can be significantly lower.

- Sample fee for one-year synch license for exclusive use (in advertising) of song in a national television commercial: $100,000

- Sample fee for five-year synch license for use of a song in television programming:

    o $750 to $1,000 for background use
    o $1,000 to $1,200 for foreground use
    o $1,500 to $2,000 for use as theme or over credits

- Sample fee for synch license in perpetuity for use of a song in a motion picture:

  o $12,500 to $15,000 for background use
  o $20,000 to $25,000 for foreground use
  o $50,000 to $75,000 for use as theme or over credits

Master Use License. Same range as synchronization license fees listed above.

License to Print Lyrics. A few hundred dollars to $1,000+, depending on the popularity of the song and your intended use.

Library or Production Music. Royalty-free music might be as low as $30 to $40 per track. You can purchase an entire CD of royalty-free tracks from $10 to $150 or more. A needle-drop fee might be $65 to $1,200 or more depending upon your intended use. Here are sample needle-drop fees for specific uses:

- $400 to $750+ for use in a feature film

- $400 for use in a national television commercial

- $250 for use in a regional television commercial

- $60 for use in a local radio commercial

- $350 to $700+ for use in a television program

A.2.4. Sample License Fees for Audio-Visual Materials

Popular Film and Television Programs. License fees for popular television and film productions can be very high. It is not uncommon for a rights owner to quote $1,000 per second or more, depending upon the rights requested.

To clear a clip, the producer may also need to obtain permission and make payments to actors, writers, directors, and other rights owners. Here are general guidelines for guild payments; there are numerous exceptions. The rates provided are those in effect as of this writing. The rates change periodically. You should consult with the applicable guild to verify current rates:

- AFTRA. Payment to each recognizable AFTRA actor varies depending upon type of production using the clip. The rates range from approximately $200 to $1,400.

- DGA. $251 to $1,057+ per clip depending on the length and source of the clip and the type of production in which the clip will be used.

- SAG. Minimum payable to each recognizable actor is the SAG day rate which is $759.

- WGA. $173 to $1,049+ per clip depending on the length and source of the clip and the type of production in which the clip will be used.

Stock Footage. Per-use licensed footage might cost approximately $25 to $75+ per second with a ten or fifteen second minimum depending on the specific license terms.   Rates for use in television commercials and feature films may be higher at approximately $100 to $150+ per second.   Stock houses may also offer royalty-free clips for $100 to $250 per clip.

A.3. Collective Rights Organizations

A.3.1. Collective Rights Organizations for Books and Other Printed Materials

Copyright Clearance Center, 222 Rosewood Drive, Danvers, MA 01923, www.copyright.com, email: info@copyright.com.   The Copyright Clearance Center manages the rights to over 1.75 million works and represents more than 9,600 publishers and hundreds of thousands of authors and other creators. It offers an online catalog that allows you to search for content, obtain a price quote, and obtain a license.

Syndicates. The larger news syndicates include Tribune Media Services (www.tms.tribune.com) and The Washington Post Writers Group (www.postwritersgroup.com/writersgroup.htm).

A.3.2. Collective Rights Organizations for Visual Art

American Society of Media Photographers (ASMP), 14 Washington Road, Suite 502, Princeton Junction, NJ 08550, (609) 799-8300, www.asmp.org. ASMP represents the interests of photographers and has over 5,000 members. ASMP offers a searchable database of photographs at www.findaphoto.org. The database is searchable by keyword and then points you to information for licensing.

Artists Rights Society (ARS), 536 Broadway, 5th Floor, New York, NY 10012, 212-420-9160, www.arsny.com. ARS represents over 30,000 visual artists. It acts as the liaison for obtaining rights to use visual art. It is not an image bank and does not actually supply copies of the art for your use.

Cartoon Syndicates. The larger cartoon syndicates include Universal Press Syndicate (www.amuniversal.com/ups/), Cartoon Stock (www.cartoonstock.com), and King Features Syndicate (www.kingfeatures.com).

Visual Artists and Gallery Association (VAGA), 350 Fifth Avenue, Suite 2820, New York, NY 10118, (212) 736-6666, www.vaga.org. VAGA represents the copyright interests of approximately 500 American artists and thousands of foreign artists.

A.3.3. Collective Rights Organizations for Music

ASCAP, One Lincoln Plaza, New York, NY 10023, (212) 621-6000, Fax: (212) 724-9064, www.ascap.com. ASCAP is a performing rights organization for songs. It has additional offices located around the country including offices in Los Angeles, Nashville, and Chicago.

BMI, 320 West 57th Street, New York, NY 10019-3790, (212) 586-2000, www.bmi.com BMI is a performing rights organization for songs. It also has offices in Nashville, Los Angeles, and Atlanta.

Harry Fox, 711 Third Avenue, New York, NY 10017, (212) 834-0100, www.harryfox.com. Harry Fox issues mechanical licenses on behalf of over 30,000 music publishers.

SESAC, 55 Music Square East, Nashville, TN 37203, (615) 320-0055, www.sesac.org. SESAC is a performing rights organization for songs. It also has offices in New York and Los Angeles.

SoundExchange, 1330 Connecticut Ave., NW, Suite 330, Washington, DC 20036, (202) 828-0120, www.soundexchange.com. SoundExchange is a performing rights organization for sound recordings. It issues statutory licenses for the non-interactive digital transmission (*e.g.*, internet streaming) of sound recordings.

A.3.4. Collective Rights Organizations for Films

Motion Picture Licensing Corporation (www.mplc.com) offers a blanket license for the non-commercial exhibition of motion pictures. It issues licenses to numerous entities including corporations, government agencies and non-profit organizations.

A.3.5. Collective Rights Organizations for Live Theatre

Play licensing services include Samuel French (www.samuelfrench.com), Rodgers & Hammerstein Organization (www.rnh.com), and the Dramatists Play Service (www.dramatists.com). Several offer searchable online catalogs.

A.4. Resources for Locating Rights Owners

A.4.1. General Resources for Locating People

The internet offers general resources for finding people including Switchboard White Pages Directory (www.switchboard.com), the Yellow Pages (www.yellowpages.com), and Yahoo people search people.yahoo.com). You can locate specific addresses using an internet service such as Mapquest (www.mapquest.com),

WhoRepresents.com is a fee-based service offering a searchable database for entertainment industry professionals including actors, agents, managers, publicists, and attorneys.

A.4.2. Resources for Locating Publishers and Authors

Copyright Clearing House (CCH). For full information on CCH, see the listing above under collective rights organizations in Section A.3.1.

Literary Marketplace is an annual directory with listings of publishers, literary agents, and other book publishing companies. Most public libraries have a copy. You can purchase a copy at a retail or online bookstore. You can also search an online version of the directory at www.literarymarketplace.com.

A.4.3. Resources for Locating Visual Artists

American Society of Media Photographers (ASMP) offers a searchable database of photographers through its website. For ASMP's full contact information, see the listing under collective rights organization in Section A.3.2.

The Virtual Library (vlmp.icom.museum) offers a searchable directory of museums with an online presence.

A.4.4. Resources for Locating Music Rights Owners

Resources for locating music rights owners include the music collective rights organizations - ASCAP, BMI, SESAC and Harry Fox. Each offers a searchable database containing contact information for its affiliate songwriters and music publishers. For full contact information for each of these performing rights organizations, see the listings above under collective rights organizations in Section A.3.3.

All Music Database (www.allmusic.com) offers information on all genres and styles of music. Album and artist information offered includes title, tracks, genre, label, credits, release date, and cover and artist images.

A.4.5. Resources for Locating Film and Television Rights Owners

The Hollywood Creative Directory (www.hcdonline.com) lists information on entertainment professionals from the film, music, and television industry.

Internet Movie Database (www.imdb.com) compiles data on the cast and crew of film, television, and other media productions.

The Screen Actors Guild (SAG) offers the CAST SAG tool on www.sag.org and an actors locate service through (800) 503-6737. For SAG's complete contact information, see the listing below under entertainment guilds.

The Writers Guild of America (WGA) offers a searchable database of its members with agency contact information when available at www.wga.org. For WGA's complete contact information, see the listing below under entertainment guilds.

A.5. Entertainment Guilds

American Federation of Musicians (AFM). New York Headquarters: 1501 Broadway, Suite 600, New York, NY 10036, (212) 869-1330. www.afm.org. AFM also has offices in Washington, DC, Los Angeles, and Ontario, Canada.

American Federation of Television and Radio Artists (AFTRA). Los Angeles location: 5757 Wilshire Boulevard, 9th floor, Los Angeles, CA 90036, (323) 634-8100. New York location: 260 Madison Avenue, New York, NY 10016, (212) 532-0800.

www.aftra.com. AFTRA has additional offices located throughout the United States.

Directors Guild of America (DGA). Los Angeles location: 7920 Sunset Boulevard, Los Angeles, California 90046, (310) 289-2000. New York location: 110 West 57th Street, New York, New York 10019, (212) 581-0370. www.dga.org. DGA also has an office in Chicago.

Screen Actors Guild (SAG). Los Angeles location: 5757 Wilshire Boulevard, Los Angeles, CA 90036, (323) 954-1600. New York location: 360 Madison Avenue, 12th Floor, New York, NY 10017, (212) 944-1030. www.sag.org. SAG has additional offices located throughout the United States.

Writers Guild of America (WGA). Writers Guild of America, West: 7000 West Third St., Los Angeles, CA 90048, (323) 951-4000, www.wga.org. Writers Guild of America, East: 555 West 57th Street, Suite 1230, New York, NY 10019. (212) 767-7800, www.wgaeastorg.

A.6. Other Useful Rights Clearance Resources

A.6.1. Search Engines

Popular search engines include Google (www.google.com), Yahoo (www.yahoo.com), Lycos (www.lycos.com), and Altavista (www.altavista.com).

A.6.2. Unofficial Lists of Public Domain Works

Bartleby.com offers several searchable databases of literary, reference, and verse materials, many of which are in the public domain.

www.firstgov.gov is the United States government's official web portal. The reference section of the website includes a listing of the government agencies that offer images and graphics, many of which are in the public domain.

The Literature Network (www.online-literature.com) offers searchable online literature including over 1200 full books and 2000 short stories and poems, and 8500 quotes. Many of the works are in the public domain.

Mini-Encyclopedia of Public Domain Songs, published by BZ/Rights & Permissions, Inc., 121 West 27th Street, Suite 901, New York, NY, 10001, 212-924-3000. www.bzrights.com.

Wikipedia.com is a free internet reference website. It includes a listing of websites that offer public domain materials. You can find the listing on the Wikipedia page titled "public domain image resources".

A.6.3. Stock Houses

The list below includes only a few of the larger stock houses. There are hundreds of additional individuals and companies offering stock materials. You can find many sources for stock materials by running a search in an internet search engine. Suggested terms to help you locate stock houses using internet search engines are included under each of the headings below.

Cartoon Banks. Stock houses that offer cartoons include Political Cartoons (www.politicalcartoons.com), The Cartoonist Group (www.cartoonistgroup.com), and The Cartoon Bank (www.cartoonbank.com) which features cartoons from the New Yorker archives. To locate additional stock houses offering cartoons, use the term "cartoon bank" in an internet search engine.

Production and Library Music. To find sources of library music in addition to those listed below, use terms such as "stock music", "library music", and "production music" in an internet search engine.

- The Music Bakery, 7522 Campbell Road, Suite 113, Dallas, Texas 75248, (800) 229-0313, www.musicbakery.com. It offers a large catalog of royalty-free music.

- Associated Production Music. Los Angeles location: 6255 Sunset Boulevard, Suite 820, Hollywood, CA 90028, 323-461-3211. New York location: 381 Park Avenue South, Suite 1101, New York, NY 10016, (212) 856-9800. www.apmmusic.com.

- Valentino Production Music & Sound Effects Library, 500 Executive Boulevard, Elmsford, NY 10523-0534, (914) 347-7878, www.tvmusic.com.

Stock Images and/or Stock Footage. To find sources of stock images and footage in addition to those listed below, use terms such as "image bank", "image library", "stock library", "stock footage", and "stock image" in an internet search engine. Also, internet search engines offering video and image search include Google (www.google.com) and Yahoo (www.yahoo.com).

- BBC Motion Gallery. Los Angeles location: 4144 Lankershim Boulevard, Suite 200, North Hollywood, CA 91602, (818) 299- 9720. New York location: 747 Third Avenue, 29th floor, New York, NY 10017, (212) 705-9399, www.bbcmotiongallery.com.

- Corbis Headquarters, 710 South Avenue, Suite 200, Seattle, WA, 98104, (800) 260-0444. www.corbis.com.

- Getty Images Headquarters, 601 North 34th Street, Seattle, Washington 98103, (800) 462-4379. www.gettyimages.com

- Jupiter Images, 8280 Greensboro Drive, Suite 520, McLean, Virginia 22102, (703) 770-5350. www.jupiterimages.com.

A.6.4. Companies Providing Copyright and Title Reports

CT CORSEARCH, (800) 732-7241. www.ctcorsearch.com.

Government Liaison Services, Inc., 200 N. Glebe Road, Suite 321, Arlington, VA 22203, (703) 524-8200. www.trademarkinfo.com.

Thomson Compumark, 500 Victory Road, North Quincy, MA 02171-3145. For copyright and title services, call 800-356-8630. www.thomson-thomson.com.

FORMS

B

These sample forms and contracts are provided for illustrative purposes. They have not been verified for compliance with the law of any particular state. No one form contract is appropriate for all situations. Please do not use a sample form unless you understand the consequences of its terms and have determined that it is applicable to your particular situation and circumstances. If you have specific legal problems, questions, or concerns, you should consult an attorney.

B.1. Permission Request Letters

B.1.1. Sample Permission Request One

William Writer
100 Main Street
Anywhere, USA 00000

Dear Mr. Writer,

I am the publisher of *Fabulous Country Living*, a regional magazine with a monthly circulation of 25,000 in the southeastern United States. *Fabulous Country Living* would like to reprint your poem entitled "Georgia Sunrise" which appears on page 27 of *Anthology of American Contemporary Poems*. The poem will be included in its entirety with an article entitled "Vacationing in Georgia" scheduled to appear in the March 20XX edition of *Fabulous Country Living*.

We request non-exclusive (i) rights for the one-time publication of your poem in a print edition of *Fabulous Country Living* as well as (ii) electronic rights for posting of the article (and the poem therein) on our website, www.fabulouscountryliving.com. Our website receives approximately 5,000 unique visitors per month.

We offer you a $200 license fee for these rights to be paid within fifteen days of your returning to us a copy of this letter with your signature. Our offer expires on February 15, 20XX. If you are willing to grant us the requested permission, please sign this letter where indicated below and return it to my attention by February 15, 20XX. Your signature below will also confirm that you have the right and authority to grant permission for the reprinting of "Georgia Sunrise" in *Fabulous Country Living*.

Sincerely,

Pauline Publisher

Permission Granted For
The Use Requested Above:

_____   _____

William Writer   Dated

B.1.2. Sample Permission Request Two

Email to Kaleidoscope Comics, Permissions Department
Subject: Quote for Use of Cover Art in CD-ROM

Dear Sir or Madam,

Brainiac Publishing is the producer and distributor of a forthcoming CD-ROM reference, *The History of Comic Art: From Prehistoric Man to the Power Rangers*. We would like to include a copy of one of the *Admiral Vertigo* comic book covers in the section of the CD-ROM that discusses the impact of world events on comic books. The initial print-run of the *History of Comic Art* CD-ROM is 5,000 copies and the release date is scheduled for October 20XX.

The *Admiral Vertigo* cover we desire for the CD-ROM is the September 1983 (issue no. 54) cover that depicts Admiral Vertigo and Lieutenant Mirth at Mount St. Helens. We request a non-exclusive license allowing distribution of the CD-ROM in English and Spanish within North America in perpetuity.

Please reply with a quote for the license fee Kaleidoscope Comic would charge for this requested use. If Kaleidoscope Comic is not the copyright owner, or if additional permission is needed for the requested use, please so indicate in your reply.

Sincerely,

Raymond Sikes,
Brainiac Publishing

B.1.3. Sample Permission Request Three

Francine McDonald
Via Facsimile

RE: Quote Request for Use of Film Clip in Upcoming Feature Film, *Political Fire*

Dear Ms. McDonald:

I am requesting a fee quotation for use of a 15-second clip of your 2003 documentary *Depths of the Ocean*. The clip would be used in *Political Fire*, a feature film being produced and distributed by Orange Hill Films.

Political Fire is a romantic comedy that chronicles the 20-year political rivalry between Mark and Rachel, two US Congressional members who were previously college sweethearts. *Political Fire* stars Clifton Port ("Midnight Train" and "Camera-Ready Copy") and Kaye Fletcher ("French Dessert") and comes out this summer.

The 15-second clip we would like to use is from the scene approximately 20 minutes into the documentary in which divers observe the family bonding rituals of whales. Mark and Rachel watch the clip on television as each sits alone in his or her respective living room, depressed about the impact of their careers on their personal lives.

We request worldwide, perpetual broad rights including a buy-out of all forms of audio-visual devices intended for home use. Please fax your license fee quotation to me at (999) 555-1212.

Sincerely,

Brenda Glass
Orange Hill Films

B.2. License and Rights Agreements

B.2.1. Sample License Agreement One

The following sample license agreement is appropriate for licensing several categories of materials including text, visual art, props, and audio-visual clips. It is not the most appropriate form for licensing music. For licensing music, see section B.3 below, Rights Agreements and Forms for Music.

License Agreement
Dated: _____, 20___

Copyright Owner of Material ("Rights Owner"): _____

Description of Material ("Material") Being Licensed:

[ ] Lyrics   [ ] Text   [ ] Photograph(s) - number _____

[ ] Film or TV Clip   [ ] Prop   [ ] Other _____

Brief description of Material to be used (title, source, duration, reference number, *etc.*): _____

_____

Description of Production ("Production") in which Material Is to Be Used:

[ ] Book   [ ] Website   [ ] Audio-Visual   [ ] Other _____

Production Title: _____

Producer Name ("Producer"): _____

Producer Address: _____

Duration or Length of Production (if applicable): _____

Brief description of Production (*e.g.*, subject matter): _____

_____

License Fee: _____ Dollars ($_____)

Credit for Use of Material ("Credit"): _____

_____

Rights Owner grants Producer permission to use the Material described above in the Production pursuant to the following terms:

1.   Non-Exclusive License. Rights Owner grants Producer an irrevocable, non-exclusive, perpetual, worldwide right and license to incorporate the Material into the Production. Producer may (or license others to) reproduce, modify, translate, distribute, perform, and display the Material in connection with the Production (and any versions or sequels thereof) and the exhibition, production, exhibition, advertising and publicity for the Production in any form, media, language or technology, now known or later developed.

2.   License Fee and Credits. Producer shall have no obligation to use the Material in the Production. However, if Producer uses the Material in the Production, Producer shall (a) pay Rights Owner the License Fee as full payment for all the rights granted and representations made by Rights Owner in this License Agreement, and (b) give Rights Owner a credit in a format substantially similar to the format set forth in the Credit section above. No casual or inadvertent failure to provide Rights Owner with a credit shall be a breach of this License Agreement by Producer.

3.   Representations and Acknowledgments. Rights Owner makes the following representations, warranties and acknowledgments to Producer:

(a)   Rights Owner has the full right and authorization to license the Material to Producer and Producer is free to implement or use the Material as set forth in this License Agreement, without obtaining permission from any other person.

(b)   Rights Owner understands and agrees that Rights Owner shall have no copyrights or other rights to the Production or any benefits derived from the Production.

(c)   Rights Owner understands that Producer is relying on Rights Owner's representations and agreements. Rights Owner agrees to indemnify and hold harmless Producer for any loss suffered by Producer as a result of a breach in the representations and agreements Rights Owner has made in this License Agreement.

(d)   Rights Owner's remedies in the event of a breach of this License Agreement shall be limited to a recovery of damages in an action at law. Rights Owner shall not have the right to enjoin or restrain any exploitation of the Production.

4.   Applicable Law. This License Agreement shall be governed in accordance with the laws of the state of _____ (*insert state*), applicable to contracts made and to be performed wholly

in _____ (*insert state*), without regard to principles of conflicts of laws.

Producer

_____
(Printed Name of Producer)

By: _____

Title: _____

Rights Owner

_____
(Printed Name of Rights Owner)

By: _____

Title: _____

B.2.2. Sample License Agreement Two

This Sample License Agreement Two is written for the licensing of television news footage for a documentary. It can be adapted for the licensing of a commercial television clip or film clip.

Agreement for Licensing of Footage
Dated _____, 20__

_____ ("Producer") has requested permission from _____ ("TV Station") to use footage on or about _____ _____ (the "Footage") for possible use in a documentary film Producer is producing on the subject matter of _____ and tentatively entitled _____ (the "Production").

Producer and TV Station agree as follows:

1.   License Fee and Grant of Rights. For the sum of _____

_____ Dollars ($____) per minute of Footage used (rounded off to the nearest fifteen seconds) and other good and valuable consideration (the receipt and sufficiency of which are hereby acknowledged) TV Station grants Producer the non-exclusive right to incorporate the Footage in the Production and to use the Footage in connection with the Production and the advertising and promotion thereof. Producer may exploit the Production (and the Footage therein) world-wide, in perpetuity, and in any form, media, language or technology, now known or later developed.

2.   Selection of Footage. Producer shall review the archival records of TV Station and select clips for screening. TV Station shall deliver selected clips to Producer for a fee equal to TV Station's actual cost. Upon completion of the Production (prior to any public screenings) Producer shall notify TV Station of the Footage used, and shall pay TV Station the amount specified above within sixty (60) days. Producer shall provide TV Station with an accounting of all Footage actually used in the Production as well as a VHS copy of the completed Production for verification. Producer's access to TV Station's archives as set forth in this paragraph 2 shall be from January 1, _____through December 31, _____.

3.   Producer Representations. Producer warrants and represents that Producer has obtained or shall obtain all necessary clearances and/or permissions from third parties, specifically including all persons depicted in the Footage or their heirs and/or legal representatives, as applicable, as well as all union, talent, music and copyright clearances and permissions. It is specifically understood that this License Agreement does not grant nor shall it in any way be interpreted to constitute the consent of any persons appearing in the Footage. Producer shall be solely responsible for any and all payments to third parties which may be required for Producer's use of the Footage. Producer further warrants and represents that any commentary or other material accompanying the exhibition of the Footage will not be defamatory to TV Station, or to any person appearing in or connected with the Footage.

4.   TV Station's Representations. TV Station does not make any representations or warranties with respect to the Footage or Producer's intended use of the Footage other than that TV Station has the full right and authority to make the grant of rights contained herein.

5.   Credit. Producer shall provide a courtesy credit to TV Station, for having allowed the use of the Footage; provided, however, that no casual or inadvertent failure to provide such credit shall be deemed a breach by Producer of this License Agreement.

6.   Governing Law. This License Agreement shall be governed in accordance with the laws of the state of (*insert state*), applicable to contracts made and to be performed wholly in (*insert state*), without regard to principles of conflicts of laws.

Producer

By: _____
    (Signature of Authorized Representative)

_____
(Printed Name of Authorized Representative)

Title: _____

TV Station

By: _____
    (Signature of Authorized Representative)

_____
(Printed Name of Authorized Representative)

Title: _____

B.3. Rights Agreements and Forms for Music

B.3.1. Sample Permission Request for Use of Song

Fred Morgan
Maximus Publishing
99 Central Place
Anyplace, Anystate 00000

Dear Mr. Morgan:

I understand that Maximus Publishing is the music publisher and administers rights for "Heartburn Sally". I am requesting a quote for a synchronization license to use the song in a television and radio commercial campaign to promote Buchanan Pharmacies, one of the largest drugstore chains in the United States.

The initial scripts for the television and radio commercials are attached for your review. Please contact me at (999) 555-1212 with your quote for the following use:

> Song: "Heartburn Sally"
> Songwriter: Gene Composer
> Publisher: Maximus Publishing
> No. of Spots: Unlimited
> License Term: 1 year
> Territory for Use: United States only
> Media: Television (free and pay) and radio
> Exclusivity: Exclusive use for advertisements of pharmaceutical products and services and retail stores

Very Truly Yours,

Samantha Kane
For Real Advertising

B.3.2. Sample Permission Request for Use of Sound Recording

Heather Reynolds
Atrium Records
99 Main Street
Anyplace, Anystate 00000

Dear Heather,

Exercise Machine, Inc. is producing a dance exercise dvd and would like to use the Rain Hill Trio's master recording of "Zany". We have already obtained synch rights in the underlying song from Maximus Publishing.

The dvd title is *Hip-Hop Aerobics with Jayne Kole*. Its run-time is forty minutes and it includes five choreographed dance routines performed to a variety of contemporary, upbeat music. The video targets active women between the ages of 18 – 30, similar to the demographics of the Rain Hill Trio's fan base.

The video/dance leader is Jayne Kole, a professional dancer who has toured internationally with The San Francisco City Group Dance Company. Jayne is also a certified aerobics instructor who regularly appears as a commentator on fitness for XYZ News.

"Zany" would be heard as a background vocal during a three-minute dance sequence on the dvd. The scheduled release date for the dvd is _____, 20XX. We anticipate distributing 300,000 copies. We request a three-year master use license for home video/dvd distribution in North America. We can offer a royalty of 12¢ for each unit sold. Photography starts next month so I would appreciate receiving your master use license fee quotation as soon as possible.

Very Truly Yours,

Monica Grant,
Exercise Machine, Inc.

B.3.3. Sample Composer Agreement

Composer Agreement
Dated: _____, 20__

This Composer Agreement is entered by and between _____ _____, ("Producer") and _____ ("Composer").

Producer and Composer hereby agree as follows:

1.   Services. Producer hereby engages Composer, and Composer hereby agrees to compose, record, produce, orchestrate, and mix approximately _____ minutes of original score music ("Score") for the film with the working title, _____ ("Production"). Composer shall also perform such services as are normally performed by composers of music for audio-visual productions. Composer shall deliver to Producer by _____, 20___, the completed Score in a format reasonably designated by Producer.

2.   Payment. In full consideration for all services rendered by Composer hereunder and all rights granted by Composer herein, Producer shall pay Composer a package fee of _____ ($_____) (the "Package Fee"). Fifty percent of the Package Fee shall be payable within five days of execution of this Composer Agreement with the balance due within five days of Composer's delivery to Producer of the Score.

3.   Royalties. In addition to the Package Fee, Composer shall also be entitled to receive the following royalties with respect to exploitation of the Score: (a) the writer's share of public performance royalties which Composer shall receive directly from the performing rights organization with which Composer is affiliated, (b) print royalties equal to Ten Cents (10¢) for each piano copy and ten percent (10%) of the wholesale selling price for each folio, and (c) fifty percent (50%) of net income actually received by Producer for mechanical licenses, for

synchronization licenses, and for income from uses of the Score not connected with the Production. In the event Producer releases the Score on a soundtrack album, Composer shall be entitled to receive royalties equal to ___ percent (__%) of the retail price of the soundtrack album, calculated consistently with royalties received by Producer through its soundtrack album deal. Producer shall pay royalties to Composer on a semi-annual basis. Producer shall prepare and submit to the applicable performing rights organizations within 45 days of the release of the Production a cue sheet containing all necessary information concerning the title, composer and publisher of all music used in the Production.

4.   Recording Costs. Composer acknowledges that the Package Fee is designed to cover all costs necessary for completion and delivery of the Score including costs for musicians, vocalists, studio rental, recording engineers, and payments required by the American Federation of Musicians, American Federation of Television or Radio Artists, or any other collective bargaining organization. Composer is responsible for costs in excess of the Package Fee.

5.   Ownership. Composer's services provided hereunder shall be deemed a commissioned work, and Composer acknowledges and agrees that all services provided hereunder are a work made for hire, as that term is defined in the Copyright Act of 1976, as amended. To the extent that Composer's services are not properly characterized as a work made for hire, Composer hereby irrevocably assigns to Producer all of his right, title and interest in and to the Score throughout the universe in perpetuity, in all languages and media (whether now known or hereafter devised). Composer agrees to cooperate in the preparation of any documents necessary to demonstrate this assignment of rights.

6.   No Obligation. Notwithstanding any other provision of this Composer Agreement, Producer shall have no obligation to incorporate the Score into the Production or to make any other use of the Score.

7.   Representations. Composer hereby represents, warrants and agrees that Composer has the full right and authority to grant to Producer the rights granted hereunder and that no material provided by Composer to Producer hereunder shall infringe any intellectual property rights of any person or violate any laws. Composer shall obtain all permissions from instrumentalists, vocalists and other third parties who contribute to the completion of the Score so that Producer may exercise all rights granted hereunder. Composer shall indemnify and hold Producer harmless for any loss suffered by Producer as a result of Composer's breach of this representation.

8.   Credit. If the Score is used in the Production, Producer shall give Composer a credit in substantially the following form:

(insert format of credit)

No casual or inadvertent failure to provide Composer with a credit shall be a breach of this Composer Agreement by Producer.

9.   Miscellaneous. This Composer Agreement shall be governed in accordance with the laws of the state of _____ *(insert state)*, applicable to contracts made and to be performed wholly in _____ *(insert state)*, without regard to principles of conflicts of laws.

IN WITNESS WHEREOF, the parties hereto have executed this Composer Agreement.

Producer

By: _____

Title: _____

Composer

_____

(Signature of Composer)

B.3.4. Synchronization and Master Use License Agreement

This Synchronization and Master Use License Agreement form is appropriate if you are licensing music from a rights owner who owns the copyright in both the song and the sound recording of the music you wish to use. This particular form is for the non-exclusive use of music on U.S. free television. It can be adapted for other media and geographic locations.

Synchronization and Master
Use License Agreement

This Synchronization and Master Use License Agreement ("Agreement") by and between _____, ("Musician") and _____ ("Producer") is effective as of the ___ day of _____, 20XX .

Whereas, Musician is the owner and/or administrator of all right, title and interest in and to the following musical compositions and master sound recordings (collectively "Licensed Music"):

(*List songs and recordings*)

Whereas, Producer desires to license the Licensed Music for the purpose of synchronization with the production described below ("Production"):

(*Insert title, length and brief description of Production*)

Musician and Producer hereby agree as follows:

1.   Grant of Rights: Musician grants to Producer the perpetual, non-exclusive right and authority (but not the obligation) to synchronize, embody and incorporate any part or all of the Licensed Music with the Production, to make unlimited copies of such embodiments and to distribute, sell or otherwise exploit such copies, subject to the terms and conditions of this Agreement.

2.   Media and Territory: Producer may exploit the Production (and the Licensed Music therein) on free television within the United States only.

3.   License Fee: In exchange for the rights granted hereunder, Producer shall pay Musician a license fee of _____ Dollars ($_____), payable within fifteen days of complete execution of this Agreement.

4.   Delivery of Materials: The parties acknowledge that Musician has delivered to Producer at Musician's cost digital copies of the Licensed Music.

5.   Performing Rights: Producer shall not broadcast or cause to be broadcast any of the Licensed Music unless each local station, system or entity broadcasting the same has an appropriate license with a performing rights organization having the right to license the performance and broadcast of the Licensed Music ("PRO"). Within thirty (30) days of release of the Production, Producer shall prepare and submit a cue sheet to the applicable PRO and provide Musician with a copy of the cue sheet.

6.   Musician's Representation and Warranties:

a. Musician represents and warrants that Musician is the sole owner of the Licensed Music and all rights granted hereunder. Musician has not done and shall not do any act or enter into any agreement which would impair any of the rights granted to Producer.

b. Musician represents and warrants that the Licensed Music is 100% original in all respects; that it, nor any part thereof, is not taken from or based upon any other musical, dramatic or other material; that it in no way infringes upon the copyright or any other right of any other person, firm or corporation; and that the use of the Licensed Music by Producer hereunder will not in any way directly or indirectly infringe upon the rights of any person, firm or corporation whatsoever.

c. Musician shall indemnify and hold Producer harmless for any loss suffered by Producer as a result of Musician's breach of the representations and warranties herein.

7.   Use of Name/Credit: If the Licensed Music is used in the Production, Producer shall give Musician a credit in the following form:

(insert format of credit)

No casual or inadvertent failure to provide Musician with a credit shall be a breach of this Agreement by Producer.

8.   Miscellaneous: This Agreement, which incorporates the introductory Whereas clauses, represents the entire agreement between the parties with respect to the subject matter hereof. This Agreement shall be governed in accordance with the laws of the state of _____ [*insert state*], applicable to contracts made and to be performed wholly in _____ [*insert state*], without regard to principles of conflicts of laws.

Producer

By: _____
       (Signature of Authorized Representative)

_____
(Printed Name of Authorized Representative)

_____
(Title of Authorized Representative)

Musician

_____
(Signature of Musician)

B.3.5. Sample Cue Sheet

Cue Sheet

Production Title/Episode Title (if applicable): _____

Duration of Production: ____   1st Air Date/Release Date: _____

Distribution: [ ] TV [ ] Radio [ ] Theatrical

Specify station or network if TV or Radio Distribution:_____

Name of Production Company: _____

Address of Production Company: _____

Phone Number: _____   Fax Number: _____

Cue No.	Song Title	Composer (Society)	Publisher (Society)	Time	Use
1	Tell Me Again	Cyn Smith (ASCAP)	Access Music (ASCAP)	:23	T
2	Twilight Rain	Joe Brown (BMI)	Solo Songs (BMI)	:40	BV
3	Succotash	Mark Ringer (ASCAP) – 50% Janet Wyn (ASCAP) – 50%	Crystal Music (ASCAP)	:18	BI

4	Here's To You	Philip Styles (SESAC) – 50% Martin Bates (SESAC) – 50%	Retro Publishing (ASCAP)	1:02	VV

Legend for Cue Sheet: Main Title (MT), End Title (ET), Theme (T), Background Vocal (BV), Background Instrumental (BI), Visual Vocal (VV), Visual Instrumental (VI)

B.3.6. Forms for Compulsory Mechanical License

These are forms you can use to obtain a compulsory mechanical license under Section 115 of the Copyright Act. Harry Fox offers an easier alternative to compliance with Section 115. Harry Fox issues a mechanical license which, other than relaxing the notice and statement requirements, substantially mirrors the compulsory mechanical license available under Section 115 of the Copyright Act. However, if you need a compulsory mechanical license for a song that is not in Harry Fox's catalog, you may need to rely on and follow the terms of Section 115 of the Copyright Act.

Notice of Intention for a Mechanical License. You may list multiple songs on one notice as long as all the songs have the same copyright owner, or in the case of any song having more than one copyright owner, any one of the copyright owners is the same.

You may send the notice to the name and address of the copyright owner of the song as listed in the Copyright Office's public records. If there are multiple copyright owners, you need send the notice to only one.

Normally, it is not necessary to file the notice with the Copyright Office. If you cannot identify and locate the copyright owner through the Copyright Office's records or otherwise, you may send the notice to the Copyright Office accompanied by the fee specified ($12 per song at the time of this printing) in Copyright Office regulation 201.3(e) (37 C.F.R. §201.3(e)).

Since you may need to prove that the notice was sent on time, you should send it via certified or registered mail or via a courier service that provides delivery confirmation.

Notice of Intention to Obtain a Compulsory License for Making and Distributing Phonorecords

Dear Song Copyright Owner:

Please accept this letter as notice of our intention to obtain a compulsory mechanical license. The information required by Section 115 of the Copyright Act and Regulation 201.18, is as follows:

Full Legal Name of Person or Entity Intending to Obtain the Compulsory License: XYZ Corporation (the "Licensee")

Fictitious or Assumed Names Used by Licensee: The XYZ Band

Address of Licensee (must be street address unless post office box is only usable address for location): 123 Meadow Lane, Plainsboro, Indiana 55555

Names and Title (*e.g.*, chief executive officer, managing partner, member, etc.) of Individual Managing Licensee's Business Operations (if Licensee is not an individual): John Smith, President

Fiscal Year of Licensee: Calendar Year

Title of Musical Work ("Song") Being Licensed: Opting For Jubilation

Author(s) of Song: Freda Jones

Copyright Owner(s) of Song: Freda Jones

Types of phonorecord configurations already made, if any, and dates of such manufacture: None

Types of phonorecord configurations expected to be made: CDs and digital phonorecord deliveries

Expected date of initial distribution of phonorecords already made, if any, or expected to be made: June 15, 20XX.

Name of recording artist or group to perform song: XYZ Band

Catalog number and label names to be used on phonorecords: INDX003; The XYZ Label

The information provided above is given in good faith and on the basis of the best knowledge, information, and belief of the undersigned.

Use this signature block if Licensee is an individual:

_____

Signature

_____

Date

Use this signature block if Licensee is a partnership, corporation, LLC, or other type of entity:

The person signing below affirms that he/she is authorized to execute this document on behalf of the Licensee.

XYZ Corporation

By: _____
   (Signature of Authorized Representative)

_____

Printed Name of Authorized Representative

_____

Date

Monthly Statement of Account. You must send a separate Monthly Statement of Account for each month you have sales activity for the licensed song. The monthly statements are to be filed on or before the 20th day of the immediately succeeding month. For example, June's statement must be filed by July 20. See Copyright Office Regulation 201.19 (37 C.F.R. §201.19) for additional guidance on calculating the royalty amount.

Monthly Statement of Account Under Compulsory
License for Making and Distributing Phonorecords
For the Period _____, 20__ (the "Monthly Accounting Period")

Section One. Basic Information.

Full Name of Person or Entity with the Compulsory License: XYZ Corporation (the "Licensee")

Fictitious or Assumed Names Used by Licensee: The XYZ Band

Address of Licensee (must be street address unless post office box is only usable address for location): 123 Meadow Lane, Plainsboro, IN 55555

Title of Licensed Musical Work ("Song"): Opting For Jubilation

Author(s) of Song: Freda Jones

Types of phonorecord configurations involved: CDs

Name or recording artist or group performing song: XYZ Band

Catalog number and label names to be used on phonorecords: INDX003; The XYZ Label

Playing time of Recording: 3 minutes; 42 seconds

Section Two. Identification and Accounting of Phonorecords:

No. of Phonorecords Made During Monthly Accounting Period:

_____

No. of Phonorecords that during the Monthly Accounting Period:

- distributed for purposes other than sale: _____
- distributed on non-returnable/non-exchangeable basis: _____
- distributed on returnable/exchangeable basis: _____
- returned to licensee for credit or exchange: _____
- placed in a phonorecord reserve: _____
- dpd's never delivered due to a failed transmission: _____
- dpd's retransmitted to complete failed transmission: _____
- for which revenue recognized: _____

Section Three. Royalty Payment and Accounting:

Step 1. No. of phonorecords shipped on returnable/exchangeable basis during Monthly Accounting Period:

_____

Step 2. Minus no. of phonorecords placed in reserve:

_____   -   _____   =   _____
(Result of Step 1)

Step 3. Plus no. of phonorecords shipped on non-returnable/non-exchangeable basis or distributed for purposes other than sale:

_____   +   _____   =   _____
(Result of Step 2)

Step 4. Adjustments as necessary for sales revenue recognized, lapsed reserves, reduction of negative reserve balance, incomplete dpd transmissions, and retransmitted dpd's:

_____ +/- _____ = _____
(Result of Step 3)

Step 5. Multiply by statutory royalty rate

_____ X statutory mechanical = _____
(Result of Step 4)   royalty rate

Royalties due for Monthly Accounting Period: _____
                                              (Result of Step 5)

I certify that (i) I am authorized to submit this document on behalf of the Licensee and (ii) I have examined this document and that all statements of fact contained herein are true, complete, and correct to the best of my knowledge, information, and belief, and are made in good faith.

(Use same format of signature block as used
for the Notice of Intention in Section B.3.6)

Annual Statement of Account Under Compulsory License for Making and Distributing Phonorecords. The annual statement must be delivered to the song's copyright owner on or before the 20th day of the third month following the end of the fiscal year. That would be March 20 if your fiscal year is based on the calendar year. You are not required to file the annual report with the Copyright Office. Note that the Annual Statement must include a certification by a certified public accountant.

Annual Statement of Account Under Compulsory
License for Making and Distributing Phonorecords
For Fiscal Year January 1, 20__ to December 31, 20__

Section One. Basic Information.

Full Legal Name of Person or Entity Relying on the Compulsory License: XYZ Corporation (the "Licensee")

Fictitious or Assumed Names Used by Licensee: The XYZ Band

Address of Licensee (must be street address unless post office box is only usable address for location): 123 Meadow Lane, Plainsboro, Indiana 55555

Names and Title (e.g., chief executive officer, managing partner, member, etc.) of Individual Managing Licensee's Business Operations (if Licensee is not an individual): John Smith, President

Title of Musical Work ("Song") Being Licensed: Opting For Jubilation

Author(s) of Song: Freda Jones

Copyright Owner(s) of Song: Freda Jones

Name of recording artist or group to perform song: XYZ Band

Playing time of Recording: 3 minutes; 42 seconds

Catalog number and label names used on phonorecords: INDX003; The XYZ Label

Section Two.   Identification and Accounting of Phonorecords. This information must be separately stated for each phonorecord configuration.

A.   No. of phonorecords made through end of Fiscal Year, including any made during earlier years: _____

B.   No. of phonorecords never distributed by Licensee through end of Fiscal Year: _____

C.   No. of phonorecords involuntarily relinquished (as through fire or theft) during Fiscal Year and any earlier periods and cause of such involuntary relinquishment: _____

D.   No. of phonorecords voluntarily distributed during all years prior to the Fiscal Year: _____

E.   No. of phonorecords distributed for sale during Fiscal Year but returned and in Licensee's possession at end of Fiscal Year: _____

F.   No. of phonorecords voluntarily distributed during the Fiscal Year: _____

A - (B+C+D+E) should equal F. If not, the Annual Statement must explain the discrepancy.

Section Three. Payment of Royalties

A.   Amount of Royalties Payable for Fiscal Year:

_____   X   statutory mechanical = _____
(Result of Section   royalty rate
Two, Part F)

B.   Total Sum paid under Monthly Statements of Account during Fiscal Year._____

C.   Royalty Payment (if any) due with this Annual Statement: _____

*(Use same format of signature block as used
for the Notice of Intention in Section B.3.6)*

Section Four. Certification by Licensed Certified Public Accountant (CPA)

We have examined the attached Annual Statement of Account Under Compulsory License for Making and Distributing Phonorecords" for the fiscal year ended December 31, 20__ of XYZ Corporation applicable to phonorecords embodying "Opting for Jubilation" made under the provisions of section 115 of title 17 of the United States Code, as amended by Pub. L. 94-553, and applicable regulations of the United States Copyright Office. Our examination was made in accordance with generally accepted auditing standards and accordingly, included tests of the accounting records and such other auditing procedures as we considered necessary in the circumstances.

In our opinion the Annual Statement of Account referred to above presents fairly the number of phonorecords embodying each of the above-identified non-dramatic musical works made under compulsory license and voluntarily distributed by XYZ Corporation during the fiscal year ending December 31, 20__, and the amount of royalties applicable thereto under such compulsory license, on a consistent basis and in accordance with the above cited law and applicable regulations published thereunder.

_____

(City and State of Execution)

_____

Signature of CPA

_____

Certificate Number

_____

Jurisdiction of Certificate

_____

Date of Opinion

B.4. Releases and Consents

B.4.1. Interview Release

Interview Release

I understand that _____ ("Producer") is the producer of the production described below (the "Production"):

*(Insert title, length, and brief
description of Production)*

By signing below, I give Producer, its licensees, successors and assigns permission to interview me on or off camera and to use the interview (including my image and voice) in connection with the Production (and any versions or sequels thereof) and in any promotional materials for the Production. I agree to the following:

- The rights I grant to Producer are irrevocable, perpetual, worldwide, and include the right to use the interview in any form, media, language or technology, now known or later developed.

- Producer may edit, reproduce, modify, adapt, or otherwise use the interview or any part thereof either alone or in combination with other material including text, images, animation, graphics, and video.

- I shall have no copyrights or other rights to the Production or any benefits derived from the Production.

- I waive any right to inspect the Production and the use of the interview therein.

- I waive any claim against and shall not file or participate in a lawsuit against Producer in connection with the use of the interview including claims alleging libel, invasion of privacy, right of publicity violaiton, or copyright infringement.

- Producer shall have no obligation to use the interview.

I am signing this release to encourage Producer to conduct and use the interview. I understand that Producer will incur substantial expense in reliance on the representations and agreements I make in this release. I represent that I am [ ] under [ ]over (*check one*) the age of 18 years and that I have read and fully understand the meaning of this release.

_____   _____

(Signature)   (Date)

_____

(Printed Name)

_____

(Address)

_____

(Phone)

Signature of Parent or Guardian
(*required if Interviewee is under 18 years of age*):

I represent that I am the parent or guardian of the above-signed minor, and that I have the authority to execute the above release on behalf of said minor. I have read and fully understand the meaning of this release.

_____   _____

(Signature of Parent or Guardian)   (Date)

_____

(Printed Name of Parent or Guardian)

_____

(Address of Parent or Guardian)

_____

(Phone or Parent or Guardian)

B.4.2. Life Story Rights Agreement

This particular form of a life story rights agreement is non-exclusive. That means the subject can also grant rights in his/her life story to other producers.

Life Story Rights Agreement
Dated _____, 20__

Individual Granting Life Story Rights ("Subject"): _____

Address of Subject: _____

Description of Production ("Production"):

[ ] Book   [ ] Article   [ ] Audio-Visual   [ ] Other _____

Production Title: _____

Name of Producer ("Producer"): _____

Producer Address: _____

Brief description of Production (*e.g.*, subject matter.)

_____

Producer desires to depict all or some of the events of the Subject's life ("Life Story") in the Production described above. By signing below, the Subject grants Producer permission to use, fictionalize and/or exploit the Subject's name, likeness, experiences, anecdotes, statements, and Life Story events. The Subject agrees that Producer may exploit (and grant permission to others to exploit) the Production depicting the Life Story world-wide, in perpetuity, and in any form, media, language or technology, now known or later developed.

Subject understands and agrees that Producer may portray Subject's Life Story in any manner including adding to, subtracting from, modifying, or fictionalizing the depiction of events.

Subject waives any claim against and shall not file or participate in a lawsuit against Producer in connection with the use of the Life Story including lawsuits alleging libel, slander, invasion of privacy, invasion of right of publicity, and/or copyright infringement.

Producer shall pay Subject the amount of _____ _____ Dollars ($_____) as full payment for all the rights granted and representations made by Subject in this Life Story Rights Agreement. Subject shall receive no additional compensation in connection with the Production. Subject shall have no copyrights or other rights to the Production or any benefits derived from the Production.

At Producer's request, Subject shall provide Producer with access to all information in Subject's possession relating to Subject's Life Story and shall relate to Producer all Subject's observations and reactions relating to the events in Subject's Life Story.

Subject has the full right and authorization to make the grant of Life Story rights hereunder and Producer is free to exercise such Life Story Rights without obtaining permission from any other person.

Producer   Subject

_____   _____
(Printed Name of Producer)   (Printed Name of Subject)

By: _____   _____
                                    (Signature of Subject)

Title: _____   _____

B.4.3. Consent Sign-Up Sheet

Consent Sign-Up Sheet

Consent Sign-Up Sheet for appearance in _____
___ ("Production"), a _____
(*insert brief description of Production*).

By signing below, I give Producer, its licensees, successors and assigns permission to interview me on or off camera and to use all or
part of the interview (including my image and voice) in connection
with the Production (and any versions or sequels thereof) and in
any promotional materials for the Production. The rights I grant
to Producer are irrevocable, perpetual, worldwide, and include the
right to use the interview in any form, media, language or technology, now known or later developed.

Printed Name Signature   Signature of Parent/
                                 Guardian (if under 18)

1. _____ _____   _____

2. _____ _____   _____

3. _____ _____   _____

B.4.4. Crowd Release

For productions that take place in an area where the camera might
pick up passerbys or audience members, you can post a warning.
This would be posted in the area in which you are filming or taking pictures.

Crowd Release

A Production of *Final Days* is currently being filmed in this area.
If you remain in this area, it is possible that your image and/or

voice will be captured on camera and used in the Production. By remaining in this area, you consent to your appearance in the Production and authorize Producer to exploit the Production throughout the world, in perpetuity, and in any media, language, or technology. If you do not want to appear in the Production, please do not enter this area.

B.4.5. Location Release

Location Release

Dated: _____, 20___

_____ ("Owner") grants to _____ _____ ("Producer"), its successors, licensees, and assigns permission to photograph and reproduce the interior and exterior of the property located at _____ ("Location") in conjunction with a production tentatively entitled, _____ ("Production").

Photography at the Location shall take place on the following days: _____. If photography is impossible on these days due to a reason beyond Producer's control, photography shall take place on alternate dates mutually agreeable to Producer and Owner. Upon completion of the photography, Producer will remove all equipment and will return the premises to their original condition.

Permission granted includes the following rights with respect to the Location: (i) Producer may bring personnel, equipment, and set decorations onto the premises; (ii) Producer shall have the right (but not the obligation) to photograph signage and other materials with the name associated with the Location and use such photography in the Production; and (iii) Producer may use the photography of the Location in the Production and with the promotion, exhibition and advertising thereof world-wide, in perpetuity, and in all languages, and all media, now known or hereafter developed.

Producer shall pay Owner a one-time fee in the amount of _____ _____ Dollars ($_____) as full payment for all the rights granted and representations made by Owner in this Location Release.

Owner makes the following representations: (i) Owner is the owner or authorized representative of the owner of the premises, (ii) Owner has the authority to grant permission for the use of the Location contained herein, and (iii) Producer is free to use the Location as set forth in this Location Agreement without obtaining permission from any other person.

Owner waives any claim against and shall not file or participate in a lawsuit against Producer in connection with the use of the Location including lawsuits or claims alleging libel, slander, invasion of privacy, invasion of right of publicity, trademark infringement, and/or copyright infringement.

Producer   Owner

_____   _____
(Printed Name of Producer)   (Printed Name of Owner)

By: _____   By: _____

Title: _____   Title: _____

B.5. Disclaimers

B.5.1. Disclaimers for Productions Based on Fiction

Sample Disclaimer One. This is a work of fiction. Names, characters, places and incidents either are the product of the author's imagination or are used fictitiously. Any resemblance to any actual persons, living or dead, events or locales is entirely coincidental.

Sample Disclaimer Two. The stories on this website are works of fiction. All events, locations, institutions, themes, persons, characters, and plots are completely fictional inventions of the author. Any resemblance to people living or deceased, actual places, or events is purely coincidental and entirely unintentional, unless otherwise indicated.

B.5.2. Disclaimer for Production Based on Fact

This story is based on actual events. In certain cases incidents, characters and timelines have been changed for dramatic purposes. Certain characters may be composites, or entirely fictitious.

B.5.3. Disclaimer for Fanzine Production

This website is an unofficial fansite made by a fan of *Firefly* for the enjoyment of other *Firefly* fans. This site is NOT authorized by or affiliated with Fox, Universal Pictures, or anyone involved with the television production, *Firefly*, or with the motion picture, *Serenity*. *Firefly*, its characters, and all related images and content are the proprietary material of Twentieth Century Fox Television and its related entities. Images and content related to the motion picture *Serenity* are the proprietary material of Universal Pictures.

B.5.4. Disclaimer for Production Containing Trademarks Owned by Others

All incidentally referenced trademarks are the property of their respective owners.

B.5.5. Disclaimers for Production with Material That May Be Objectionable

Sample Disclaimer One. The purpose of this website is to promote the erotic fiction of author Wayne Writer. The excerpts provided may contain explicit words or passages that are unsuitable to minors or possibly prohibited in some localities. Anyone who is uncomfortable with the discussion of physical relationships between consenting adults, or who is not legally able to read such fiction, is warned against browsing the pages on this website. The author assumes no responsibility for the actions of any person visiting this site.

Sample Disclaimer Two. The web pages you are about to view contain material that is intended for responsible adults who are over 18 years old and over the age of legal consent in the locations in which they live and are accessing these web pages. If you are not more than 18 years old and are not also over the age of legal consent in these locations, you are NOT permitted to access these web pages. These web pages may include images, text, graphics, sounds, illustrations, or descriptions of nudity and sexual activity. If you do not wish to access material of that nature, then you should not access these web pages.

Sample Disclaimer Three. Parental Advisory. Explicit Content. Strong language. Sexual and Violent Content.

B.5.6. Disclaimers for Productions That Offer Information

Sample Disclaimer One. This book is a basic guide only. It will introduce you to the wonderful world of business. It will explain business terms and help you understand general business concepts. It will enable you to ask more intelligent questions when you meet with your CPA, lawyer and other professional advisors. This book is not meant to be a replacement for professional accounting, legal, financial planning or other advice. Always seek the assistance of a qualified professional before proceeding with any business venture.

Sample Disclaimer Two. This site is provided by Producer on an "as is" basis. Producer makes no representations or warranties of any kind, express or implied, as to the operation of the site, the information, content, materials or products, included on this site. To the full extent permissible by applicable law, Producer disclaims all warranties, express or implied, including but not limited to, implied warranties of merchantability and fitness for a particular purpose. Producer will not be liable for any damages of any kind arising from the use of this site, including but not limited to direct, indirect, incidental punitive and consequential damages.

Sample Disclaimer Three. Following certain links on Producer's pages will take you outside of Producer's website. Producer has no authority to vet the materials contained on externally linked pages. Producer further notes that the contents of an externally linked page may change from time to time without notice to Producer, and that the reasons for an initial decision to link to that page may no longer hold true. Producer cautions readers that certain recitations of "facts" within externally linked pages may be inaccurate in whole or in part. Furthermore, deductions, conclusions and opinions expressed in those externally linked pages represent the views of their authors, and are expressly not endorsed by Producer.

INDEX

ABOUT THE AUTHOR

Joy R. Butler is an entertainment, intellectual property and business attorney. Her legal expertise includes copyrights, trademarks, commercial licensing, entertainment law, private equity financing, and mergers and acquisitions.

In her entertainment practice, Ms. Butler regularly advises clients on the proper use of copyrighted and other protected materials. Additional entertainment legal services she provides to producers of all media include contract negotiation, business entity formation, joint venture arrangements, guild compliance, and private investor financing.

Ms. Butler is also the author of *The Musician's Guide Through the Legal Jungle: Answers to Frequently Asked Questions About Music Law*, a three-hour professionally-narrated audiobook presentation that explains the music industry in the format of an informal conversation between a "musician" and an "expert".

A frequent speaker and writer on entertainment and business issues, Ms. Butler has been quoted in publications such as the *New York Times*, Forbes.com, *Vibe Magazine*, and *The Independent Video & Film Monthly*. She has a law degree from Harvard Law School and a B.A. degree in economics from Harvard College.

Ms. Butler can be contacted through the website:
www.joybutler.com